WISDOM
OF THE ANCIENT SEERS

Mantras of the *Rig Veda*

WISDOM
OF THE ANCIENT SEERS

Mantras of the *Rig Veda*

DAVID FRAWLEY

MOTILAL BANARSIDASS PUBLISHERS
PRIVATE LIMITED • DELHI

3rd Reprint: Delhi, 2016
First Indian Edition: Delhi, 1994

First Published : South Lake City, 1992

ISBN: 978-81-208-1159-1 (Cloth)
ISBN: 978-81-208-1160-7 (Paper)

Also available at:
MOTILAL BANARSIDASS
41 U.A. Bungalow Road, Jawahar Nagar, Delhi 110 007
8 Mahalaxmi Chamber, 22 Bhulabhai Desai Road, Mumbai 400 026
203 Royapettah High Road, Mylapore, Chennai 600 004
236, 9th Main III Block, Jayanagar, Bengaluru 560 011
8 Camac Street, Kolkata 700 017
Ashok Rajpath, Patna 800 004
Chowk, Varanasi 221 001

Printed in India
by RP Jain at NAB Printing Unit,
A-44, Naraina Industrial Area, Phase I, New Delhi–110028
and published by JP Jain for Motilal Banarsidass Publishers (P) Ltd,
41 U.A. Bungalow Road, Jawahar Nagar, Delhi-110007

To the modern Vedic teachers that have helped me in my research, without whom the ideas in this book would not have taken shape.

M. P. Pandit
Kapali Shastri
Sri Aurobindo
Swami Rama Tirtha
Swami Sri Yukteswar
Lokamanya B. G. Tilak
Vasishta Ganapati Muni
Swami Dayananda Sarasvati

OM! Reverence to both the ancient and the modern seers!

CONTENTS

FOREWORD
BY SUBHASH KAK

Should time or nature, or necessity or chance, or the elements
be considered the cause? — Svetasvatra Upanishad 1.2

Our deepest questions find new resonance in each age. Beyond the pale of mundane knowledge, these questions seem intractable to logic and advances in science. Yajnavalkya expressed these paradoxes very well when he said *paroksa priya iva hi devah, pratyaksa dvisah* or "the gods love what is mysterious and dislike what is evident." The *Rig Veda*, the earliest book of Sanatana Dharma, the Philosophia Perennis, deals with these mysteries. Not surprisingly, the *Rig Veda* has appeared too difficult a book to most scholars, and its translators have been baffled by a considerable portion of its contents. To read the *Rig Veda* superficially is akin to reading laws of quantum mechanics literally and getting perplexed by inherent contradictions like why an electron is sometimes a wave and at other times a particle.

Tradition has recognized these difficulties and emphasized intuitive insight and a search for the meaning behind the words. Those who understand the mystery of words and appearances are seers, the rishis. David Frawley is a modern rishi who in his translations and interpretations from the *Rig Veda* shows with great clarity the vision of the ancient rishis. Frawley shows clearly that the *Rig Veda* is not about anthropomorphic gods competing with each other; each god is every other god and in reality just a metaphor for a universal principle. Frawley shows how the *Rig Veda* is to be read to make one ask questions, which is the first step in the discovery of its meaning.

We live in an age of style and manners. Our trades have become so specialized that we are fearful of asking basic questions. If there can only be one science of the physical world, surely there cannot be more than one science of the spiritual world. This science of consciousness must be just one unique truth. Sanatana Dharma is the way of this truth. In reality "the highest being is truth," says the *Chandogya Upanishad.* But to reach truth one must continually transcend early meanings. One must be like a caterpillar, who to reach a new leaf at the end of one draws itself together towards it.

Many paradoxes of the *Rig Veda* are about time and consciousness; but there are others as well. Frawley shows us how these paradoxes can be resolved through a process of synthesis. Scholars have often forgotten that the act of bringing 1028 hymns together required a certain purpose. So while one can read individual hymns for their insights, one should never forget the whole architecture of the *Rig Veda* to comprehend its different dimensions. The different hymns must be seen through the mirrors of other hymns and those of the *Brahmanas, Upanishads,* Sutras, and science. It has been said that the *Rig Veda* is nectar and the *Upanishads* are the *guhya adesah,* the nectar of nectar. Just as there is a continual interplay between the general and the specific within the *Rig Veda,* there is also an interplay between the *Rig Veda* and the later books. The books that followed the *Rig Veda* cannot be completely understood without understanding it.

"Sight is inseparable from the seer," says Yajnavalkya elsewhere. And also "They who know the life of life, the eye of the eye, the ear of the ear, the mind of the mind, they have comprehended the ancient primeval Brahman. By the mind alone it is to be perceived." So poetry or prose cannot describe this meaning directly, and one needs to know the meta-language *(paribhasa)* of the *Rig Veda* in order to understand it. The *Rig Veda* is a celebration of mystery and it does not explicitly provide its own metalanguage. David Frawley's book is a guide to the elements of this metalanguage and he brings to it a rare transparence.

The *Rig Veda* is a mirror to the world and the thesis of the ancient rishis was that you comprehend the mystery of the world through mirrors that open on doors. Frawley shows how this is done in the *Rig Veda* through word play, through metaphor, through paradox. This requires that one look at all aspects of life: the cosmic, the sacred, the fearful, the passionate. These sideshows can be serious pitfalls for one who seeks just the literal.

To know ourselves we must explore all frontiers: those of space, function, and form. To know ourselves we must also know our past. The *Rig Veda* is a marvelous book in code that describes the insights of ancient sages and the wonderful thing is that these insights are still of great validity. It has often been said that all later Indian philosophy is at best an amplification on ideas already spelt out in the Vedas.

The Vedas should be viewed at three levels. First is the philosophical level where it is asserted that the mystery of the world is beyond logical analysis but it is nevertheless comprehenisible by intuition. This is the reason why the hymns are full of paradoxes and riddles; indeed, the text is all wrapped up in an air of mystery. At another level the Vedas deal with the representation of the mystery of reality in the framework of the theater of ritual. This leads to the realm of sacrifice. The third level deals with astronomical phenomena which are often described in the garb of myths. Naturally it is the first level that has proved to be of enduring interest.

The hymns repeatedly proclaim a unity that lies beyond categories of opposition such as *sat* and *asat*, being and non-being, death and immortality, knowledge and ignorance. Born out of a creative principle, this radical oneness is beyond all duality and it is unutterable and unthinkable. By implication it can only be seen in a mystical awareness. The differentiated aspects of this oneness are the everyday distinct categories. These images are supposed to apply to the universe as well as the human mind.

The potentiality that underlies nature is seen to emerge through the paradoxical process of sacrifice. The word sacrifice (*yajna*) has several meanings, including creation through transcendence, the one most appropriate in these philosophical hymns. The whole universe is the altar of sacrifice out of which its potentialities emerge. Yet, according to the Rigvedic rishis, the mind's eye can comprehend the nature of this creation.

Purusha, the cosmic Being, is visualized in a human image in the *Rig Veda*. Does that have any implications for our understanding of people with different characteristics? Using the well-known terminology from the Vedic era itself, it means that each person is to be viewed as being partly a brahmin, a kshatriya, a vaishya, and a shudra. One's predispositions may be inclined toward one task or another, but each one of us has a mixed character. However, certain tasks do require a one-pointed concentration that makes us perform pure roles. Thus when seeking answers to basic questions of meaning each one of us is a brahmin; when fighting each one of us is a kshatriya; and so on.

What were the implications of the Vedic world view on the cultural and the literary life of the Indians? The viewpoint that the duality of everyday life is subsumed under a higher unity was used as a framework for all activities, including art and literature. The purpose of life was to know the mystery of existence. Symbolic representation of the universe in the shape of the primeval man gave rise to a distinctive approach to architecture, sculpture, and literature. Each composition was to be a symbolic image of the universe in some aspect while simultaneously intimating the larger unity.

It is a very auspicious time to do a fresh interpretation of the *Rig Veda*. Recent archaeological researches have compelled the abandonment of that view of the Vedic civilization which was popularized by European scholars of the 19th century and their successors. According to that view the Vedic people entered India only in the 2nd millennium BC and the traditions of the Vedic religion go back at best to this epoch. Academics held on to this dogma in spite of considerable evidence within the Vedic literature that pointed to epochs going back to the 4th millennium BC and earlier. New archaeological and geological research has shown that the Sarasvati river, which originally flowed somewhat parallel to Indus, dried up around 1900 BC. Now the *Rig Veda* speaks of a mighty Sarasvati and it is in much later literature that we hear of the disappearance of the river. This indicates that the *Rig Veda* itself could not be much later than the 3rd millennium BC.

The most recent archaeological evidence points to a dispersal of the Indo-European people toward Europe, and an expansion within India starting about 7000 BC. The spread of agriculture appears to have been at the basis of this expansion. David Frawley has recently brought together this evidence as well as a new analysis of the literary evidence in another book called *Gods, Sages and Kings* to provide a new synthesis of our knowledge of the Vedic age. This book reviews the astronomical references in the Vedas and describes the geography of Sapta Saindhava, the original home of the Indo-Aryans. This region lay roughly between the Indus and the Ganga rivers, although the periphery of the Aryan world stretched all the way to the steppes of Central Asia, to the Caspian sea and the Oxus river. The Rigvedic hymns were composed mostly on the banks of Sarasvati and its tributary Drishadvati in the Aryan heartland called Brahmavarta. My own study of Indus writing, used during 2600-1900 BC, and that of Vedic science is in general agreement with the new longer chronology.

I first heard about Frawley in the Hanuman temple at Taos in New Mexico on a stop during a pilgrimage to the national parks of the desert West. Frawley lives nearby in the enchantingly beautiful city of Sante Fe. The geography of this part of the United States provides interesting parallels to the Himalayan ranges of India. In both regions desert, rivers, high plateaus, mountains and canyons are to be found in close proximity. It is fitting perhaps that the labors of the Himalayan sages should now be continued in the mountain ranges of the Americas.

Frawley has now written a series of books on different aspects of Vedic civilization. His books illuminate through common sense and logic. Frawley is always equipoised and rational; his books are very useful guides to understand the variegated complexity and yet the fundamental unity of Indian civilization. In view of the fact that the Vedic or Indo-European heritage lies at the basis of contemporary European and American as well as Far Eastern civilizations, these books are of universal relevance. Frawley's deep knowledge of the various aspects of Vedic society gives him the ability to walk that narrow path of fidelity to the original where one is not using later categories to interpose imagined meanings. Frawley has made the *Rig Veda* accessible to the informed layman. Undoubtedly, these books will serve as torchlights to those who wish to chart their own ways in the dawning new age.

Subhash Kak, Ph. D.
Baton Rouge
December 3, 1991

PREFACE

Though many of us in the West are familiar with the great gurus or teachers of the East and practice yoga and meditation, few of us have studied the great ancient teachings, the *Vedas*, which are the oldest portion of this tradition. Though translations for the *Vedas* do exist, they are inadequate as they are largely the product of academic scholarship rather than spiritual insight.

Of the *Vedas*, the *Rig Veda*, the oldest and most central Vedic teaching, remains the most inaccessible and enigmatic. Even in India today this book is rarely studied and hardly understood, mainly owing to its extreme antiquity. Though it is highly revered and in fact sometimes worshipped, though millions of people chant verses from it daily, few know what its hymns really mean or the yoga that is hidden within them. There is a general recognition that the mantric or sound power of the Vedic chants is the greatest in the Sanskrit language but there is seldom an effort to penetrate into the teaching encased within these sounds.

While a number of groups speak of Vedic knowledge, they usually mean Vedanta, the *Bhagavad Gita* or one of the *Puranas*, which though based on the *Vedas* are not part of the actual Vedic mantras (Samhitas). They are seldom speaking from an actual study of the mantras of the *Rig Veda* itself, though it is the real book of revelation (Shruti) from which all Vedic teachings derive.

The *Rig Veda* is the fountainhead of Vedic science, the ancient spiritual science of the Himalayas from which such systems as Yoga, Vedic Astrology (Jyotish) and Ayurveda (traditional Indian medicine) arose. It is the basis of the Sanskrit language and of the culture, the arts and sciences of traditional India. It is also the oldest book in any Indo-European language, and, if recent archeological finds in India prove correct, it may be thousands of years older than the current estimation of it (1500 BC).

Wisdom of the Ancient Seers attempts to reveal the spiritual secrets of the *Rig Veda*. As part of a series of books in which I address the field of Vedic science from a modern perspective, this book is the most central of them. The version of the *Rig Veda* presented here is a radical affirmation of its spiritual meaning or significance in terms of Self-knowledge. The inner sense of the Vedic terms has been pointed out, which relates to the practice of yoga and meditation.

Most available versions of the *Rig Veda* aim at sociological or psychological meanings, often with little sympathy or knowledge of its spiritual basis. Compared to these, this work may appear daring and provocative. What makes it so is not the inappropriateness of the spiritual sense, which would be expected in a book deemed to be a scripture, but rather the superficiality with which the book has been approached elsewhere.

I have often given the spiritual meaning of the mantras directly without much explanation of the outward sense, as this is available elsewhere and inclusion at every point would make the presentation cumbersome. I have avoided most Sanskrit terms to make the book more accessible to the general audience, providing a Sanskrit glossary as an appendix. I have in other books and articles done translations and commentaries of Vedic hymns, with a word by word analysis of the Sanskrit. There is yet, however, no real popular demand for these. But those looking for such a detailed examination of the chants can contact me for further information on this issue.

My concern in this book is with the inner truths of consciousness and its transformation from the practical standpoint of the spiritual life. These eternal truths are presented powerfully in the universal language of mantra in the *Rig Veda*, and the attempt here is to intimate this in the English language, insofar as it may be possible. Naturally, as with any poetry, particularly that which is very ancient, this requires bending our language to another direction, and at best it can only intimate the real power of the chants.

Wisdom of the Ancient Seers is an alternative to the versions of the *Rig Veda* presented by the narrow mentality of nineteenth-century European scholarship, with its materialistic bias and spiritual naivete. It also differs from more recent studies which, though an improvement, still use a sociological, anthropological or psychological approach that does not adequately yield the meaning of the mystic symbols of the *Veda*. Yet this book is based on the original meanings and usage of the mantras, a strict knowledge of ancient Sanskrit, and my own personal practice of a Vedic spiritual life, and is hopefully, therefore, closer to the actual meaning of the hymns than other versions. What we discover in this way, through both intuitive and scholarly methods, is that the original meaning of the Vedic mantras reflects not a primitive culture, but the highest spiritual realization and most profound knowledge of the entire cosmos, both visible and invisible.

I have written a separate book — *Gods, Sages and Kings: Vedic Secrets of Ancient Civilization* — which deals with the outer, cultural and historical implications of the *Rig Veda*. This present book is intended to show its spiritual and yogic meaning.

The reader will find typical hymns to the main Vedic Gods — Agni, Indra, Soma and the many forms of the Sun God — as well as some hymns to the Dawn, Heaven and Earth and other Goddesses. There are a number of other Vedic deities, such as Rudra and collective or group Gods like the Vishvedevas or Ribhus, not included here, primarily owing to space. These deities are not necessarily less important, but those here are more commonly mentioned in the hymns. I hope to deal with these other Vedic Gods in another book.

Included are the main line of Vedic hymns, which begin with hymns to Agni, then to Indra, then to the Sun Gods, and then have a special book, the ninth mandala, for Soma. In this regard the usually translated cosmological hymns (like Purusha Sukta) and the story hymns (like those of Pururavas and Urvashi) have not been included. Though embedded with Vedic symbolism, they are not part of the main line of Vedic hymns. Hence the habit of presenting them as representing the *Rig Veda* can breed some misconceptions.

I have chosen hymns from all the mandalas or books of the *Rig Veda*, but have not done as many from the tenth book as have most translators. This is because I wanted to show that the spiritual meanings I see in the hymns are everywhere, particularly in the main Vedic hymns, and are not exceptions found only in the so-called later books.

This book was originally published under the title *Hymns From the Golden Age: Selected Hymns of the Rig Veda with Yogic Interpretations*, by Motilal Banarsidass (Delhi, India, 1986). It was written in a period between 1981 and 1983. The Indian publication has received many favorable reviews from both spiritual and scholarly circles in India, for which I am grateful. The book was revised slightly for American publication, and this revised edition is also being reprinted in India by Motilal Banarsidass.

I approach the *Rig Veda* here as a universal language of pure mantras, as perhaps the music of Life itself. I hope it does not take the reader the great amount of time and effort that it took me to make the transition of thought and language necessary to uncover these meanings. It is difficult for the modern mind to go beyond its preconceptions and world-view to connect with the vision of the ancient seers, though this effort may contain the keys of our redemption. Until we have regained the legacy of the spiritual humanity from which we have fallen, we may not be able to find a truly humane and happy future.

> May the vision of the ancient seers arise in the minds of all beings on this planet today!
> May the great deities that underlie creation again be honored and worshipped in the world!
> May we once more come to recognize the sacred powers of the Godhead and of our deepest consciousness!

David Frawley
Sante Fe, New Mexico
August 1992

I

INTRODUCTION

This is the upheaval of the heaven-kissing summits whose streams shall feed the furthest generations.   — *Swami Rama Tirtha*

Our Fathers ordained the majesty of the Gods. As Gods they placed the Spirit in the Gods.

They encompassed all ruling powers and made them brilliant and merged them again into their own Selves.

They strode with their conquering force through all realms, measuring in themselves the original immeasurable laws.

They embraced all the worlds within themselves and streamed forth their progeny in manifold ways.   —*Rig Veda X.56.4–5*

This homage is to the ancient-born Seers, to the ancient makers of the Path.
                    —*Rig Veda X.14–15*

1
THE *RIG VEDA,*
THE BOOK OF MANTRA

The Veda Reexamined

The *Rig Veda* is regarded by many as the oldest book in the world.It is the best preserved of all ancient writings and our most authentic document of the languages of the ancient world. Even the original accents and pronunciations are known. Since we have so little from early times to draw on, the *Rig Veda* represents our most direct communication with our ancient ancestors.

The *Rig Veda* is a compendium of poetry, legend, mythology, ritual, ancient science and culture, and, above all, ancient religion, yoga and spirituality. It contains much of the beauty and the simple joy of a life in harmony with nature, as in its hymns to the beauty of the dawn. Yet it also contains much that is mysterious, enigmatic and strange, reflecting the deep and primal side of the mind.

Modern man has lost touch with this realm of the sacred and finds it difficult to understand, even disturbing. The *Rig Veda* presents many challenges for us, but also offers a doorway to a side of our nature with which we may require contact in order to understand the full scope of who we really are. The *Rig Veda* contains the same profound myths and archetypal images of man and nature that many of us are exploring today in psychology, anthropology, shamanism and in yoga practices such as Tantra. It has relevance, therefore, for understanding our deeper psyche and for connecting us with our ancient origins. To go forward we must always connect deeply with our origins. It is perhaps our loss of this connection with our ancient soul that has brought us into our present crisis. The return to it may provide much of the cure we need.

While ancient Egypt left us the pyramids, ancient India left us the *Vedas* — the pyramids of the mind. Much of the language and symbolism of the *Rig Veda* reflects the same profound mentality as ancient Egypt. It shows a world of great Gods and demons, a life filled with the sacred, the awesome and the terrible in which man is just a field for mysterious cosmic forces often beyond his comprehension, though not beyond his inner being. In this sacred realm nothing is as it appears or as it is given on the surface. The teaching is often purposely veiled from the outer mind. The ancients did not try to convert others to their teachings. They felt truth had to be earned by our own individual experience and direct perception. They preferred to protect the truth by making certain that only those who were open to it would be given any access to its pathways. The *Rig Veda* as a document of the ancient mystery religion of India and the Himalayan region has many such secrets. To uncover them requires not only patience, but a great subtlety and sensitivity of mind and language. The *Rig Veda* is the oldest scripture of India, the land where throughout the centuries religion and spirituality have been most emphasized. Therefore, it contains many keys to the origins of all the great teachings of India. The *Veda* is called the "Shruti," the revelation or scripture, of which such texts as the *Upanishads* or *Bhagavad Gita*, well known for their philosophical and spiritual profundity, were a late appendix. The Hindus consider the *Rig Veda* to be the oldest book in the world and the source book of all human civilization. Even those of us who would not agree with this judgment would have to be cautious in too quickly judging a teaching considered to be so old and important by such a large and spiritually developed portion of humanity. Many great modern teachers and yogis of India, great Self-realized and God-realized souls, have attested to its profundity and antiquity. These include Paramahansa Yogananda and his teacher Sri Yukteswar, Swami Vivekananda, Swami Rama Tirtha, Sri Aurobindo and Ganapati Muni, to mention but a few.

The *Rig Veda* is the source book of the Sanskrit language, the oldest most continually used language in the world, containing what is perhaps the largest literature in the world, particularly in the spiritual realm. Both Hindu and Buddhist teachings have their main texts in this language. Sanskrit is one of the most scientific of all languages and the most etymologically consistent. Much of modern linguistics has developed from the study of Sanskrit.

Sanskrit is also important because it is perhaps the most ancient of Indo-European languages, and so shows much about their origin. Such languages include most of those of Europe and Iran and many of Central Asia, as well as those of north India. The ancient Persian religion of Zoroaster (Zarathustra) is given in a language like that of the *Rig Veda*, with many of the same deities and practices. Much that later came to be part of Judaism, Christianity and Islam has connections with Zoroastrianism and hence, indirectly, with the *Veda*. As such, the *Rig Veda* may be the most central document to world religion.

The *Rig Veda* shows a very ancient form of Indo-European language and culture. We can see in it an earlier or alternative form of many Greek, Roman, Germanic, Keltic or Slavic gods, as well as similar cultural practices. In this light we can look on the *Rig Veda* as the oldest book or scripture of our European forefathers, centuries or millennia before the advent of Christianity. Hence a proper understanding and appreciation of the *Rig Veda* is one of the most important issues in world scholarship and in the understanding of human history today.

The Vedic religion, with the *Rig Veda* as its oldest document, was called the "Arya Dharma," the teaching of noble souls or the Aryans. The Buddha also called his religion Arya Dharma. Zoroaster of ancient Persia called his teaching Aryan. As such the Arya Dharma has been the most widely developed and practiced of all religions throughout human history.

Most of the translations and interpretations of the *Rig Veda* used today were produced by nineteenth century European scholars. Their work often reflects the bias of their times; the imperialism, materialism and Christian missionary spirit, the tendency to look down upon Asia and its culture as inferior, to even blame the spiritual traditions of Hinduism and Buddhism for the political decline of these cultures. Such writers were quite unappreciative of the spiritual life, of yoga and meditation. Even their psychological or sociological concepts are archaic or biased by more recent standards. Their interpretations of such ancient texts are quite superficial. They often reflect simplistic political ideas, like wars between light and dark skinned people to explain the Vedic clash between light and darkness or truth and falsehood in the human soul to which all religions attest. They mention little or nothing of yoga, meditation or mantra or the cosmic meaning of ritual, though these are the main topics in the *Vedas*. Unfortunately, these nineteenth century works are still followed and our historical and philosophical judgment of the *Rig Veda* remains based upon their limited views.

If the *Rig Veda* is a spiritual document, we cannot expect that it can be understood by an interpreter who has no sense of the spiritual. To examine an object, we must have a sensitivity for what it is. We don't look to a chemist to judge a great painting. Hence we should not look to intellectual scholars to understand the mystery religions of the ancient world. Nor should we be surprised if they fail to appreciate them or even degrade them.

These same modern scholars tend to date *Rig Veda* from around 1500 BC. This is the time that the Vedic people or Aryans are supposed to have entered into India; and the *Rig Veda*, at least in part, shows aspects of the land and climate of India. However, Vedic Gods like Indra do appear in a treaty of 1500 BC between two Indo-Iranian people, the Hittites of Anatolia (modern Turkey) and the Mitanni of Syria, quite far from India. As these Gods could not have been invented overnight, they must have existed many centuries before this date. Hence a few scholars speculate that the Gods of the *Rig Veda* may date as early as 2000-3000 BC, though perhaps not in India.

An old civilization has been found in India, the so-called "Indus Valley" culture or "Harappa and Mohenjo-daro" from its two main cities; it generally dates from around 2600-1800 BC. It has now been found to have extended from the coast of Iran through Gujarat in India and east past Delhi and the Ganges, making it the largest civilization in the ancient world of that time, covering a larger area than the whole Egypt-Mesopotamian cultural base put together. It has been thought by most modern authorities to be pre-Vedic or non-Aryan, though its language has yet to be definitively deciphered.

Many scholars in India and a few in the West, however, have contested this view. For example, they point out the existence of many fire altars, water tanks, ritual sacrifices and other aspects of the Vedic religion, as well as such Vedic symbols as the swastika found at various Indus valley sites, thus showing an Aryan influence.

The so-called Indus culture has primarily been found to exist along the now dried banks of the Sarasvati river, between the Yamuna and the Sutlej, which is described as the main river of the Rig Vedic culture. However, it appears that the Sarasvati went dry before the end of the Indus culture. This would also indicate that the Indus culture was Vedic or Aryan. Why would the Vedic people eulogize a dried river as the source of their culture if they had not lived on its banks when it was flowing?

In the early eighties an important new archeological site was found in India, at Dwaraka, the site of the legendary city of Krishna. According to a legend in the *Mahabharata*, Dwaraka was submerged by the sea right after the death of Krishna. This was regarded as a grandiose metaphor, part of a story filled with great myths. Now it has been discovered that the whole coast of western India sank by nearly forty feet around 1500 BC and a number of submerged cities have been found. At the supposed site of Krishna's city the ruins of a great stone port have been found, one of the largest in the ancient world.

The Dwaraka site has revealed characters intermediate between the Indus Valley script and the Brahmi alphabet used for the Aryan languages of north India in ancient times. Dwaraka also shows trade objects from Mesopotamia of this era, from the Indo-European Kassites who ruled Babylonia. Dwaraka has been scientifically dated at 1500 BC. This site thus shows that not only were the Aryans in India by 1500 BC, but they also had already reached the ocean, had built massive stone cities, were engaged in maritime trade and possessed a written script. It shows a level of culture much higher and at a much earlier date than modern Western scholars have imagined. Previously, cities and a written script for the Aryan were thought to have started around 900 BC. This would have to be pushed back a thousand years or more. The Dwaraka site shows that the Indus Valley culture either included the Aryans or was an Aryan culture. The Aryans could not have reached the sea without having passed through the Indus Valley culture and during the time that it was flourishing.

Such finds attest to the antiquity of the *Rig Veda*. By ancient Indian historical accounts in the *Puranas*, Krishna came at the very end of the Vedic period. Many kings and dynasties are listed before him. By his time the *Rig Veda* was very old, a document of great antiquity that few understood at all. If this is the case then the *Rig Veda* must be much older than 1500 BC, perhaps by millennia.

According to the ideas of a number of Hindu scholars the *Rig Veda* is thought to date to 4000 or 6000 BC. This is based on references to astronomical positions of these eras as a basis for the calendars used in the *Vedas*. It agrees with the Vedic description of the Sarasvati as the greatest river of India, which indeed it was in very early ancient times. As such the *Rig Veda* may indeed be the oldest book in the world. It may provide our most authentic view of the ancient spiritual culture which prevailed across the globe.

If this is the case our whole view of the ancient world and the origins of civilization has to be changed. We find through it that there was an Aryan culture in India as old and as sophisticated as those of the Middle East and Egypt. It shows that our own Aryan ancestors may not have been as primitive as we would tend to think, or as unspiritual. The Aryans may not be late comers into the ancient civilized world but may have been present at its very origin. This agrees with the research of such modern Western scholars as Colin Renfrew, who proposes that the Aryans were the original people who brought agriculture to Europe, beginning around 6000 BC. It may mean that Aryan India is the origin and point of diffusion of all Indo-European peoples, their languages and cultures. If this is true, we should look to India rather than to the Middle East for our own cultural origins or for the origin of human civilization as a whole.

The new interpretation of the *Rig Veda* presented here thus has a special meaning. It is intended to start a new era of examination of the Vedic and other ancient teachings with a sensitivity to their spiritual meaning. It hopes to initiate a new era of study of such teachings as the *Rig Veda* and a whole new way of examining the ancient world — in light of the new knowledge of yoga and meditation we have today. Therefore, it is not just another version of the *Rig Veda*. It is the *Rig Veda* seen in the light of consciousness, not as picked apart by some scholarly brain. It is an attempt to bring the *Rig Veda* back to life and make it relevant for today, not just to present some half-preserved relic for our curiosity.

Ancient and modern man may not be as different as we think. Certainly we all still contain our ancient ancestors within the depths of our psyche. The spiritual, religious and occult nature of ancient culture is as much a part of our humanity as is the materialistic, technological, scientific side we have today. As this inner side is deeper and older, we can only assume that it must rise up again. Now that we are reaching the limits of expansion in the material world, many of us are looking inward again. In this renewed quest for the spiritual meaning of life such ancient insights are not only helpful but show us that this quest is the very essence of our true nature in life and the key to our purpose on Earth.

The *Rig Veda*

The *Rig Veda* is said to be the original book of mantras from the ancient seers and sages of the Himalayas who set forth the ways of truth for mankind at the beginning of this world-age many thousands of years ago, apparently at the end of the last Ice Age. It became the basis for the entire ancient Hindu culture, its living oral tradition of hymns, songs, myths, legends, ritual, philosophy and yoga, all intermixed in a mantric language with many levels of meaning. From it not only the systems of yoga derived but also the sciences of ancient India like mathematics, astrology and Ayurveda (medicine). The *Rig Veda* is used and quoted by many ancient Indian writers including those who established the original laws and social order. Even the poets, dancers and musicians looked back to it. Its mantras are still recited at most important ceremonies or sacraments done in India. Hence it remains at the core of modern Hinduism, which has developed from it in many directions.

The *Rig Veda* was passed down orally for thousands of years according to set rhythms and patterns which continue to the present day. It was the great fountainhead of Hindu culture, the guiding document of its earliest era, its mythical Golden Age of spiritual civilization to which the later ages looked back in awe and reverence. It preserves the original hymns of many of the most famous and legendary of the sages of India, like Vasishta or Vishwamitra, from whom many later teachings derived. These sages were as renowned as Buddha or Krishna were in later times, and well known long before them.

Yet to reiterate, the *Rig Veda* is not merely of interest relative to Indian spirituality. As the oldest book in an Indo-European language, it has a unique relevance for Western culture as well. Our European ancestors shared not only a similar language, but also had many cultural and religious affinities with the Vedic people. For example, the great Sun-God of inspiration Apollo of the Greeks corresponds to the Vedic Sun-God of inspiration, Savitar, lauded by the Vedic people at the rising and the setting of the Sun. The *Rig Veda*, therefore, also represents the original roots of Western culture and may be its original scripture as well. It reveals a spiritual potential our Western culture has not so extensively developed. Looking back at the *Rig Veda* is thus looking back at a forgotten heritage of our own, uncovering another cultural potential we also have.

To enter into the *Rig Veda* is a journey into the spiritual roots of civilization. Through it the ancients speak directly to us and tell us how they viewed reality. This is quite different from our interpretation of who the ancients were and the level they reached relative to our preconceptions. Through the *Rig Veda* the ancients speak in their own voice and their own language. By opening up to it, we can cross the barrier of time and culture and feel once more the profound wonder and joy of the ancient seers. We can touch the magic and mystery of that earlier spiritual humanity from which we have not so much advanced as fallen. Our material advancement parallels a spiritual fall, a growing loss of the sense of the cosmic being in life, the glory of the universe overflowing in wonder everywhere that the ancients felt, to which we now must return to survive as a species.

I do not look upon the hymns of the ancient seers of India according to our accepted historical interpretation of them: that they were obscure magic spells and rituals with some genuine poetry mixed in of a very local and primitive ancient culture, not advanced enough to be called a real civilization at all. I see them as probably the most extensive and exalted spiritual teaching the world has ever known — the records of numerous enlightened seers from an earlier and more spiritual age which, in terms of cosmic awareness, dwarfs our own. They are the hymns of the mythical original sages to which all the ancient cultures from Mexico to Egypt, India and China attribute the real origin of their civilizations. Here we will approach the Vedic hymns from a poetic, mystical and spiritual stand-point, not through the materialistic intellect of today which does not have the basis to understand the Vedic mentality. Those who are sensitive to the higher intuitive knowledge that proceeds through mantra, symbol, myth and archetype will be able to share in this.

The *Rig Veda* is the great book of mantra behind ancient Indian spirituality, the original basis of the Sanskrit language. It is written, or more correctly, spoken in a purely mantric language, an archetypal proto-language of sound-symbol-ideas with multiple levels of meaning.

It is a language more proper to a deeper level of consciousness than the
rational intellect, a language we touch in art, dream, creative insight and
meditation. This spiritual language sees all things as expressions of the
Divine Word, notes a cosmic significance everywhere, each thing as a
manifestation of the great totality. This capacity allowed the ancients to
see in the simple phenomena of nature like fire, wind, sun, the cow, the
bull or the horse, archetypal images of the entire universe, powers of our
own psyche and keys to its transformation from mortality to immortality.
Yet this sense of great truth in the simple and organic, possible only
through a great sensitivity to life, also became the basis for pronouncing
these hymns to be primitive by the modern intellect that sees advancement
not in oneness with life but in domination over it. It is back to that more
simple and unconditioned vision which reveals the cosmic being of all
things that the journey of this book proceeds.

The Golden Age

All the cultures of the ancient world look back to a mythical Golden
Age, an era of profound inner awareness and simple outer living in which
men lived in the presence of the Gods. We find this myth everywhere from
classical Latin and Greek writers to the Bible and to the mythical legacy
of the ancient Near East, Egypt, Assyria, Babylonia and Sumeria, to Persia
and India, to China and even to Mexico and the cultures of the American
Indians. It is central to all the ancient scriptures including the Bible, the
Persian *Zend Avesta*, the Hindu *Vedas*, Lao Tzu and the *I Ching* in China.

The ancients look back to this earlier era for their guidance, for the
basis of their culture, its laws and prototypes. Even the first civilizations
we know of, Egypt and Sumeria, speak of their cultures as being very old,
as going back thousands of years before the time we say civilization first
began. The first civilizations we know of do not project themselves as
original cultures, a new era, but look back on long ages before them,
regarding their cultures as old and declining. By modern accounts, this is
all a baseless mythology — but it is hard to believe that the ancients were
so misinformed about the origins of their own culture that they could
invent civilization and yet somehow imagine it had been around on a much
higher level before them.

The Hindu spiritual tradition, like others of the ancient world, talks
of the four great ages of civilization: The Golden, Silver, Bronze and Iron
ages (Satya, Treta, Dwapara and Kali Yugas). They claim a continuity of
their culture through all four ages and to have preserved the spiritual
teachings of the respective ages. The *Rig Veda* is stated to derive from
these earlier ages. Their exact time or duration, however, is a matter of

dispute. The last, the dark Iron Age or Kali Yuga, was known to have begun before the time of the Buddha, and the earlier ages were of longer duration. Yet whether this Golden Age was mythical or actual, it remains the background of the hymns, the great symbol they invoke and the context that comprehends them.

In any case, we invoke here that symbol and that aspiration, the sense of the Golden Age the *Rig Veda* transmits. It is the vision of a spiritual humanity not toiling outwardly for transient wealth, fame, pleasure and power, but living a simple life and giving their greater energy to the worship of the Divine. It is humanity living in a cosmic vision with a sense of reverence for the Divine permeating all life. It is the rising Sun every day being lauded with mystic chants as the visible image of the Godhead of enlightenment. It is all life as a worship arising spontaneously from the heart towards the Being within the heart that is everywhere. It is creation irradiated with the beneficent light of truth and human society ruled by men of seeing, sages who ordain all things according to their nature, who rule not by a rigid pattern but by a principle of creative freedom for all. It is an era in which human beings live in harmony with the will of God. This does not mean a time in which everyone is enlightened, but when the inner and outer states of people correspond; when rulers are really noble, the priests really spiritual, and the masses of people docile to the rule of men of knowledge.

Though we may not think that such an age ever really existed or may not be possible at all, this is merely the measure of our own distance from it, our own lack of understanding of our past or future, and consequently of our present. It is that aspiration we wish to awaken here, the aspiration to a spiritual humanity, a society once more founded on the higher knowledge. This is not to laud an oppressive priestly class who are only merchants or politicians in disguise, but once more to reverence the true seers and the sages. This means that we as individuals must give precedence to the state of seeing in our lives, that we once more value being itself and not just our own personal or collective becoming. The Golden Age we look back to, our true utopia, is the age of the sunlight of self-knowledge that a few people must always incarnate so there can be any world at all. It is to such spiritual values — a society based upon the cosmic, the infinite and the eternal — that we must return for there to be any age of light for humanity.

The Solar-Dawn Religion of Enlightenment

The ancients worshipped what we call Gods, but which are, more properly speaking, principles of light. This is not light as an outer power, but the principle of illumination which is consciousness itself. For them, worshipping the Gods meant manifesting the powers and principles of enlightenment in our own thought and action. This requires acknowledging the sacred unity of all life. The ancient symbols of light are symbols of enlightenment which function to draw forth from the depths of our psyche its hidden Divine light. The Sun is the symbol of the enlightened Mind, the mind of light free of the darkness of unconsciousness and egoism. The Dawn is the symbol of the wisdom of awakening. The Gods were not images but the forms of light, the laws of truth.

The ancients revered light in the outer world according to their intuition of light in the inner world. They saw the outer luminaries as manifestations of the inner light. Theirs was the religion of light. Yet this was not a religion like our religions today, which are a worship of the Divine as something beyond ourselves and largely apart from our lives. It was a religion of the transformation of man by the light, a symbolic religion of meditation. The light was in the heart. The Sun was that of our own heart, not our conditioned thoughts and emotions, but the light of the soul behind and beyond them. The outer Sun was to the ancients only the visible image, the reminder of the inner Sun of the Heart in which all the universe, all creation ever exists in the state of oneness.

The work of the ancient seers was to find that Sun, to purify it and to enable it to rise within our hearts and illuminate the darkness of the psyche, our interior night of ignorance and egoism. It was the sunlight of unity they sought, not some God of superstition and division. It was not just the unity of man with man, which in itself is impossible, nor the unity of man and nature that by itself is regressive. It was our own internal unity, the integration of our nature in the knowledge of the Divine Self, the Godhead in which there is unity with all. It was the unity of thought-free awareness no longer bound by name or form that regards all names and forms as plays of a single light of truth.

This Solar-Dawn religion or religion of light was the universal religion of the ancient world. It is found in all ancient cultures and their great cults of sun worship. We find it in Egypt, Sumeria, Babylonia and Assyria, in India and Persia, and in the religions of the American Indians. We find it among the Scythians of central Asia and our own European ancestors before Christianity. We even find it in Christianity itself, whose savior is born on the winter solstice like the Sun, who is the Divine Son like the Sun, that is sacrificed, dies and is reborn for the salvation of all beings. Christ himself was the last in a long line of solar resurrection, compassion-enlightenment figures that dominated the ancient Near East. This sense of the Divine, of mystery, awesomeness and reverence that we see in the monumental and hieratic cultures of the ancient world came from that original solar religion, the religion of sacrifice in which all life is an offering, a giving of each to all and all to each.

That sunlight of enlightenment we find in the teachings of the Buddha who proclaimed once more the Aryan religion, the religion of noble wisdom and sunlight perception in which all is one. It is that Sun we find enshrined in the *Upanishads* as the Self in the heart of all beings. The ancient teachings speak of themselves as derived from the Sun, as different rays or radiances of the Sun of truth. The scriptures we have from the ancients, upon which all our religions are based, are rays of that Sun, the inner shining of truth perception in which all barriers between beings melt away.

As light is the basic language of life, the solar religion is eternal in its symbolism. It reflects the experience of all beings in an intuitive translation. We may not understand our respective and culturally conditioned customs, but we all have a sense of the meaning of light and darkness, life and death, knowledge and ignorance. This symbolism of light underlies all poetry, mythology, symbolism and alchemy. It prevails in the inner psychic realm as it does in the outer realm of nature. We could, therefore, call it the universal language, as in this respect the Sun does not represent a particular star but the psycho-cosmic principle of life, light and consciousness. What we contact in the *Vedas*, therefore, is the primeval language of the ancient world and our own cosmic being; not a cultural message, but the unconditioned song of light of our own solar soul.

The Aryan Seers

This spiritual culture of India's mythical Golden Age called itself "Aryan," and it is from here that this term originally derives. Aryan originally means noble; people of noble character, inner values, integrity and honesty, the nobility of self-knowledge. It was in this sense that even the Buddha (who criticized much of the Vedic religion which by his time had degenerated from its spiritual base) called his religion Aryan (Arya Dharma), his wisdom Aryan (Arya Prajña) and his path Aryan. This original sense of Aryan has little to do with the Germanic sense of the term invented by nineteenth-century European thinkers and further warped by the Nazis. Aryan is a term for a higher spiritual humanity based on the principles of truth, giving, self-sacrifice and the consciousness of unity and universality. It is unfortunate that it has been debased and that these negative and inappropriate associations, which are really ignoble, unspiritual and un-Aryan, should be projected upon it. Yet this is often the way of the world, as the *Vedas* say, wherein the dark forces take upon themselves and use falsely the powers and appellations of the light.

The highest human type in Aryan society, the culture bearer and guide, is the seer and sage. Aryan society was ruled by men of spiritual knowledge, the enlightened and illumined who lived in cosmic awareness. The values of Aryan society were arranged hierarchically to lead all human beings to become seers. Material and commercial values were regarded as inferior and kept in check. The prime value of Aryan society was the worship of the Divine, outwardly and ritualistically for the ignorant, inwardly in meditation for the wise.

The Aryan seer is a higher order of human being, a man of spiritual knowledge like Buddha or Christ. At that time such seers were not rare individuals outside of society, but the highest level of the society whose place was recognized and revered by the culture as a whole. These seers manifested the love of truth, a free and open creativity, and a great ardor of life and awareness. In stature they were like great mountains, in movement like mighty rivers. Their powers of perception extended through all the realms of cosmic existence. Their creative force manifested in many worlds. Yet they were as yielding and serviceable as a cow, as impartially beneficent as the sun. Reaching in mind the highest heavens, they remained as humble as the earth. Knowing the supreme beyond, they could still revel in the simple beauties of life in the here and now. They were men of the greatest simplicity yet of vast comprehension, which is why their hymns frequently become too multiple and magical in meaning for us to grasp. They were our spiritual fathers, the makers of civilization, and as long as civilization upheld their inner and spiritual values, there was true harmony on earth.

The Vedic hymns are, in a way, merely a means of introducing us to our seer ancestors, that we might comprehend the heritage of spiritual humanity we also possess. Our true human legacy is not just of violence and sorrow. At the origins of our civilization are the seers and their great meditations. Recognizing them again, we can once more call up their power within us and again become true human beings, men of cosmic awareness, instead of animals or machines out of control. A true understanding of ancient culture discovers the work of these seers and a true vision of the future shows their influence returning again.

Our present idea of man as a purely physical entity with purely material drives and our idea of history as the development of material tools and capacities is false and degrading. Our true and original human heritage from which we have fallen is as seers, cosmic beings of spiritual awareness. A proper understanding of the *Rig Veda* restores this original and higher heritage of ours and returns to us that capacity of seeing in which alone we can realize our potential, a condition more happy and wise than anything modern culture has yet to imagine. It is to bring the Aryan seer out in us that this book is written, to stimulate our true nobility of character and capacity to perceive the truth. It is not for some mere cultural or intellectual interest, but to link us upwardly to the ancient spiritual forces that once had great power on earth and are needed again today for us to survive this difficult transitional period of the race.

The Gods

The thought of the Gods arouses certain feelings in us. On one hand we sense something mysterious, unknown and primeval, a sense of the original life, the magical faces of cosmic being. On the other hand, we think of idols and images, superstitions, fetishes and crude sacrifices. It is important, therefore, to discover what the ancients really meant by their Gods.

First of all, there is nothing rigidly defined about the ancient Gods. They are not idols or images each separated from the others. The term God, apart from its poetic sense, would be best rendered as "Divine." There is no sense of any fixed multiplicity in the ancient meaning of the term. It has more of a generic sense. Each God is God — the Divine in one form or aspect or another. The names of the Gods are not names of different Gods but different names for the Divine. A God is the Divine generally and there is no real difference between one God and another. Each God is all the Gods, as each God is an all-encompassing universal principle. The Gods flow in and out of each other as the One Divine in its various powers and principles, each of which contains the whole. Behind each usage of the term God is the sense of the unity and universality of the Divine, its infinite powers of manifestation, each of which reflects the being of the totality.

The ancient Gods are both one and many, many in one and one in many. They are unity, duality and multiplicity, totality as a single fact. They are a unity that contains within itself, without contradiction, an unlimited creative diversity. They are the unity of universality in which nothing is excluded. In the ancient Gods monism, monotheism and polytheism exist together in mutual harmony. They reflect not an idea of the mind and its artificial limitations, but the fact of life and existence, which is a unity that the mind can never limit, define or exhaust. This comprehensive nature of the Gods we find equally in the *Rig Veda* as in ancient Egypt, wrongly interpreted as pantheism or polytheism.

The diversity of the ancient Gods is not according to a real multiplicity or polytheism, but according to a universal creative vision that sees one in all and all in one, that comprehends unity in multiplicity and multiplicity in unity; the integration of all views and ideas in the multidimensional being of consciousness. It is a synthetic intuitive perception beyond the dichotomies of intellect, not a primitive imagination beneath it. The Gods are the organic comprehension of the Divine in the state of seeing, in the true glory of life. They are the impression on the human mind and speech of the powers and principles of the Divine nature. They are the lightning that requires no system but moves with a spontaneous, all-illuminating unfolding.

The imagistic character of the ancient Gods, their human, animal or naturalistic forms, is similarly not any kind of idolatry. The Gods, though they have a human facet, are not anthropomorphic. Their human facet is intertwined with other forms and images and abstract senses. The Gods reflect not the Divine in the image of man but rather man in the image of the Divine, in the image of all creation. Their animal forms similarly have nothing primitive or totemistic about them. They are numinous psychic symbols of the powers of the universal life. They are more like the swan of the French poets, the horse of painters; grand aesthetic spiritual symbols, like the cosmic Cow. Without a sense of these associations, what these terms evoked and connoted for the ancients, not just as concrete images, but as sound and idea forms (i.e. the Cow as the nourisher or nourishment in general), we will only superimpose upon them our much less sensitive sense of the simple life and the natural world. The ancients often preferred the animal over the human symbol as it more reflects the primeval and unknown character of Being itself. It has a greater appeal to the unconscious, and it was the work of the seers to bring that unconscious and its proto-language of symbols into consciousness for the integration and transformation of our entire nature.

Nor was the ancient religion what we would call pantheistic. In it Nature is seen as existing in the Divine, but the Gods are also referred to as transcending the world by their very nature. The natural imagery of the ancient teachings reflects not the Divine reduced to the natural world but the natural world as a reflection of inner truth — nature resurrected into the Godhead as its self-expression in manifestation. The forms of nature are symbols for the Godhead, faces it takes or masks it wears, yet no more reducible to them than is a painter to his painting. This leads us to the main sense of the Vedic Gods: it is impossible to say what they are or are not. They contain everything, including each other, but are not reducible to anything. One cannot even give them a name. A name is merely a means of their intimation and evocation, nothing that can define, delimit or explain them. They have all names and no names. They are the principle of naming but not a thing that can be named. When we name them it is only a symbolic gesture to point out their general character which is never to be taken literally.

Agni, called the God of Fire, is not a fire in the sense we normally use the word. He is the energy of transformation, which is essentially the energy of consciousness. He is whatever burns, penetrates, perceives, labors, creates, envisions, wills, aspires and ascends with force. He is symbolically a fire, for example, the way we speak of the fire of genius. He is like fire but not simply a fire, even as seen by a fertile but primitive imagination. As the principle of light and energy in general, Agni is the Sun by day, the Moon by night, the fire in the home, the stars in the sky, the wind in the atmosphere or lightning in the clouds. As whatever manifests power, strength and spirit, he is the heroic man, the swift stallion, the strong bull or the soaring eagle. In terms of our faculties, he is wakeful awareness and mindfulness, the will to truth, consciousness, the state of seeing, the Self, the soul, the intelligence, listening, chanting, the voice and so on. In short, Agni is whatever in us manifests the essential light and power of the Divine which is consciousness and creative being. And he is all the Gods according to time, according to quality. Shall we then call him the God of fire? He is fire only in a Jungian, an alchemical, a yogic, a poetic, a mystic or a Zen sense. He is the energy of awareness that flames upward in a primeval spiral transformation from the depths. And all the other Vedic Gods are of the same nature and interpenetrate at many points.

The ancient seers apprehended creation, the natural world, as a kind of language, as the manifestation of Divine Word. They apprehended all objects as names, appellations of the Divine in its various powers and qualities. To them a man, a cow, a horse, the sun, are certain archetypal images of the Divine or cosmic being. Every being is a microcosm and reflects some truth about the universe, its way of being and action, its self-formulation. They felt the cosmic presence in all life. As such, the wonder we feel today with a quasar, a galaxy or a black hole, they felt with the earth, the sun, the rain, a cow, not by a more primitive imagination but by a profounder intuition of the cosmic being of all life.

We have scientifically explained away many of the mysteries of nature, but have we really ascertained the real origin and reality of existence? Does that not remain a sacred wonder one can only commune with but never define? Our knowledge, apart from its practical benefits (and even these are often dubious), has profaned the sacred but not understood it. It has separated us from the mystery, which means we must only seek it at a greater distance. The ancients faced that mystery in life and lived it. They opened up to that being of wonder, reverence and awe and found it to be their own original and immortal nature. They saw creation as its voice, filled with magical intuitive sound-symbols of the transcendent. This is the original sense of the mantra.

The seers did not apprehend things as entities in themselves. They saw connections, interrelationships, mutualities. Each being for them was a window on the entire universe, a unique way of apprehending the totality anew. All beings were seen as notes in a Divine song, sounds in a Divine poem, to be understood in their mutual harmony and interrelated movement. As such all objects were Divine Words and archetypes to be understood, to be grasped not separately but as a common fabric, currents of a common stream. It was in this vision, this sense of sacred immanence that the ancients revered the cow, the bull, the horse, lion, hawk or man. They saw them not as creatures of the world but as mantras of the spirit, archetypal incarnations of Divine qualities, pages in the book of Nature showing the mystery of the Absolute, the Godhead everywhere.

The Gods, then, were the Divine principles, the cosmic presences, the spiritual archetypes the ancient seers apprehended working through the forms of things. Their Gods were not personifications of forces, imaginations about the world they could not scientifically understand. Rather, on the contrary, they saw the forces of nature as workings on an outer level of the Gods or Divine principles from an inner level. The Gods were the cosmic archetypes that manifested through the forms of nature, the ideals which informed the actual. It was the external world that was a symbol for the Gods, not the Gods who were symbols for forces of external nature. It was the world and its creatures that were imaginations of the Gods, not the Gods who were products of men. The Gods were the product of the Divine Man who is the Self, but the mortal creature and his sensate mind is far below them. These Gods are the archetypes of seeing, the beings of the light of conscious laboring at the secret heart of the world. They are the natural laws of truth which all beings find in truth-perception. Though given different names in different epochs, they are most revealed in the mantric language of the seers that manifests the vibrations of the Divine Word on which they move.

For us the term "the Gods" invokes primarily some imagination of primitive polytheism, yet also a freedom of spiritual formulation that appeals to us as through something aesthetic. The term "God" evokes the sense of a rigid monotheism that we find either stifling to our creativity or comforting to our need for faith and belief. It is a word on which our mind often closes, accepting or rejecting, but not inspiring us further in the creative adventure of living. For the ancients, the Divine meant the Being of light and play, the light of consciousness and the play of delight. It was the magical being of the play of consciousness, a liberated creativity burgeoning into the uncreate Godhead. It was the universal, eternal, open and free truth that our intelligence seeks, the state of undivided seeing. It is this sense of the Divine we must invoke in order to understand the ancients and our spiritual roots and potentials within their legacy.

The ancient Gods are part of a language of truth through which the symbolic, archetypal and Divine nature of all life can be understood. Through them we learn to see the spiritual powers and principles operative in life, of which material forms are only a lower manifestation. What is really taught through the figures and the stories of the Gods is the symbolic comprehension of reality — that all things are symbols in one supreme intelligence, facets of its own self-revelation.As such, no symbol or God is ultimate or an end in itself. All are only a means of indicating what is beyond form and expression.

Through this sense of the symbolic we apprehend life without idolatry. We worship no objects. We take no material things as final or real in themselves. We reverence all things as symbols of a reality beyond form. We see all things as only masks of one inexhaustible creative reality. We are no longer hypnotized by mere words into thinking that different names indicate any real division in things. We realize that all names are of one nameless being, facets of an unbounded creativity without divisions. We do not just look at things anymore. We perceive them as a message, a truth of all life, of the cosmos itself. We see in each being an expression of the totality. Behind the apparent division of form we see divine principles, Gods, through which there is an original unity. The Gods are only unifying archetypes to return the mind to a state of unity, symbols of transformation into the oneness, not idols of belief in multiplicity. Their multiplicity only indicates the vastness of this creative unity that is not a mere fixed concept of unity but a perception of oneness through universality, by uniqueness everywhere.

The great freedom and fluidity of the ancient mantric language, its free identification of each God with all, is to teach this great truth of oneness. Hence in the end, all terms become synonymous and all the Gods indivisible. The Gods are the inner principles and archetypes of enlightenment, which is why their primary character is light. It is not ancient superstition they reflect, but unconditioned cosmic awareness. They are the principles of a creative intelligence and objective awareness free of all egoism and ignorance, beyond all illusion and idolatry, free of every bias and prejudice of preconception. They are principles of the highest philosophy of the direct perception of Being itself. They are principles of an all-comprehending synthetic knowledge in which the abstract and the concrete, the archetypal and phenomenal, thought and action, are integrated into a single reality and self-aware self-determination.

The ancient seers worshipped no Gods of superstition, idolatry or duality. They were not below a religion of monotheism but beyond it, in a religion of creative monism in which unity and multiplicity are harmonized by the sense of the Divine in all as the Self of all beings. Such a creative comprehension of the Divine requires the transmutation of our consciousness in the fires of truth perception. This sense of the Divine as creative freedom is the essence of the Vedic Gods. It reflects the spiritual freedom which is the true freedom we are all seeking. This is the freedom not of egoistic achievement that leads to bondage and sorrow, but of self-knowledge and surrender to the Divine in which we find our freedom as Life itself. The principles of that true and eternal Life became the ancient Gods. It is in this light that they are offered here again today in this book that we may discover the deeper truth of what we are.

The ancient multiplicity of Gods in every form — animate and inanimate, concrete and abstract, human and nonhuman — was merely a device for teaching that everything is Divine, all life sacred, that each thing is a shrine for the sanctity, the purity of awareness which is Being itself, the Self of all creatures. It is this sense of the universality of the Divine that the ancient Gods were meant to instill, not some sectarian dogma, idolatry or superstition. This universality goes beyond monotheism and its separation of creator and creation to pure monism, the oneness of the Godhead everywhere that is the culminating realization of the ancient path of light.

Gods and Goddesses

The ancient deities are not merely anthropomorphic entities, Gods and Goddesses in the image of men and women. The ancient Gods represent the cosmic masculine force of which the human male is only one manifestation. The ancient Goddesses represent the cosmic feminine force of which the human female is only one manifestation. The ancients did not merely mirror their relationships between men and women into those between the Gods and Goddesses. Rather, they sought to organize society around organic and spiritual lines with men incarnating the cosmic masculine force and women the cosmic feminine force. They sought to have human sexual relations mirror the relationship between the Gods and the Goddesses, the cosmic archetypes operative at the depths of our psyche. They recognized the place and value of both forces, the cosmic masculine and feminine, and the need for their proper balance both in society and in the individual. Yet this balance was not seen as a simplistic equality. It was the organic harmony of heaven and earth, the mountain and the valley, fire and water, a profound complementarity.

The Vedic Gods and Goddesses are represented by many forms and ideas that go far beyond our sense of the human male and female. Their forms include the phenomena of nature, implements and tools of human activity, aspects of worship and many abstract ideas. Generally speaking, any feminine term is a form of the Goddess and any masculine term is a form of the God, whether it be an animal, a weapon, a luminary or an idea. In fact, none of the Vedic Gods or Goddesses are primarily men or women at all. They all have one side of their symbolism that is anthropomorphic, but this is secondary to other aspects. The main Goddess is more the Dawn than a woman, and the symbolic Dawn of aspiration more so than the dawn as a natural phenomenon. The main God is the Sun more than a man, and the symbolic Sun of the solar Self, the enlightened consciousness, rather than the mere Sun of the natural world.

As the English language, unlike Sanskrit, does not have word endings that indicate masculine and feminine cases, most God and Goddess terms from the *Rig Veda* are neutralized in translation. This is compounded by the lack of understanding by most translators that case ending was not an inessential custom but an important means of delineating the dual cosmic powers and their qualities. The effect of this has been to obscure and limit the place given to the Goddesses in the hymns.

The Goddess is the hymn itself. She is our soul which alone has the power to invoke the Gods. She is the word and the God is the meaning or song. Hence the Goddess is always present and revered in the hymns. She is the very process of worship, the chant itself and its rhythms. Yet for this same reason the Goddesses are seldom invoked separately. As hymns are usually to the Gods, it has been thought by many scholars that the Goddess had little place in the Vedic religion and by this that women held little esteem in the culture. Yet in these hymns to the Gods we usually find numerous forms of the Goddess and numerous feminine terms, which have an integral importance and equally complex association as the terms for the Gods. A hymn said to be only to a God may have many such feminine associations with which the God is combined, perhaps identified with or made secondary to.

Some of the most abstract terms for the Godhead in the *Veda* are of the feminine gender and even the most masculine Gods can be invoked in terms of feminine qualities and symbols. The seers themselves frequently compare their spiritual work with that of a woman; mother, sister, wife, or lover of the Gods. If we restore these major feminine terms, as listed in the glossary, to their sense as the Goddess, we will find as great a place for the Goddess in the *Rig Veda* as at any time in the history of India.

For the ancients, all life was a manifestation of two forces, the cosmic masculine and feminine, what could also be rendered as the electric and the magnetic and which have many different levels of manifestation. Their purpose in setting forth these two powers was not to fixate us on an original and unresolvable duality. They reduced all things to two complementary forces like inhalation and exhalation as an intermediate step to their resolution into unity. The ancients' preoccupation with the two forces was not a fixation on sexuality but the working of an organic intelligence which, through seeing the complementary nature of all dualities, brings us to the consciousness of unity in which the mind expands into the Godhead. They saw all nature as the manifestation of two complementary forces through which there is an original and inviolable unity. Their language and its science of giving masculine and feminine appellations to all manner of terms is a means of instilling in us the perception of complementarity through which there is unity. That is why in the end the two forces are combined, united or intermingled or merged into the neuter sense, the Godhead beyond duality. That is why there is no strict division between the two and why, through their full extension, like inhalation and exhalation, they generate a single energy of life.

Yet that supreme Godhead is not presented only as a neutral term. It can also be thought of and approached as the supreme God or Goddess, or as both in their state of union. It is not merely neutral but the essence of all beings, the essence of the male, the maleness of the male and the essence of the female, her femininity itself. There is only one essence that makes unique all things. So, too, the masculine and the feminine reflect a certain truth of the Godhead itself, certain qualities within it. As Being or will (Sat), the Divine has a masculine quality; as Consciousness or force (Chit-shakti), it has a feminine quality. These constitute the twofold, all-encompassing nature of the Absolute; a complementarity within unity which is the natural expression of that unity.

The Goddesses are everywhere in the ancient hymns. They are the qualities complementary to those represented by the Gods and all that has been said about the Gods is also true of the Goddesses, what they represent and how they are presented. The Goddesses are the powers through which the Gods manifest and by which they are invoked. The hymns aim at the greatest sense of universality, which the creative multiplicity of Gods and

Goddesses intimates. In the hymns, the Gods and Goddesses move back and forth through each other and each becomes the other. It is this unity or universality that the hymns teach, not the primacy of a single God or Goddess. It is the primacy of an infinite creative reality they teach, not the ultimacy of any form or quality.

Mantric Language

Mantra is the original form of all language, the original language from which all others derive. Mantric language, to define it succinctly, is language in which sound and meaning correspond. It is like poetry wherein the sound of words reflects their meaning and aids in its manifestation. More than this, it is a science of sound wherein the meaning and force of all sounds is known and developed towards mergence in the Divine Word.

To the organic logic of the intuitive mind, words are not mere arbitrary designations for various objects, with sound and meaning corresponding only through the incidence of custom and usage. Rather, the sound projects the meaning, partakes of it and is not separate from the object it names. Such names are not mere words that veil the being or essence of things with the memory associations of the externally directed mind. They are not names in our ordinary sense at all. They are the essential sound-idea behind the object that evokes its being, which becomes the tool whereby its essence comes forth and is grasped. They are the mantric names of objects which arise within the mind in meditative perception, as the mark of entry of the being of the object into the fabric of the mind.

Such mantric names cannot arise when we cast our labels and titles upon things, when we place our arbitrary values, judgments and determinations upon them. These reflect our manipulation of objects rather than what they are in themselves. Mantric names arise spontaneously when we open our minds to the being of things in choiceless observation. They are the vibration of the mind uniting to the being of the object in the unity of seeing. As such, they serve to invoke and to become that state. Mantric names, by their psychic connection in being, arouse in us the essence or archetype behind the object, serving as a catalyst to allow it to come forth in its spiritual significance. In the mantric sense, therefore, to name is to know the nature of a thing, to touch its essence.

Such mantric names do not reflect merely an arbitrary cultural usage. They reflect the archetypal vibrations behind all phenomenal objects, the vibrations of the Divine Word itself. This is not a religious belief, but the vibratory energy of cosmic intelligence that informs all things. Such words are ways of contacting the Word of God, which is not the word of some anthropomorphic deity, but the creative vibration at the heart of life in which all life is a unitary movement. Mantric language is the Word of God made manifest, which is not a set of moralistic commandments but the cosmic principles in all things, whereby their unique nature is comprehended. This Divine Word is the Word of Life, in which rest the organic laws of creation. It is the word that lets things be, which enables the soul of things to come forth by receptivity. It is the word-law of the essence, of which all nature is an effusion and evil is only the attempt to selfishly limit its flow. Such a language is a cosmic language that attunes us to the cosmic creative vibration which we are isolated from by the inertia of our animal and social conditioning. It is this language alone that can comprehend life and its fluid harmonies, that can qualitatively extract the essence of things, whereas our present rigid languages shadow life in artificial concepts and quantitative values in which all things are reduced to some manipulative or material value that denies their soul or timeless significance.

Such a mantric language is called a revelation or scripture. All the world's great scriptures have some sense of it. It is a multidimensional intuitive language that combines symbol, myth, legend, ritual, alchemy, yoga, philosophy and theology — all inner and outer ways of knowing. In it everything becomes archetypal and takes on a cosmic meaning, reflecting the universal, the eternal and the infinite. Mantra is the language of the soul wherein we feel all life as cosmic and sense each thing as a unique revelation of the all. It is the language of truth realization which reveals the vibratory structure of all objects within the unitary field of consciousness, unveiling their eternal being. Mantra is the basis of all religion, language and culture because it alone can manifest the eternal laws by which anything can endure or have any real order and harmony. Only through such mantric language can real change be possible for humanity because it bears the ascending creative vibration that brings about all transformations. All true creativity, thinking and perception partakes of this mantric language whose most original, extensive and primal manifestation for the human race came with the ancient seers of the Himalayas, through which they brought forth human culture in the beginning.

To understand the *Rig Veda* or any ancient teaching or scripture requires this sense of mantra, this different approach to language that takes all things as evocations of the cosmic being. Such words become means of unification for ourselves and our environment with our true nature. Their meanings are not artificially limited, but expand creatively towards a universal comprehension. Such a language really has only one word, which is the cosmic word of truth and harmony. It has only one message: that all is Divine, all a formation of the Divine Word. It has no practical message for the mind, nor any social, political or intellectual meaning or bias. Its purpose is to break all the barriers of the mind and merge it into the unity of cosmic intelligence — to break all our limiting constructs and dissolve the mind into the direct seeing of unconditioned being.

Mantric language develops organically from various roots which are its prime mantras. In later Tantric texts these were called "seed-syllables" or "bija mantras." As such, mantric language can always be consistently understood in terms of its prime root meanings. It is always etymologically decipherable. These roots do not possess rigid meanings. They are currents of meaning that unify. They reflect a way of being that manifests on all levels, a quality of energy, a spectrum or vibratory range of meaning that has a certain characteristic but no single indication. They are like prime numbers from which complex equations can be evolved, but into which they are always resolvable. Such root sounds can never quite be put into words or defined in any final manner.

There is the root "Vas," for example, which has three major sets of meaning. In the first, it means "to shine," like the light of the sun as it rises in the morning. In the second, it means "to be," as in the sense of to remain (English "was" being a derivative of it). In the third, it means "to put on," as to wear something. Yet we find that all these meanings are related under the common idea of what is pervading or encompassing. Light is what fills, pervades and manifests being. It is also what encompasses, defines, invests or clothes us. Hence illumination, being and investiture merge into a single yet more primordial idea. As such, in its deepest sense "Vas" means the plenary light of being and in the general sense it means the Divine itself (Vasudeva). Such mantric root meanings are designed not to give us precise, rigidly defined terms with exclusive meanings, as does our current analytic, intellectual language. They are meant to instill in us a sense of the universality of meaning in the prime value that is being itself and which is the Divine. They are the tools of a synthetic and organic comprehension designed to lead us into the oneness.

We can find such roots remaining in English also, though randomly dispersed and less systematically developed. There is the Sanskrit root "Stha," meaning to stand, to be, to be present, to endure, to stop or be still, also what stands, is hard or firm, and so on. English has this root as its "st" sound with a similar meaning; to stand, be stable, to stop, be still or to stay. We have things which are hard or firm as stone or steel; things which stand as a stick, a stake, a staff, a stalk, a stamen. As a place to dwell or to stay we have a stall or a stadium. To step is to take a stand, make a stand or go from stand to stand. Closely related are such words as strong or sturdy and hence the strong or male animal as the steer, stallion or stag. Negatively, as what has stood too long, we have stagnant or stale, or related terms as stiff or sticky, or even to stink. To be sterile is to be stagnant, to be incapable of creative change. To stare is to stop one's vision and fix it on something. A stoic is a philosopher who can stand or endure all the vicissitudes of life. By similar extensions and modifications, according to the vowels and consonants added to the "st" root, we can use it to comprehend nearly all our "st" words. Combined with prepositions or in the middle of words, we can use it to comprehend many more words such as establish, exist, ecstasy, install, system, which all have a determinative "st" sound.

We see, therefore, that language does not develop arbitrarily but organically according to root-sound-meanings. The artificial usage and development of our language has obscured this, but cannot efface it, for without it no real language is possible, no poetry and nothing scriptural.

The ancient seers developed their language consistently along these lines. They remained conscious of these broad sound-symbol-idea correlations with multiple plays on words. A typical hymn may have dozens of such associations. These our language cannot produce, and we can hardly imagine them to be possible according to our more precise sense of meaning. Hence, most translators miss them altogether. The ancient language has much more depth than ours. Its meanings are much more fluid, intricate and subtle, with abstract and concrete, spiritual and material senses combined. It is like a multidimensional gestalt pattern that can be read on many different levels. With a shift of perspective, we can change levels and elicit a whole new strata of meanings. We open up an entire new domain of knowledge by understanding its symbols; for example, now in terms of myth, now in terms of alchemy or yoga, now in terms of astrology, ancient history or the highest spiritual truths. The *Rig Veda* is like the Glass Bead Game of Herman Hesse's novel *Magister Ludi* — a musical mantric system upon which we can play the essence of all knowledge. Yet unlike the intellectual sterility that limited the Glass Bead Game, it has an intuitive creativity that opens us up to the domains of cosmic intelligence and unconditioned perception. The depth and variability of meaning that can be read into these mantras is beyond the conception of most of us. They contain universal analogues which comprehend all forms and levels of knowledge — the creative power and myriad strata of the Divine Word itself. The ancients saw in them and through them the awe, magic, mystery and wonder that only distant quasars may still evoke in our more conditioned intellectuality.

Through these prime roots, all terms of the Vedic language resolve themselves into unity, not by overt philosophical statements, but by the natural coalescence of their meanings into the Divine. The ancient seers employed an intuitive language designed to open up the depths of our being to the oneness of existence. The language itself is the secret teaching, hidden in the sounds of the words and letters. The complexity of symbol, metaphor and even riddles we find in the *Veda* is the reflection of this sense of one in all and all in one. The meaning of the mantra is oneness in which all words resolve themselves into the Divine Word of the silent mind, the mind vibrating in harmony with all life. To understand the ancients and the spiritual roots of our civilization, we must remember the mantric form and meaning of their language.

Method of Translation

This translation differs radically from most Vedic translations, particularly those of scholars or intellectuals who have no real mystical background or understanding of mantra. The language is taken here in an inward, spiritual and abstract sense, whereas most other translators aim at the most concrete, literal meaning, even to the point where it often becomes incomprehensible. This translation is not literal. However, the ancient language itself, consisting of mantric sound-symbol archetypes, is never literal either. Literal translation is often not possible, and all translators are compelled by the fluidity of the language to shift their translations of the same term even in the same hymn. Vedic words are expansive in their meaning, not restrictive as is modern language. They have whole ranges of meaning both abstract and concrete. Here, the inner, more abstract sense is given its place and priority. It regularly makes perfect sense, is consistent etymologically and reveals various word plays within the hymns, which otherwise would be inexplicable.

The term "Vrka," for example, appears to mean a wolf. Etymologically it means "what tears," from the root "vrasch," to tear. Yet in one passage it clearly means a "plow." Our word wolf could certainly not also mean a plow. The Vedic term could because the general etymological sense still predominated. By this sense of root meanings, the ancient language has a more abstract sense and is only symbolically or superficially concrete. Vrka is "a tearer," by image a wolf, but also anything that tears, including not only an evil man but the Gods as destroyers of darkness. To take all these terms concretely and literally — wolf, cow, horse, etc. — does violence to the language and makes it seem primitive when it is really the organic language of a higher intuitive intelligence. Another example is the word "Prthivi," which usually means "the Earth" and is almost invariably so translated. Etymologically it means what is wide or broad. Yet the only hymn to Prthivi is not to the Earth but to the power of the atmosphere, as again the abstract sense of wideness prevails over the concrete connotation.

Most notably is the case of the famous Vedic Cow, "Gau." Its range of meaning is so great, we have nothing even close. Gau is symbolically a cow. Generally, it is anything that comes from a cow, is made from a cow or is somehow cow-like. From the cow as the basic wealth of the ancients, it meant wealth, nourishment and value generally. Yet even this is only the beginning. It means a ray of light; the rays as the cattle of the Sun, its wealth and nourishing force. As such, it more generally means light (which is the best equivalent for it most of the time). Light for the seers was also consciousness. The Cow was the receptive mind, the tame or docile soul (as the Vedic herdsman was like the good shepherd of the Bible) or wisdom that gives nourishment and propagates itself like cattle. The herds of the seers, the cattle they milk are their truth-perceptions, words or mantras. The Cow is the soul that is the being of perception whose field is that of the senses. The Cow is the Divine Word-Wisdom at the heart of the soul which yields all boons. As such, the cow is the Goddess, who is inwardly consciousness and outwardly the sky, the dappled cow being the night sky with its stars. Or the cow in the masculine tense can be a general term for the Gods as powers of light and the wisdom-word. The variegated cow is the Sun and its manifold rays.

There is an additional root "Ga," meaning "to sing." The Cow is the singer, as is the soul. Yet it is also a note in the song. The cow in its most correct sense means an archetype, word, note or number, the essential unit. It is knowledge that is the measure of all things and which grows and overflows organically. This sense comprehends all the other meanings of the word. The Cow is the basic archetypal symbol of reality that is the beneficence of consciousness. How, therefore, can we translate Gau as Cow? It reduces and violates the actual usage of the term and ignores many deeper implications and etymological word-plays. All translators are compelled to render the term Gau as cow, milk, leather, a ray of the sun, the sky, the earth, a word or chant. Why should we accept only the broad range of concrete connotations when the abstract ones are equally applicable and relevant?

This same trend applies to all Vedic terms. There is the word "Pasu," from the root "Pas" meaning to fix or bind. It is usually rendered as cattle, which are bound or kept in a stall. But there is also the root "Pas" meaning to see. These are not two separate roots. To see is to fix in form; to pierce, penetrate and possess. The cattle of the seers are their perceptions. The hymns play upon this dual meaning of the root: "Yours is all this that can be seen (pasavyam, or relating to cattle), which you see (pasyasi) by the eye of the Sun" (VII.98.6). As the Sun is elsewhere the Self, the sole Seer, we can hardly suspect such abstract implications not be have been intended. In giving the inner or spiritual meaning of the text, perception is more accurate than cattle, which is only the metaphor. It is also as etymologically literal and justified.

Another example is "Ghrta," which means literally "what is heated or clarified" and by image is clarified butter. Yet in its usage, it fills Heaven and Earth, drips from the Gods and so on. Inwardly Ghrta means clarity, the clarity of awareness transmuted by the heat of concentration. This sense is quite consistent with its cosmic implications and also is as etymologically sound. To render it only as clarified butter is like calling the Milky Way (our name for the galaxy, a term also found in the *Rig Veda*) not a galaxy but a stream of milk.

There is the frequent solicitation in ancient teachings for cows and horses (if we insist on a merely concrete sense of these terms) and other forms of outer wealth. This is understandable to our idea of the ancients as primitive people. We imagine them praying to their nature Gods for the forms needed to sustain their simple lives. Yet it does not do justice to the connotations of these words. They can generically mean wealth or prosperity outwardly, or inwardly as measures of abundance. This also ignores the fact that the Vedic Cow is usually light and the Vedic Horse is usually the Sun. In the mystic sense it is the cosmic cow and cosmic horse that are sought, which are spiritual knowledge and energy.

In fact, the ancients really had nothing that we would consider as a substantive noun, no word that meant only a specific object like a cow and only a cow, or a man and only a man. Their words retain a general adjectival character that can be related to several objects, as Vrka, wolf and plow. We find this in some older languages that exist today, like that of American Indians such as the Hopis, which are similarly generally adjectival in nature. Yet we cannot translate Vrka as a tearer. It would not make sense to us. What is necessary is to bring in both the abstract and concrete senses of the Vedic words and relate them to the spiritual meaning and orientation of a scripture. This is what I have attempted here. It has been done with consistency to etymological meanings, and to grammar and phraseology insofar as English allows. The translation has been done directly from the original Sanskrit text of the *Rig Veda*, and it is not based on any other translation. It has more in common with the modern spiritual translations of hymns of the *Rig Veda* coming from India, like those of Dayananda Sarasvati or Sri Aurobindo, than any Western versions.

Anyone familiar with the Sanskrit of the text knows the variability of the language, its broad and, by our sense, sometimes bizarre metaphors, the multiple meanings of single words and the apparent large number of synonyms. There is nothing definitive or authoritative about any Vedic translation, and to arrive at their more primitive sense of the book, translators will often change or ignore grammar and etymological meanings of terms. They translate the same term in different senses in the same hymn or in different hymns. Even so, they label some passages as hopelessly or wilfully obscure. To get their more literal, primitive and concrete meanings, they have to take as much freedom with the language as is done here — only theirs is a negative freedom that reduces the meaning of hymns which everywhere expand into cosmic proportions. It is possible to show word by word, according to grammar and etymology, the meanings set forth here, but it takes too much space and is not of interest to the general reader (I have done this elsewhere for more specialized publications). To this end I have included a glossary of key Sanskrit terms and their range of meanings.

The basic method I have employed is to go to the etymological meaning of the root in both its abstract and concrete senses and set forth aspects of each for an integral comprehension with, however, the more inner, abstract sense predominating over the outer, concrete connotation. Each term or mantric word represents a stream of archetypal sound-symbol-meaning of which we can only indicate the current. To fix the meaning artificially as with the words of our own language is to ignore and violate the ancient usage of language itself, which was radically different than our own. It is not enough merely to translate their terms into our terms, as their linguistic background and usage was of an entirely different order. Some sense of that background has to be translated also to make their full stream of associations understandable. This accounts for the variability and complexity of some translations I have given here, which is to some extent unavoidable given the radically different nature of ancient language.

It is not a matter of merely finding equivalent terms in English, which seldom exist, but of revealing a totally different, more spiritual, mantric language — which English must be stretched considerably to even intimate. It is not a case of simply translating from one contemporaneous language to another, like French poetry into English, which itself can be difficult. It is translating from one kind of mentality to another, from one world-age to another, from a creative and intuitive language of open meanings to a fixed and intellectual language of closed meanings. There is no simple meeting of these two languages and mentalities. The ancient mantras cannot be reduced to modern English. English has to be expanded to incorporate them, which is what is attempted here. Vedic phraseology has been preserved where possible, which accounts for some unusual sentence formation and syntax.

The ancient language appears primitive at first with its endless references to cows and horses and solicitations for food and wealth. However, as we get to know it better, we find a wealth of deeper associations emerging, multiple meanings of words justified by manifold word plays in the hymns themselves. We find these terms used with abstract and cosmic connotations we would never associate with them. Finally, we reach a point where the ancient language spreads its wings for us and we find an inexhaustible depth of meaning, etymological associations of vast proportions moving on multiple levels. After this, we find the English language to be a much poorer, more rigid and less expressive tongue. It is like the difference between organic food from the garden and junk food from a fast food restaurant. We understand why the ancient language was called mantra and said to be the language of the Gods.

Constant in appearance today, constant to-
morrow. They follow the eternal nature of the
Lord of Heaven.

Blameless throughout the thirty regions, one
after the other in an instant they encompass the
Spirit.

She knows the nature of the first day. Luminous, from the dark she is born turning bright.

The maiden does not diminish the nature of
truth, day by day reaching the source.

As a young girl beautifying her body, Goddess you go to the God who adores you.

The resplendent young lady, smiling from
the east, reveals her bosom,

As a beautiful bride adorned by her mother,
you reveal your body for the vision.

Auspicious Dawn, shine for our furtherance.
No other Dawns can attain this splendor of
yours.   — Rig Veda I.123.8–11

2
CHANTS TO HEAVEN AND EARTH
AND CHANTS TO THE DAWN

Heaven and Earth as the Divine Father and Mother I.159
Seer — Dirghatamas Auchatya

1. I laud with sacrifices at the sessions of knowledge great Heaven and Earth, wise in consciousness, who flourish in truth, parents of the Gods, who with the Gods through most wonder-working intelligence bestow all boons.

2. And I meditate with invocations upon the Father's harmless, undeceiving Mind and the Mother's mighty Self-power, prolific parents who made the world for their children, with all-around wide immortality.

3. Your sons, perfect in their work, most wondrous in action, generated the Mighty Mothers for the Original Consciousness. To uphold the law of all that is stable and moving, you guard the station of your son who knows no duality.

4 Those of magic wisdom power, most wise in consciousness, have measured out of the Sisters of common origin, the twins of common home. The most luminous Seers have extended in Heaven, in the depths of the sea, a continuity that is ever new.

5. That today is the adorable grace of the solar creative Spirit. We meditate in the creative impulse of the Divine. For us, Heaven-Earth, with benevolent awareness, found a hundredfold luminously rich splendor.

Heaven and Earth as the Divine Father and Mother I.160
Seer — Dirghatamas Auchatya

1. These two, Heaven and Earth, are bliss-giving to all. They are the truthful pair, the two seers and upholders of the region. The wise twins of perfect birth, be-

tween these Goddesses the God, the bright Sun, travels
by the law.

2. Widely spacious, mighty, inexhaustible, the Father and Mother guard the worlds. Heaven and Earth are
most daring and beautiful because the Father has ever invested them with forms.

3. The Son of the parents, the carrier-flame, the purifier wisely intelligent, purifies the worlds with his
magic wisdom-power. He milks out forever for his luminous milk the myriad-colored Cow and the prolific Bull.

4. Among the skillful Gods he was most skillful,
who generated Heaven and Earth that give bliss to all,
who with the perfect will measured out the two regions
and with undecaying pillars united them.

5. Thus sung, mighty Heaven-Earth, found for us a
great inspired knowledge, a vast lordly power, whereby
we may forever extend over all the peoples of the work.
Infuse in us the most wonderful vigor.

Heaven and Earth as the Divine Father and Mother are the basis of
ancient cosmology, Father Heaven and Mother Earth. In this sense they
are not simply the worlds, but the transcendent Divine principles which
manifest through them. The Father and his harmless, undeceiving mind
is Shiva, the supreme Being. The Mother, who has the mighty Self-power,
is Shakti, the supreme Consciousness-force. The beneficence of Heaven
and Earth rests upon them. The world of nature is their gift of vision to
us to lead us up into the immortalities of their higher nature.

Their Son is the Sun, the Divine Seer, of which our souls and their
power of perception are the rays. That Son who knows no duality, who is
the light of the twin-powers, is our own immortal Self in the heart that is
our inner Sun. Heaven and Earth exist through the vision of this Divine
Son-Sun, originating from it and giving impulse to it, in the spontaneous
stream of mutual creation that constitutes life, throughout the Heavens of
the mind and oceans of the heart. Our place on Earth is to grow in
consciousness by that creative impulse, flourishing by a creative vision
and action which is open, free and giving to all, just as the worlds
themselves demonstrate.

Yet Heaven and Earth are not just the Father and Mother, they are also
the two Mothers, the mighty Mothers of truth. It is the feminine principle
that represents the creative power, the world-nature. The masculine
principle represents the transcendent, the uncreate being. She is all the

worlds and he is the spirit that moves within her. She is the shoreless cosmic Waters and he is the Fire, the Sun which burns within her. The two Mothers are also twin Sisters, as everything earthly stems from a heavenly archetype. As such, they are Heaven-Earth, the dual world, as a single entity.

To the ancient seers, all life was good, all creation beneficent. The difficult ignorance and darkness of the material world they viewed as a daring adventure for the spirit. This assumption of form by the spirit in Heaven and on Earth they did not see merely as a veil on its formless being, but also as a free expression of it. The seers lived in the beauty of the first day of creation in which the Heavens are on Earth. All who similarly learn to see, to cleanse their minds of the darkness of memory and self-centered thinking, will find that first day forever, in which the inherent beneficence of creation puts all doubts about the meaning of life to rest.

Resplendent with Clarity VI.70
Seer — Barhaspatya Bharadvaja

1. Full of clarity, resplendent over the worlds, wide, vast, honey-yielding, beautifully formed, Heaven and Earth, by the law of the Lord of Heaven are up-pillared, prolific, undecaying.

2. Inexhaustible with an abundant stream, rich in milk, they yield clarity to the perfect worker whose vow is pure. Rulers of all this world, Heaven-Earth pour in us the seed that is auspicious to men.

3. Wise Heaven-Earth, he who apportions the offering to you for right action, that mortal reaches perfection. Through his creativity he is born from the law. From you are poured diverse forms of a common nature.

4. Heaven and Earth, encompassed with clarity, resplendent with clarity, sprinkling clarity, who increase by clarity, wide, vast, placed foremost at the worthy invocation — the sages adore them as bliss for furtherance.

5. Mix the honey-bliss for us, Heaven and Earth, you who pour honey, who yield honey, whose law is sweet. As the Godhead holding the sacrifice and the treasure for us, grant us a great inspiration and an heroic vigor.

6. Heaven and Earth, Father and Mother who know all, magic-workers, overflow a rich energy for us. Heaven and Earth, who give bliss to all, in common delight infuse in us the vigor, the splendor and the victory.

Heaven and Earth are filled with clarity and sweetness for the seer. The clarity, literally "what is clarified," is symbolically the clarified butter. The sweetness is the honey or the honey-wine. The beauty of the natural world is to instill in us the clarity of perception, in which the essence, the honey-bliss of nature, comes forth overflowing from every side. Our whole life through them can be a milking out of that Divine bliss of truth creation.

✳✳✳

HYMNS TO THE DAWN, USHAS
Human Aspiration as the Spiritual Dawn

All human life rests upon a fundamental aspiration to know the truth. The human being is the spiritual being in creation and it is our real human nature to seek the true, the eternal and the infinite. Human life, in its proper quality and dimension, is a prayer, an aspiration to manifest the Divine light. The real action of Man is to generate the Dawn of truth in creation. The soul of man is the Dawn, the yearning for the light. His is the labor of awakening to the universal being. The Dawns of aspiration are the strivings of humanity. They are our lives and the secret work of our soul behind them to discover the truth of creation hidden within and around us. Each of our incarnations is a day of our soul, as it strives for a greater and greater unfolding of its light towards the eternal day, the perpetual Dawn of immortal life. We are given in each birth a new dawn to take us to the inner light. This whole science of rebirth was symbolized by the ancients in the stream of days and nights, the risings and settings of the Sun as our soul towards an eternal day.

The soul of man loves the truth, for the soul is the wisdom that is the prelude to the manifestation of the Divine within us. The soul of man loves and attends the light as the Dawn loves and attends the Sun. All life, all creation is a great and universal Dawn, the unfolding, the flowering of being to being, light to light, in the glory of the ever new. The truth of the Dawn, therefore, is that each moment is a new creation and a new flowering towards the Divine. The life of the true man, the seer, is lived at the heart of the Dawn, in a perpetual day, with each nuance of the dance of life a new revelation of the overflowing light of Divine beneficence. We are each in our own way striving towards our Dawn, struggling to awaken, to express our true Self, to manifest the light within us and unite it to the light around us.

To be in harmony with life, with the Divine dance that it is, is to be awake at every Dawn. This is to see the Dawn that is everywhere, in all things, the unfolding and the aspiration, the burgeoning splendor of existence. This is the Vedic Dawn, the Dawn of noble wisdom. It is Ushas, which means to aspire, to burn, and to bloom. She is the ardor of the wisdom that seeks ever to grow. She is wherever the light comes forth and gives us a sense of our deeper aspirations, our longing for something immutable beyond the distracting affairs of our everyday life. The Dawn, that aspiration within us all, is something holy. It is the power of the Gods, the energy of the Divine to rediscover itself in the cosmic dream. This primal state of prayer and aspiration, which is the Dawn, is the pure mind, our own mind in its clear and purely receptive state as an awakening of love. She is the virgin who gives birth to all the Gods, as it is through the pure, innocent and open mind that all Divine powers are able to manifest. As we yearn for the Divine, so it comes into being within us. Whatever we aspire to most completely in our being, that we become. We are the magic of the Dawn. She is the virgin of pure mind that gives birth to the Divine Son, Sun of enlightenment, the Universal Self who is all the Gods — the Oneness in which there is wholeness and Divinity.

To proceed along the path of light, to enter into the ancient and eternal religion of light, we must first invoke the Dawn. We must invoke the Dawn within ourselves by allowing our secret aspiration toward transcendence to manifest itself. Life is short. We cannot forever set aside the voice of our soul and its longing for the Divine, its vertical aspiration to go beyond all mundane concerns if only for a moment. We must nourish that aspiration which is often a discontent with ordinary attainments. Whatever we have achieved, we must be willing to set aside that we might continue to grow, for life is in the growing; what has been accomplished is its shadow. This longing of human beings for the Divine Light is as old as man. It is the origin of our being and our culture. To open up to it in the hymns of the ancient seers is to discover the unity of all men in the labor for the truth. It is to look into our most distant past and find ourselves.

There is nothing really foreign to us in all humanity, in all creation. In all is the same aspiration to live, to grow, to love and to know. It is the same Dawn struggling to emerge behind all of our labors, however confused. In these ancient hymns we see the innocent, original aspirations of humanity in the early days of our world-age. That sense of the Dawn, of the direct and simple life of the Oneness, remains always. We have become more complicated only in our thought and the environment it has refashioned for us. Life is always in that primordial simplicity, the innocence and ever-newness of the Dawn. This the seers saw when our race was still new and young, still in the Divine glimmer of its own childhood.

Goddess Human in Mortals VII.75
Seer — Maitravaruni Vasishta

1. Heaven-born by truth the Dawn has shone out. Revealing her majesty she has come. She has concealed the unwelcome, hateful darkness. As the foremost of the flaming seers she has set the paths in motion.

2. Be awakened today for our great and happy journey, oh Dawn, into a great auspiciousness extend us. Goddess human in mortals, hold in us a wonderful splendor and glorious revelation.

3. The wonderfully clear immortal radiances of the Dawn have come for the vision. Generating the Divine laws, filling the interior realms, they have spread afar.

4. When she is yoked from the beyond, she travels around the five races of men in an instant. Surveying the ways of knowledge of men, she is the daughter of Heaven, the queen of the world.

5. Full of power, the maiden of the Sun, possessing a wonderful beneficence, she is the ruler of the plenitude of splendors. Lauded by the seers, giving maturity, the beneficent Dawn shines, sung by the carrier-flames.

6. Wonderfully bright radiant horses appear conveying the flashing Dawn. She travels luminous by her chariot of the universal form, as she grants the ecstasy to harmonious mortals.

7. The truth with the truth, great with the great, the Goddess with the Gods, holy with all the holy ones, she broke down the firm limitations and dispensed the radiant mornings, as her rays roared to greet her.

8. Now hold for us an ecstasy made of nourishing rays and heroic force, oh Dawn, the all enjoyment made of swift energy. May our mere humanity not stain this altar. Protect us with the powers of well-being forever, oh Gods.

The Dawn is the Goddess human in mortals, our true humanity of loving aspiration and awakened sensitivity which leads us on our path to the Divine. She unites all men in a common spiritual labor and breaks down all the barriers between ourselves and life. She is the Divine love in our true humanity which manifests all the Gods or Divine powers, and prepares the way for the Sun of enlightenment. Man is the dawn of the Gods. Until we are willing to return to the Dawn of creation, we shall fail to be really human or humane.

The Birth of the Eye of the Gods VI.76
Seer — Maitravaruni Vasishta

1. The universal Man, the Divine creative Sun, has spread aloft his immortal all-generating light. By the will of the Gods, the eye is born. The Dawn has revealed the entire world.

2. The paths of journey to the gods have appeared to me, unhindered, perfected by the beings of light. The illuminating ray of the Dawn has come into being from the east, returning from the west, from the mansions of warmth.

3. Abundant were the days which were before in the rising of the Sun, when as playing with a lover the Dawn was seen as one who would never leave again.

4. The primordial seers, bearing the truth, were the feast companions of the Gods. Our Fathers found the secret light. Their mantras of truth generated the Dawn.

5. The Dawns have come together in a common wideness. They possess a common knowledge and do not against each other strive. They do not diminish the laws of the Gods, unhindered, uniting with the beings of light.

6. Auspicious Goddess, the Vasishta seers who awake at dawn, exalted in your presence, adore you with hymns. Queen of power, the guiding Goddess of the light, shine for us; Dawn, be the first to burst into song.

7. She, the guiding Goddess of the graces of the joyful truth, the shining Dawn is sung by the Vasishta. As she assumes in us a splendor of far revelation, protect us with the powers of well-being forever, oh Gods.

The Dawn of aspiration gives birth to the eye of the Sun of knowledge. She is the Divine lover of men who seek the truth. This Dawn of our human aspiration was generated by the ancient seers, recorded in the *Vedas*, but remains hidden in our own hearts, wishing to unfold again and fulfill its promise of true humanity for all in the spiritual light. The Dawn is the true man who sees and sings the truth. It is to her we must return for a new creation. The Vasishta seers, which means "most full of light," are the seers of these seven hymns to the Dawn. Our ancient fathers with the mantras or meditations of truth first brought forth the Divine Dawn for humanity, which remains as our spiritual legacy.

The Guiding-Goddess of the Days VII.77
Seer — Maitravaruni Vasishta

1. She beams like a young maiden as she approaches, arousing all life to motion. The Fire has come into being for the enkindling of man. She has made the light, driving away the darkness.

2. Facing all, extensive, she is arisen. Bearing a lustrous garment she shines bright. Of golden color, a most visionary presence, the Mother of the light, the guiding-Goddess of the days is illumined.

3. Now auspicious she bears the eye of the Gods and leads the visionary white horse. The Dawn appears manifested by her rays, possessing a wonderful beneficence pervasive unto all.

4. You whose presence is beatitude shine afar the unfriendly; make for us a wide and fearless field of light. Ward away duality, bear to us the plenitudes, energize the power of grace for the singer, Goddess beneficence.

5. Shine in us with your most beautiful beams, Goddess Dawn, as you deliver our souls. Hold for us, you who have all boons, an energy, a grace, made of nourishing rays, swift energy, and means of conveyance.

6. Dawn, daughter of Heaven, perfectly born, whom the Vasishta seers with their intuitions exalt, may you assume in us a vast and sublime splendor. Protect us with the powers of well-being forever, oh Gods.

The Dawn of aspiration brings the day of awareness, of clear consciousness, wherein we follow only the dictates of our soul. Once we accept our aspiration to the Divine this aspiration to greater awareness becomes our real impulse in life. Our way becomes clear and what we need to do becomes apparent. We no longer exult in our personal darkness, but accept the Divine will in life and its orientation of our life towards the light. We learn to shine in the presence rather than to dwell in the darkness of our personal thoughts and emotions based on memory. We learn to have faith in life, to love and to accept the truth, to be open and humble and giving to a reality that is pure grace.

The Beneficent Daughter of Heaven VII.78
Seer — Maitravaruni Vasishta

1. Her original illuminations appear, aloft her clear adornments open wide. Dawn, turning towards us with a vast, light-made chariot, convey to us beatitude.

2. The Fire enkindled flares to greet her. The seers welcome her singing with their thoughts. The Divine Dawn comes, driving away all darkness and error with the light.

3. The effulgent Dawns have appeared from the east, extending the light. They have generated the Sun, the sacrifice and the Fire. The unwelcome darkness has fled away.

4. The beneficent daughter of Heaven is conscious. All see the effulgent Dawn. She has mounted her chariot yoked by the Self-nature, which well controlled swift horses bear.

5. As we awaken in right-mindfulness for you today, both ourselves and our benefactors, let your effulgent Dawns be abundantly fruitful. Protect us with the powers of well-being forever, oh Gods.

The Dawn is the divine Daughter, the discernment that springs from the wise and discerning Father. It is the discrimination between truth and falsehood, between what unites us with others and what separates us from them, that heralds the Dawn. Through this she is conscious, conveyed by the Self-nature, our sense of natural oneness that is the shining of the inner light. Her light generates the sacrifice, for it is the nature of the light to give, to offer itself, in which offering is the greatest fruitfulness.

The Path-Goddess of Men VII.79
Seer — Maitravaruni Vasishta

1. Awakening the five human peoples, the Dawn has shown out as the path-Goddess of men. She has diffused her lustre with visionary, bull-like rays. The Sun with his vision has opened up Heaven and Earth.

2. They manifest their rays at the ends of Heaven. Like people at work the Dawns strive on. Your rays, oh Dawn, turn away the darkness. They extend the light like the arms of the Sun.

3. The beneficent Dawn has become the supreme power of the Divine warrior. She has generated the revelations for the blissful movement. The Goddess, the daughter of Heaven, the foremost of the flaming seers, dispenses the plenitudes to the perfect worker.

4. Such grace grant us, Dawn, as that you disclosed for those who originally lauded you. You whom they generated by the roar of the Bull opened out the doors of the impenetrable mountain.

5. Stimulating every God for grace, energizing the joyful truths for our vision, as you shine out for us hold our souls for the victory. Protect us with the powers of well-being forever, oh Gods.

All the five human races find their unity in spiritual aspiration, the seeking of the cosmic and universal. These are the five temperaments of human beings according to the predominance of the five elements in our nature. The Dawn of aspiration is the path-Goddess for all mankind. She is the lady, the loving spirit, that stimulates the male, our inner power of conscious action, to the spiritual work of unification. It is her beneficent presence that puts all men to their proper labor in harmony with their natures and with other men. This is the Aryan ideal of a spiritual society organized around the pursuit of enlightenment and its natural unfoldment.

The Dawn as the seeking of enlightenment is the passive or feminine spirit who conveys the power of the spiritual Man or Divine warrior (the Vedic God Indra), generated by the Bull of the Spirit to awaken men through love and the consciousness of service. She is the Goddess who is the key to all the Gods. She is wisdom itself that gives each thing its proper place in the cosmic order.

A New Eon of Life VII.80
Seer — Maitravaruni Vasishta

1. As she draws apart the ends of Heaven and Earth revealing all the worlds, present at Dawn with hymns of affirmation, the Vasishta seers, as the original sages, have awakened.

2. Assuming a new eon of life, having concealed the darkness, she, the Dawn, is awakened by the light. Youthful, she remains unblushing at the front, when she has made conscious the Sun, the sacrifice and the Fire.

3. Full of energy, rays and vigor, let the Dawns shine forever auspicious, overflowing, yielding clarity to every side. Protect us with the powers of well-being forever, oh Gods.

The awakening of our Dawn, our urge and impulse to enlightenment, is our entry into a new eon of life. We move from the materialistic order of the ignorance into the spiritual order of the knowledge. We move from the domain of mortal life to that of immortal life.

That Dawn is a beautiful unblushing maiden who makes everything else conscious, aware of her and her light, as she is the light of spiritual aspiration that lights up and gives color and meaning to all life. She is the purity and innocence of the soul that brings the Divine light and makes mortals conscious of their own inner lives and secret aspirations. She establishes us in our true heart and opens our joy in our creative unfoldment towards the infinite.

As Sons to the Mother VII.81
Seer — Maitravaruni Vasishta

1. The luminous daughter of Heaven appears approaching. Vast, she encompasses and drives away the darkness for the vision. The beautiful lady makes the light.

2. The Sun, the rising radiant star, releases aloft his companion rays. In your breaking, oh Dawn, and that of the Sun's, may we realize our portion in the Divine.

3. Quickly may we awaken, fronting you, daughter of Heaven; you who lovely convey all that is desirable, bliss as ecstasy to the harmonious mortal.

4. Shining Goddess, you who great by greatness create the perception of the Sun-world, as partakers of your ecstasy we implore you, may we be to you as sons to the Mother.

5. Bear to us that wonderfully bright fulfillment which is far revealing. Daughter of Heaven, that which is the mortal enjoyment, grant it also that we may experience it.

6. Granting our illumined souls the revelatory knowledge of a plenary immortality and for us a power full of nourishing rays, Goddess of the joyful truth who energizes all beneficence, Dawn, shine away all error.

The Dawn is the Mother of men. She is the aspiration in nature to manifest the spirit which has evolved the human being. She is the longing in the human heart to know the truth of things, that impels us to awaken to our true humanity as spiritual beings, as cosmic entities, lights of the universal intelligence. She is our longing for purity and clarity that makes us open to the truth. She is the ideal we form, our muse, and the impulse to realize it. Before we can know the Gods, discover the Divine powers and cosmic truths, we must first invoke her and gain her grace, not as some Goddess outside ourselves, but as the very purity and transparency of aspiration necessary to go beyond the corruptions of our conditioned nature.

We must once more establish a new dawn for ourselves and for the world as a whole. We require again that daring vision to unfold a new creation of light, no longer bound by the old materialistic groping and the darkness of selfishness and the clinging to security in outward things. We must remember and again bring to life these ancient spiritual aspirations from the childhood of our race. What have you done with your Dawn, oh Man? Where is your heart? How far have we gone astray from our original grace. We must again return to the Divine Mother, as children to the Goddess that we may regenerate our world and society in the grace of the Divine.

II

THE FOURFOLD GODHEAD

THE FOURFOLD
GODHEAD

The ancient seers recognized seven planes of existence. The *Rig Veda* is pervaded with this sevenfold symbolism. These are matter, life, mind, intelligence, bliss, consciousness and being. Matter, life and mind form the triple phenomenal realm which is all that we ordinarily know. This is the realm of the ignorance ruled by karma, whose main entity is the ego. It includes occult planes of life and mind beyond our ordinary perception, which we enter in sleep and after death. We ordinarily know life and mind as manifested in physical matter. They also have their own planes in which their characteristic subtlety and freer motion can manifest.

Of this lower triple realm the mind is Heaven, life the Atmosphere and matter the Earth. These are the three basic or lower worlds of the *Veda*. Matter (anna) is physical matter, but actually all three lower principles are material, that is, principles of insentience or vehicles of manifestation. Life (prana) is the vital force that includes emotion as we know it, wherein the subtle forms and energies of things exist. It is based on desire and fear, manifested as the impulses to expand life and avoid death. The mind (manas) is the consciousness born of memory, built of karmic reactions and evolutionary latencies, which includes the intellect. It grasps the ideas, laws and principles behind things and becomes our externally directed material intelligence which is no real intelligence at all. What we usually call the mind is not a power of conscious perception, but a kind of organic computer operating through compulsion and preconception, projecting and modifying its conditioned pattern but never free of its programming. These three principles constitute the lower, material, ignorant or undivine half of existence. Yet they are also the vehicles for the manifestation of the Spirit, and when conquered through self-knowledge become the instruments, the perfect tools of the Divine Creator to fashion the formless truth in living forms.

Being, Consciousness and Bliss (Sacchidananda) form the triple Absolute or Godhead, the transcendent, unborn and uncreate. They are also principles of a common existence, not differentiated from each other. They are a Being which is not material but spiritual, a Consciousness not based on mental conditionings but on unconditioned awareness and an intrinsic Bliss not dependent upon external pleasure.

The intermediate principle between these two great triplicities, the mediating fourth factor is Intelligence or Wisdom (vijñana). It is the causal principle and its plane is that of the ideal, archetypal or noumenal. It is the creative power, the Divine creative being, through which the universes are envisioned. Whereas the higher three principles of Being-Consciousness-Bliss are the transcendent Godhead, Intelligence is the immanent Godhead. Whereas the higher three principles are vibrationless, the Intelligence is the subtlest vibratory state behind creation. It is the realm of eternal law, of all-encompassing creative will and design. Through the eternal laws of being, this Intelligence possesses an integral comprehension and consistent right action. Through this fourth principle we can know the truth of the Absolute above and also harmonize the phenomenal realm below, changing it from an inertia that veils the Spirit, to a dynamism which manifests it. The key, therefore, to all spiritual growth and higher evolution is the bringing of this Intelligence or Wisdom into function. It brings the capacity to see the Self in all beings and all beings in the Self.

This Intelligence, along with the triple Absolute of Being-Consciousness-Bliss, is considered as the fourfold Godhead in the *Vedas*. These four constitute the higher or Divine half of existence beyond ignorance, karma, rebirth and sorrow. Intelligence is the manifestation of Being-Consciousness-Bliss, the creative and dynamic unity of the three. Consciousness, Bliss and Intelligence can also be regarded as creative or causal principles, a triple creative or causal being, with Being as the fourth, their immutable and transcendent unity. As usual, all spiritual formulations are fluid and many-sided because they reflect not a restrictive formulation of matter, but an integral being of the Spirit. As the fourth is the unity of the three, sometimes only three principles are spoken of; the laws of three and four being thus the same basic law. All four principles form an integral unity and each contains the other. They differ only in emphasis, and each can be designated in terms of the others. Hence the Gods, which symbolize them individually, can also symbolize them as a whole or can at times stand for any one of them.

These deities are not metaphysical theories of an intellectual ideation. They are truths of existence found through direct perception, choiceless observation of what is. The purpose of their explication here is not that we might have some theory for intellectual speculation. It is to give us a guideline for meditative practice that we might open to the vast integrality of existence through them. They are not principles of philosophical dialectic set forth systematically. They are an overview of the mantric logic of existence in which all is one and one is all.

Being is expressed primarily by the God Indra, the foremost and chief of the Vedic Gods. He represents the supreme truth beyond all falsehood, the ultimate entity, conscious perceiver, or spiritual Man, the sole reality in the universe. Even more so Indra represents the manifestation or realization of this truth. He is the archetype that we must energize in order to bring it forth. It was not the concern of the seers merely to give us some intellectual idea as to the ultimate truth. Their concern was, through mantric knowledge, to arouse its manifesting archetype within us — within our deeper psyche — appealing directly to the deeper levels of the mind. It is this inherent archetypal Intelligence, the mantric nature of the Divine Word, which the hymns arouse. The supreme being of the mantra is Indra, the Bull or Spirit of the chants. He is life itself in its highest aspiration as the will to always exist and triumph over all the limitations of external fate. His symbol is lightning or direct illumination.

Consciousness is expressed primarily by the God Agni, the sacred Fire. He is the supreme, immutable and inextinguishable awareness that persists through and beyond all changes, the flame which, even in the depths of darkness, never goes out. His is the force that sets everything in motion, the primal light and energy which exists behind all transformations. Vedic Fire rituals are actualizations of this supreme Consciousness-Force in its universal movement, and mirror the rhythms and right action of the energy of awareness.

Bliss is represented by Soma, the God of the mystic nectar or honey-wine, the elixir or ambrosia of immortality. His symbolic form is the Moon that gives joy to all. He is the communal essence of bliss in which all creatures partake of the oneness. He is the delight hidden in all things that is pressed out by the power of concentration and direct perception. He is the eternal happiness and unbounded love from which the creation comes and which we all must seek. Vedic Soma rituals mirror the process of the descent of that bliss in the practice of yoga.

The Sun (Surya) represents Intelligence, the illuminating and functional light of truth. As this Sun of Intelligence is the Divine creative being, the principle of multiplicity in unity, there are many different forms of Sun-Gods. The Sun is the integral Godhead, the immanent Spirit, whose various rays are all teachings, all the Gods and all the worlds.

Within the Sun exists the Moon, in which in turn exists the Fire. Within the Fire exists the point of light, the lightning or conscious Self. We find these symbols of the yogic process in much of the art of the ancient world and in Vedic symbolism. They are also common symbols in Tantric yogic texts, which derive from the *Vedas*.

While this is the general system, by their underlying unity these four principles are frequently found combined in various ways. Indra and Soma, Being and Bliss generally combine as immortal life and eternal joy. Fire and the Sun combine as Consciousness and creative Intelligence. Indra and Agni combine as Life and Light. Agni and Soma combine as Light and Joy. Soma and Surya combine as Bliss and Wisdom.

All four are principles of Self-being and powers of Self-knowledge. In their essence they are formulations of One Reality. They are principles of infinity through which all the universe, manifest and unmanifest, is resolved into the unity of our own being. The fourfold Godhead or Brahman is the fourfold Self or Atman, which is the integral comprehension of pure unity.

We may consider such spiritual ideas too grand and abstract to have been hidden in these primitive ancient hymns. We tend to ascribe philosophical ideas to a much later stage of human history. Yet we should remember that our religions come from the ancients and religion was the realm in which the ancients excelled. A simple outer life and a profound inner life go hand in hand. Spiritual truths do not require a massive technology, large cities or well-printed philosophical volumes to be understood. Complex intellectual ideas do not indicate spiritual realization as much as these powerful and primal symbols. Such sound-symbols require a direct and unconditioned perception of the cosmic life. This perception was possessed more by the ancients than by ourselves. They had the raw direct experience which became the philosophies and religions of later ages. Because they lived in the light they did not require a theory about it.

AGNI

May we abide in the right thinking of the Universal Man, for he is the Ruler resplendent over all the world.

Born from here he perceives the entire universe. The Universal Man extends himself through the Sun.

Present in Heaven, the Fire is present on Earth. His presence has entered all the plants.

The Universal Man, the Fire, by enduring force is present. May he protect us from harm by day and by night.

Universal Man, let that Reality of yours be. May beneficent splendors attend us.

— Rig Veda I.98

Energize the Word Goddess for the Fire, the Bull of the peoples. May he deliver us across duality.

Who from the supreme beyond shines across the shores,

The Spirit with his luminous heat who consumes all evil,

Who discerns all the realms of being and envisions them together,

The Fire which on the other shore of this region was born luminous — may he deliver us across duality.

— Rig Veda X.187

3
AGNI

CONSCIOUSNESS-FORCE, THE SACRED FIRE

The Flame of the Sacred

Consciousness is a Fire. It is not a concept. It is not a matter of thought, speculation or imagination. It is pure presence without issue, life without boundaries — the burning bush. It is the flame of ecstasy that puts out the half light of thought, banishes time and space, penetrates into the deepest primordial recesses of creation and endures.

The ordinary human state, the state of mind or thought, is not the conscious state. It is not the awareness of the universal life, but the dream of the ego, of the me and the mine. It is a form of sleep in which we dream in the cocoon of our separative thoughts. We are not satisfied with what we know, with what thought determines for us through its capacity to measure. We continue to try to expand the frontiers of our knowledge, to project it further in time and space that we might eventually arrive at the origin or goal, the truth of things. Yet, however far we project our mental knowledge, it remains thought — the measurable, name and form bound by time and space. It remains phenomenal and does not reach the essence. We have information and out of it project various theories, but in the end we still do not know the reality of things. We fail to see and to be. We do not touch existence, but only refine the burden of our explanations and opinions. Inside of us there is a Fire, a longing to know. We try to satisfy that longing with the fuel of external knowledge, but it consumes it all and burns more intensely. Whatever we arrive at with our minds as an answer to this burning desire to truly know is found eventually to be insufficient. The mind can reason, speculate, even conclude, but life is different, always more, always containing another dimension or level wherein our knowledge fails us and is not sufficient to give us peace.

Thought, our ordinary consciousness, is smoke, not fire. It suggests or intimates but can never really illuminate. Its half light can be blinding and breeds many illusions. It provides a sense of light and warmth, but no real heat and radiance. There comes a time, therefore, when we realize its limitations, when the Fire within us wells upward, when we open up to life itself and see how restrictive our preconceptions have been. It is only then that we begin to really see, for it is the Fire of life alone that truly perceives. Life is a movement in consciousness that thought cannot reach, but only dimly reflect. Life is not how we live or what we think about it. It is the endless and interrelated dance of the Flame of existence, in which all life is a perpetual consummation.

All life is burning. It is moving, changing and turning in transformation. Within all life abides a flame of love and creation that goes beyond all the boundaries of what thought can define. This burning is our true life, the flame of consciousness that burns inextinguishably in our hearts — the flame which is the heart. All life is but an offering into that Fire. Each being in life is not a separate entity but a portion of the fire, a twisting dance of the flame of life. This is what the ancients meant when they said that all life is a sacrifice, and why they set forth the sacrifice as the religion of light. All life is a sacrifice, an endless series of mutual offerings, a giving which is also a receiving, a complementary rhythmic exchange within the Oneness. Living is giving; a single interdependent movement in which each being partakes of the whole and the whole partakes of each being. To give is to give light because it breaks down the separative barriers of darkness and demonstrates an illumination which has no horizon. This burning state of giving which bestows warmth and radiance is the flame of life, the inner Fire of the cosmic religion of oneness.

This state of being, which is an offering of oneness to oneness, is consciousness or true awareness spontaneously awake to the unity of all things. It is life that knows itself in the giving, that in giving receives of itself in all. The basic law of the eternal religion is to give because giving is the act that demonstrates the knowledge of oneness, our reunification with the all. Consciousness is a sacrificial awareness that sees each thing as an offering to the totality — each being as a holy offering of life to life. This sacrificial awareness — this capacity to sacrifice our own preconceptions and be open to the open-ended movement of life — is the revelation of the sacred. We are all sacrificial masks for the eternal being in its play of self-manifestation. The being and consciousness of sacrifice, this deep prayer and reverence for the sacred being of all, is the Vedic Brahman, the Godhead of the Absolute. It is the supreme truth of the Fire, the pinnacle of the Flame of Life.

It is the dignity of man that he bears within himself the consciousness of sacrifice, that he has the capacity to give himself for the good of all. This is not a matter of personal virtue that some of us may be able to cultivate. It is the nature of the Divine Fire within us, the nature of consciousness itself which is beneficence. When we are willing to sacrifice our preconceptions about life and the identity we cling to, we invoke within us the Divine Fire that is our true Self. What is sacred is thus the sacrificial mind that is ever willing to set aside the accumulation of its past knowledge and look at life with open eyes, with the eyes of Fire. This state of reverence for all life, in which we set aside all our attempts to manipulate it, is the being of reverence that is the Godhead. To become conscious of the sacred nature of life is to accomplish the real sacrifice, the inner surrender of our manipulative motivations and struggles. It is to be reborn in the Fire of presence, to enter into the heart of life as a seer. This inner offering requires that we no longer think, judge, analyze, criticize or in any way try to gain some special position or advantage for ourselves. It is to know that the center and the periphery are present at every point where life sees itself.

From this choiceless consciousness, which is the sacred and inviolable nature of life, these hymns to the Fire originated. They were not invented by thought, by the cunning or imagination of the human brain. They were seen by the seers in the truth of existence which is sacred and sacrificial. They are the mantras of the state of seeing which partake of the immortality of life's vision. They are the spontaneous arising of the irrepressible flame of the heart, the Fire of inspiration, of which genius is only a spark. They are the sacredness of being, finding its own voice in transformation. They remain as a door to that eternal flame if we would see them with the eyes of life — if we would learn to have power within and inspire the world as true human beings, rather than languish in external stimulation and entertainment.

Fire is the omnipresent mystery of the Godhead that is the indefinable light in all things. It is hidden in and can manifest from all things. It is the spirit latent in the body and mind that comes forth like magic when our thoughts are still. All spiritual work, all yoga, is like the kindling of a fire or feeding of a flame. The alchemy of fire is the great metaphor of the yogic opus. This great God, Agni, is thus the leader of the great cosmic ritual of spiritual evolution. We all contain that Divine spark, which will begin to work within us when we seek the truth, not as a speculative venture but as a real yearning for the light no thought can encompass.

An Ocean of Oneness X.5
Seer — Trita Aptya

1. An ocean of oneness, the foundation of splendors, he perceives the manifold births from our heart. He holds to the breast in the lap of the two secret ones, in the midst of the fountain-source, the hidden seat of the bird.

The Fire of Consciousness is the eternal sea of the oneness. This Fire grows in the Waters. It is the light that blossoms in darkness when we see the unity of the opposites, of subject and object, man and nature in the eternality of existence. That universal being of the flame is our own Self, the dweller in the heart, who perceives all our births, all existences. The two secret ones are Heaven and Earth which are hidden within us as the creative powers of our own mind. The fountain-source is the heart that is the hidden abode of the bird, the eagle of the soul.

> 2. The mighty ones who dwell in a common lair, the strong horses have come together with their powerful mares. The seers guard the seat of truth. They hold in secrecy the supreme names.

This is the image of the unification of our life-energies in the flame that is the seeing of life. The seers speak the language of the Fire, of symbol and mantra, not to hide anything from anyone. It is simply that the truth of life is a matter of inner awareness, a secret of the heart which can be alluded to but never definitively put into words.

> 3. The two truth-bearing Sisters of magic wisdom power conceive him. Having formed the child, increasing him they give him birth. The center of all that is stable and moving, the seers weave by the mind the thread of the seer.

The twin Sisters are Heaven and Earth as the dual creative power without and within. They are also the dawn and the night of the sacrifice, our births and deaths, our awakenings and our states of peace. They are the complementary dualities of life, like inhalation and exhalation, that between them generate the energy or intensity of awareness which is the Divine Son or Fire. He is the center, the wordless source, around which the seers weave the tapestry of their mantras to invoke him within us.

> 4. Born perfectly from the paths of truth, the energies of earlier Heaven hold to him for vigor. Heaven and Earth, wearing him as their investing power, have increased him with the clarity and substance of their honey-bliss.

Earlier Heaven is the causal or archetypal world that manifests through the Divine Son or spiritual man. Heaven and Earth increase him as their beloved child, as the world exists for the birth of the Spirit, the coming forth of the Fire. He is the child who when born consumes his parents, the Spirit who reabsorbs both the worlds into his pure awareness.

> 5. Desiring the seven radiant Sisters, the knower
> bore up their honey-bliss for the vision. The ancient
> born labored in the atmosphere, searching he found the
> covering of the fostering Sun.

The seven radiant Sisters are the Goddess-powers of the seven levels of existence. The Divine Son, the seer, absorbs their bliss. They are the energies of the seven chakras or spinal centers wherein spiritual knowledge dawns in man. The atmosphere is the world of manifestation between the two polarities of Heaven and Earth or mind and body. The spirit works to spread apart Heaven and Earth, to open up the atmosphere for the greatest extension of life. It is only in this fully open life that the Divine can manifest. The covering of the fostering Sun is the veil of light, the light of truth which blinds the ignorant but which the wise turn open like a door, seeing it as the radiance of their own Self.

> 6. The seers fashioned seven frontiers. Along only
> one of them the straight and narrow path will go. He is a
> pillar of immortal life in the lair of the supreme. Where
> the paths diverge he stands in the upholding laws.

The seven frontiers are the seven realms of existence, the three Heavens and three Earths and the seventh realm of the Self or the Spirit, where the straight and narrow path to immortality leads. It is the origin of all the paths, the heart of all realms, their central pillar of light.

> 7. He is being and non-being in the supreme ether,
> in the birth of the discerning Father, in the bosom of the
> infinite Mother. The Fire for us is the firstborn of truth.
> He is the Bull and the milch Cow in the original eon.

What can one say after a verse like this? Such is a revelation, a scripture, the mantras of the ancient enlightened seers. The Fire is our Self, the eternal flame within our hearts. As the individual Self or Divine

Son, the Absolute or Divine Father is born into his own creation through the receptive consciousness that is the Mother of all things.

The Divine Self is both immanent and transcendent. He is the firstborn in creation, our own central being. How otherwise could we know the truth and for what other reason would he create the world? He is both the Bull, the symbol of the cosmic male or Spirit, and the milch Cow, the symbol of the cosmic female, matter or Nature. The original eon or world-age is the immortal life of the Oneness, in which the Son becomes both his parents. It is the pure life of unity with nature and our own inner nature, the original paradise of the pure mind. To that original life of pure unity, all life through man is striving to return. Therein alone is peace.

This Immortal Light in Mortals VI.9
Seer — Barhaspatya Bharadvaja

1. A day that is dark and a day that is bright, two regions revolve in ways to be known. The Universal Fire, like a king in his birth, dispels the darkness with the light.

The night is the ignorance and the day is the knowledge. They are not only day and night but the dark and bright fortnights of the Moon and the northern and southern courses of the Sun. They are life and death, expansion and contraction, unification and separation, spirit and matter. Our direction in life, whether we grow or decline spiritually, depends on how we understand these two forces and place ourselves under the rule of the light. What dispels the darkness is that flame of true perception, the wakeful seeing, in which these two forces are comprehended. He is the king of all the worlds.

2. I know not the thread, I know not the cross-thread, nor that which they weave in their coming together, moving back and forth. Whose son beyond his father below will through him speak the words to be spoken here?

3. He knows the thread, he knows the cross-thread, the words to be spoken in season he speaks. He is conscious of truth as the guardian of immortality. He descends through another, the one beyond who sees.

The thread and the cross-thread or warp and woof are the fabric of creation composed of positive and negative forces, the interplay of the two region's lights. The son beyond is the Divine or inner son of conscious perception, the offspring of our inner labor of spiritual awakening. This inner child is the flame of our aspiration, the being of our creative force. The father below is the mortal mind, the ego or separate self, that must surrender its rule to find the truth, to give the Divine son, the ever-youthful king of direct awareness, his proper domain.

The mortal mind cannot know the immortal being. Its knowledge is inherently mortal; that is, limited by time, space and duality. Whatever the mortal mind knows, even its idea of God or enlightenment — whatever is produced by thought based on memory — creates the veil of a presumption to know, obscuring the deeper reality that inherently transcends thought.

The inner fire of truth perception delivers his father, or the conceptual mind, and accomplishes his work to discover what is real. He speaks the truth in its appropriate season, for he knows the ways of light and the ways of darkness. Through the receptivity of his father, the surrender of the mortal mind, he is able to descend into the lower material world. He is given a voice, while remaining as the one beyond who sees.

> 4. He is the original invoker. Perceive him, this immortal light in mortals! Resting in the eternal he is born, the deathless one flourishing in his own Self.

The inner Fire is the power of consciousness that invokes, originates or directs all things since beginningless time. He is the immortal light through which alone any perception is possible, the ground of our mind. When we come to rest in the eternal, when our sense of values is spiritual, giving precedence to unity and to giving, we are reborn within as the Divine child who never dies. He ever lives in our heart as the magic child of Divine love.

> 5. The eternal light is placed within for the vision, the swiftest consciousness among the speeding senses. All the Gods of common mind and united perception converge perfectly in that single will.

Through the light of the eternal alone do we see, because all seeing is a cognizance of the transient or moving, which is only possible from a background center that is fixed or eternal. Unfortunately, we become so

lost in the shifting spectacle that we forget the seer on whom it depends
and which is its true being. Caught in the seen, we do not really see. Above
all we do not see ourselves, and thereby miss the ground of seeing in which
alone things are revealed as they are. Our inborn spiritual consciousness
by nature ever moves in front of our shifting thoughts and sensations. Our
faculties of perception are our Gods or powers of light. If we remain
mindful of them and their power, they all harmonize and come together
perfectly in the single will of the great high God, our own immortal Self.

> 6. My ears move wide to hear, wide my eyes to see
> this vast light that rests within the heart. My mind opens
> wide, an understanding that goes beyond. What shall I
> speak, indeed what can I think?
> 7. All the Gods surrendered to you in awe, oh
> Flame, as you endured throughout the darkness. May
> the Universal Man further us with his grace, may the
> deathless one further us with his grace!

When the light of the heart irradiates the senses, everything becomes
a vast light. The mind becomes too wide even for thought and one no
longer needs to say anything. One is immersed in the awe of the inexpressible being that is life itself, in the wonder of the flame of Divine love
which renders all things immortal in the instant.

This Divine flame of life and consciousness endures immutable
through all time and inspires all men forever. All the Divine powers and
qualities take refuge in it. All the cosmic powers stand in awe before it as
the supreme mystery of existence. This flame, the energy ever to grow, is
the working power in nature that builds up all the worlds. The Divine
flame gives light to the stars and brings the light of life to matter. This
same flame burns painfully in man and makes him seek a higher dimension of existence than time and space. It discontents him with apparent
boundaries and divisions and impels him to seek union and understanding
with all. That flame alone remains in the darkness of ignorance when all
other Divine powers are hidden or extinguished. It is the flame of the inner
will to grow and transcend, which in spite of all opposition remains true
to itself. It is the sense of ever-new life that leads us to continue regardless
of how we have suffered. It is the flame of feeling, of true sensitivity, in
which alone life is intense and meaningful. That flame of sensitivity is the
true and Universal Man through which all human beings labor towards a
common understanding. It is our sense of the deathless being in all beings
whereby we see all things as sacred and treat all beings with respect. It is

our Divine will to burn with rapture in the endless and integrated overflowing which is life.

This final verse also refers to the higher or mystic night, as the regions revolve in several ways. The mystic night is the dark night of the unknown Absolute, the pure unity beyond form, in which all the Gods and senses are put to rest and in which time, space and all creation are abolished. It is the Absolute in which the flame of Self-awareness endures immutable and alone, having absorbed into itself all the worlds. That is our true being, the role of the human being as the spiritual being in creation who bears the flame of the uncreate.

The Foremost Station of the Bird III.5
Seer — Gathina Vishvamitra

> 1. Conscious, facing the Dawn, the Fire is awakened, the sage, the guide of the seers. A wide force enkindled by God-seekers, the carrier-flame has opened out the doors of darkness.
> 2. The Fire, who is to be adored with hymns, grew through the songs and affirmations of the singers. Enjoying the manifold vision of truth, the accomplisher has shone out in the breaking of the Dawn.

At the Dawn of enlightenment, the Fire of consciousness, from its origin as the ever-present flame of aspiration hidden in the dark night of ignorance, explodes at last into the Sun of cosmic awareness. The rising of the Sun of truth is only possible if we have maintained the flame of our awareness through the long nights of our suffering and discontent.

> 3. The Fire has been placed in human peoples, the child of the Waters, the friend who brings perfection through the truth. Beloved and holy he has mounted the summit. He is the sage to be invoked by thought.
> 4. The Fire becomes the friend when enkindled, the friend as the invoker, the Lord of Heaven as the knower of all beings. He is the friend as the master of the sacrifice, the inspired lord of the house, the friend of the rivers and the mountains.

The fire of truth is the Divine friend (Mitra) in man and the friend of all life in whom is real compassion. This flame of friendship unites all

men and all life. This flame of relationship does not allow itself to be put
out, but struggles to grow into the sunlight of beneficence for all. Awareness is our true friend and the protector of all. It opens all nature to us.

> 5. He protects the beloved fissure, the highest station
> of the Bird. As a mighty stream, he guards the course of
> the Sun. He protects the seven-headed truth at its center.
> Sublime, he looks over the ecstasy of the Gods.

The Fire is the cosmic Bird, the eagle of the Spirit. The beloved fissure
is the cliff-nest of the bird, the secret recess of the summit-consciousness
of the Absolute. The seven-headed truth is the truth of the one Supreme,
present on all seven levels of existence. Our inner flame guards this truth
of the Supreme from the secret cave or source within the heart, the place
of the solar-soul.

> 6. As a magic craftsman, he fashioned the adorable
> lovely nature, the God who knows all the ways of wis-
> dom. The ground of the essence, the clarity-filled sta-
> tion of the Bird, that the Fire guards unceasing.
> 7. The Fire, aspiring, has ascended his wide extend-
> ing, clarity-filled source of aspiration. The purifier, med-
> itating clear and sublime, he has made his Mothers ever
> new.

The clarity-filled station of the Bird, his source of aspiration, is his
summit lair in the supreme, the transcendent Brahman. All creation is
renewed when we learn to return our Fire to its uncreate source in the
clarity of pure perception. Through the light of truth vision, all our doors
of perception are cleansed and we see the world made new, in its ever
pure essence of consciousness.

> 8. Spontaneously born, he grows through the plants,
> when as Waters purifying themselves down a slope, his
> Mothers increase him with clarity. Let the Fire guard us
> in the bosom of the parents.

The flame of life is present in the plant, which has received it from
the sun. In the sacrament of eating that flame passes into man wherein it
feeds his soul and becomes the flame of his inner plants, his astral growths
of thought and emotion. We are all growing a garden of aspiration to the

Divine, as this is the natural evolution of our being and of the world nature. The clarity that feeds the flame of perception is, in concrete symbol, the clarified butter that feeds the Fire, the oil distilled from all that we take in.

> 9. Lauded with kindling fuel, a mighty stream, he has radiated out to the summit of Heaven and to the center of the Earth. The Fire, the adorable friend, the spirit within the Mother, the worker will convey the Gods to the sacrifice.

Our inner flame of perception grows and streams upward, opening up for us the cosmic vision and sense of the oneness. By the laws of mystic correspondence, the summit of Heaven and center of the Earth are one, the seat of the Divine Fire. What is above is within; as at the summit, so in the depths. This wisdom of correspondence is the light of the Fire which brings the Gods for the mystic sacrifice. It is the mortal, offering itself to the immortal — offering its feeling of separation to the consciousness of unity, its private accumulation for itself to a giving for all.

> 10. Sublime, with kindling fuel, he up-pillared the vault of Heaven. The Fire is the supreme of the luminous Heavens. He is the mysterious being, whom the spirit in the Mother enkindled from the refulgent seers to become the bearer of the offering.

The spirit in the Mother (Matarishvan) is the power of being in the receptive mind, the life breath hidden in nature. It kindles the cosmic Fire from the seer-powers that preserve and protect it, the guardians of the world. His fuel is all the worlds. That mysterious being who is the supreme Heaven is our own secret Self. His play of light is our true and immortal life.

The Knower of All Births III.1
Seer — Gathina Vishvamitra

> 1. Convey me as the power of the Soma. You have made me your carrier flame for sacrifice in the sessions of knowledge. Shining towards the Gods I work the stone. I labor. Oh Fire, accept yourself.

> 2. We have made the forward-turning sacrifice. Let
> the Word grow. With fuel, with prayers of surrender,
> put the Fire to work. The Heavens have declared the ses-
> sions of knowledge of the seers. For the wise and strong
> they have searched out the way.

The human sage is himself the spiritual fire working on Earth. Man is the keeper of the cosmic fire of intelligence on Earth. So the seer prays to the Fire to accept himself as the sage in his work. He works the stone of our material nature to bring out the secret powers of immortal life.

The sacrifice is the inner offering of the ego to the Divine through the fuel of surrender, acceptance of the Divine will. That sets in motion a fire of inner transformation within us, for which the Heavens, the higher planes of the mind, have a way prepared. In this way the human being begins his true and inner work of ascending the higher planes of the mind.

> 3. Wise, of purified discernment, he holds to the ec-
> stasy, the friend of Heaven and Earth by birth. The
> Gods found the Fire in the artistry of the Sisters, vision-
> ary in the Waters.
> 4. Seven mighty streams gave increase to him auspi-
> cious, white by greatness born red. Born as a child he
> mounts the horses. The Gods marveled at the birth of
> the Fire.
> 5. Extending the atmosphere with luminous limbs,
> purifying the will with seer-purifications, encompassing
> himself with the pure life of the Waters, he has formed
> for himself vast, undiminished splendors.
> 6. He approached them, who are unconsuming, invi-
> olable, the mighty rivers of Heaven, unclothed, un-
> naked. There the ancient yet young Goddesses of
> common origin, the seven voices, conceive a single
> child.

The Fire of perception is born in the confluence of the Waters of inspiration. The Sisters are the muses, the Divine voices within us that sing celestial songs of mysterious immortalities in vast landscapes of creative vision. The Goddesses are everything and nothing, freely assuming manifold forms of splendor for the delight of the inner eye. Their vast and variable creative tapestry generates within us a single sense of pure vision, the purity of all colors in their free display. The Fire is white by nature, that is pure, but also born red, that is creative, as he is both the immanent and transcendent God. The horses are the various Pranas or life-energies over which the Divine Child or innocent mind gains power. It is the childlike awareness which is our true flame. All our energies mount that and move according to its impulse. The horses are the expression of the will of the rider.

> 7. His gathered fuel of every form is strewn at the
> source of clarity, in the flow of the honey-wine. There
> his cows, swelling with milk, have stood up, the mighty
> common Mothers of the wonder worker.
> 8. Bearing himself as the son of power, he has shone
> out, as he assumes luminous forms of beauty with pas-
> sion. Streams of clarity and honey-bliss flow where the
> Spirit by seer-wisdom grows.

The gatherings are all the perceptions gained through the flame of seeing. When we look directly at what is, at things as they are, in a state of choiceless observation, as we may by chance look at a beautiful sunset or distant mountain range with full attention, through that seeing the essence of creative joy comes out of what we see. The essence or ambrosia, the honey-bliss or mystic wine, is extracted by the clarity of perception. The Mothers of the Fire are Heaven and Earth, the worlds, which overflow with the milk of truth when they are approached with the true seeing that reveals the spiritual essence of their beauty. It is the power of concentrated seeing that distills the essence of beauty and delight out of the myriad perceptions of life.

> 9. From birth he found the udder of the Father. He
> released wide its streams, its nourishing currents. Mov-
> ing hidden with his auspicious friends, with the mighty
> streams of Heaven he has not remained hidden.
> 10. He bore the child of the Father and generator.
> Alone he suckled many overflowing streams. Protect for
> him, for the pure spirit, his common wives, his two
> human sisters.

The udder of the Father is the nourishing power of the imperious Bull, the Spirit. It is also the image of the Cosmic Androgyne, the Divine Male-Female or two-in-one Godhead, from which differentiation arises and returning to which there is the overflowing being of the Oneness. His auspicious friends are the seers or his seer-powers, in whom he pours the mighty rivers of Heaven for the cosmic vision that leaves nothing hidden.

As the Cosmic Androgyne, the Fire is also the Mother who bears the child. He is the child that bears himself, the undivided childlike awareness. Or as the Divine child, all things are his Mother and he finds the nourishing milk of oneness everywhere. He is the pure Spirit, the supreme male, the supreme female, both and neither. He is the eternal child that dreams all creation, the child who is parent to all the worlds. His two sister-wives that are human are the mind and body which bear him. We see here how the ancients used symbols and paradoxes to express the highest philosophical truths.

> 11. In unbounded wideness he increased. Manifold glorious floods united to the Fire. The house-Lord rested at the source of truth, the Fire in the artistry of his Sister-friends.
> 12. He holds himself as if inactive in the confluence of the mighty streams, whose light is straight, lovely to be seen for a son, who as the Father generated aloft the radiant mornings, the child of the Waters, the mighty, most heroic Fire.
> 13. The child of the Waters, the beauty of the plants, him the auspicious forest generated diverse in form. The Gods came together in mind at his marvelous birth and put to work his power.
> 14. Vast beams like luminous lightnings hold to the straight-rayed Fire, as they milk out the immortal one who in his self-nature, in the shoreless wideness secretly has grown.

All the creative Goddess powers in the myriad tapestries of their labor in the natural world unite to the seeing-Fire. He is the seeing which is the light of life to the world, as the world exists only for the glory of its vision. That visionary flame works everywhere, as all things seek beauty, harmony and integration. All the Gods or cosmic powers are unified and their energy harmonized when that Divine Fire of the Spirit is magically born by the power of awareness.

The lightnings are the illuminations of the seeing-Fire, which yield his milk of immortality. True seeing is always a series of lightning-like revelations. It is that seeing which is grown in secret in our own Self, as in our own nature alone is the central point of awareness, the integrity of independent being which nourishes the soul.

> 15. Your worshipper, I adore you with offerings. De-
> voted, I adore your kindness and your friendship. With
> the Gods measure out your grace for the singer, guard
> us with the presence of your law.
>
> 16. Companions in your perfect guidance, Agni,
> holding all treasures, powerful by your essential inspira-
> tion, may we overcome the godless powers that would
> assault us.
>
> 17. You became the guiding ray of the Gods, the joy-
> ous knower of all seer-wisdoms. As the lord of the
> house you gave light to mortals. As the master of the ve-
> hicle, granting perfection you go to the Gods.
>
> 18. In the gated house of mortals, the immortal has
> been sitting as king, perfecting the sessions of knowl-
> edge. Whose face is clarity, with wideness he has shone
> out, the Fire who knows all seer-wisdoms.
>
> 19. Come to us with your auspicious friends, great in
> common delight with your great aids. Accomplish in us
> an abundant, conquering splendor and for us the glori-
> ous portion of the perfect Word.

The flame of seeing is the king who sits in the center of the gated house of mortals, in our own body, in the heart. There as the master of the spiritual vehicle, the vehicle of insight that takes us into the Godhead, he perfects the sessions of knowledge which are our lives and our states of consciousness. His seer-wisdoms are the organic truths of life and cre-ation, the secret correspondences that link all things together. He brings to us all the Gods or cosmic powers and links us up to the portion of the Divine Word that we are.

> 20. These your eternal births, for you the ancient
> have I declared anew. For the Spirit these vast effusions
> have been made. In every birth is hidden the Knower of
> all births.
>
> 21. The Knower of all births, hidden in every birth,
> by the Universal Friend is enkindled inextinguishable.
> May we be in the right thinking of that holy one and in
> his auspicious right-mindedness.

The flame in the heart is the individual Self that is the reincarnating entity in man. All creation is his eternal birth, the ancient eternal being who does not die. Every moment of seeing declares this ever new birth of the eternal seer. He is the pure Spirit in which the effusions of the essence of perception are made. He is hidden in all births as the Knower of birth or Knower of all things born (Jatavedas). He is the psychic flame, the fire at the heart of our soul. To know him in all births, in all beings, is to become free of the bondage of rebirth, the compulsion through unfulfilled desire to be born again in ignorance. It is to gain the freedom to act according to our will in all the worlds.

The Universal Friend is the name of the seer of this hymn, Vishvamitra, and his family, but it is also anyone who becomes a friend of all — for it is this seeing of the Self in all beings and all beings in the Self that is this true universal friendship. This is the perpetual and inextinguishable enkindling of the Fire of consciousness. In that wakeful flame is the right thinking and right-mindedness in which there is peace with all. The enlightened maintain the fires of awareness inextinguishable through all states of consciousness; waking, dream and deep sleep. In that the universal manifests of its own accord.

> 22. You who have the good will and the power, delighted, take our sacrifice into the Godhead. Invoking Fire, extend forth now a vast energy for us, sacrifice a great reality to yourself.
>
> 23. Agni, perfect for him who invokes you the all-accomplishing speech, the perpetual victory of the light.
> Let there be a son for our continuity great in his birth.
> Let your right thinking be in us.

The son the seer prays for is Agni, the Fire of awareness as our inner son who takes our sacrifice, our life's labor into the Godhead and grants us thereby the continuity of immortal life. His right thinking, which is a feminine term, is the Goddess-power that gives birth to the flame of the Divine childlike mind, through whom we are born again forever through all the dance of creation as the Knower of all births.

The Cosmic Victory of our Ancient Fathers

The rishis or ancient seers were our original spiritual fathers and creators of our humanity. They found all the ways of truth for mankind at the beginning of this world-age. They seeded humanity spiritually and we are their diverse and manifold progeny which has wandered far. They are the original spiritual archetypes our different human types are striving to manifest. When a form of life departs too far from its seed-potential, when it loses contact with its ideal form or archetype and its potency, it begins to decay. Such is the problem with mankind today. We have lost the sense of our original spiritual humanity and have taken upon ourselves the color or conditioning of our environment, which is presently a world of machines. As such, we are losing the native dignity of our species, losing our center, and becoming more addicted to external influences and artificial stimulations for our motivation in life. We have lost faith in ourselves, in the internal world, and we throw ourselves away on the external world to try to be someone or get something. Yet whatever external recognition we get is never fulfilling, for a real sense of worth is only possible when we are true to ourselves. This mad striving for wealth and recognition creates competition and division, in which in the end no one has a good word to say about anyone else unless they are getting some special advantage in return. All this is called being contrary to reality, stifling the true man.

The true human type — and none of us can find fulfillment in anything else — is the seer, the spiritually·daring human being who works to bring a higher consciousness into the world. He works to perfect creation by sensitivity to the conscious being everywhere. Our true humanity is to recognize that all life is sacred and humane. As it is, most plants and animals are more humane than we are. The sense of spiritual adventurousness, the willingness to open up new ways of perception, makes the true man. It is to rediscover this seer within ourselves as our original human heritage that we look to the *Veda*. It is not some blind mechanical or organic force that is the true power of evolution in the world but this spiritual consciousness. The labor of consciousness is to manifest itself in all the worlds of its creation. This is the highest birth of the Divine Fire in which it reveals its true nature as complete cognition and total recognition of itself everywhere. We start in the middle of a long hymn.

IV.1
Seer — Vamadeva Gautama

> 6. Most glorious is the vision of this auspicious God, most wonderful in mortals, pure clarity as the ardor of the indestructible, the loveliness of this God like the abundance of the milch Cow.
> 7. Three are his supreme truths, the lovely births of the Divine Fire. Pervasive in the infinite, he has come pure, bright, noble and radiant.

The God in whom there is great vision is the Fire, the flame of seeing that illuminates all the worlds. His is the beauty and abundance of the wish-fulfilling cosmic Cow, the Divine Mother, or receptive consciousness of the Divine Word. His three supreme truths and births within the infinite are his triple nature in the Absolute as Being-Consciousness-Bliss. From this infinity he comes to us with all its powers that we might also return to it.

> 8. He, the messenger, the invoker, with golden chariot and blissful speech, the radiant horse beautiful and pervasive, ever delightful as a food-laden feast, desires all abodes.
>
> 9. He appeared as the sacred friend of men. By a vast rein they lead him forth. He dwells in their gated houses bringing to perfection their labors. The God has a common nature of delight with mortals.
>
> 10. Let the Fire, the Knower, lead us towards his ecstasy that is our portion of the Divine, which all the immortals made by the soul, with our heavenly Father and progenitor raining the truth.

Our fire is our will and energy that ever seeks to grow, in the sharpening of which we have interest, capacity and enjoyment. It is the horse or energy that leads us on the path of life. The key to the spiritual life is to discover the spiritual basis of our inner fire, the sense of growth, discovery and acquisition in consciousness that is enduring, rather than in material things which are fleeting.

This inner fire of seeing and aspiration is our portion of the Divine that is our door into the Godhead. It is our soul that all the Gods and our heavenly Father made in the great rain of the light of truth. It has the power to lead us back into the infinities, the freedoms of our nature to be and to see.

> 11. He was born first in bounteous habitations, in the foundation of the vast, at the source of this region, without feet or head, concealing his extremities, putting forth his intensity in the lair of the Bull.
>
> 12. His daring sent forth the first vibration, in the source of truth, the lair of the Bull. The lovely youth, beautiful and pervasive, the seven beloved Sisters generated for the spirit.

The inner fire has its native home in the Absolute, which is the lair of the Cosmic Bull, the Spirit in which it has the freedom and intensity of its own nature, where it dwells in undifferentiated oneness, without high or low. From that supreme plane creation begins as a daring, a will of the Absolute to manifest itself in form. All creation is a challenge and an adventure to express the inexpressible, to bring the transcendent and eternal being to self-knowledge and creative action in time and space. It is only the Divine which can make this possible, and it requires the Divine to accomplish it. The Divine in man takes up this work, which is our true humanity, to strive for the apparently impossible, to become the infinite and the eternal. It is this magnitude of Divine daring that is behind the difficulties of spiritual evolution on Earth, not any Divine mistake — which would be unthinkable. The seven Sisters are the seven powers of creation that bring the Divine Fire into the world to reside as the spiritual being in creatures.

> 13. There our human fathers, striving within, realized
> the truth. The Dawns they invoked led forth the well-
> yielding radiant herds who were imprisoned in the re-
> cesses of the mountains.
> 14. Breaking open the rock they purified themselves.
> Let those who see declare this deed of theirs. Having
> bound their perceptions they gave light to the singer.
> They found the light and cried with their souls.
> 15. With a light-seeking mind, they encompassed
> the massive, impenetrable mountain which held the
> rays. The inspired heroes with the Divine speech opened
> up the hard enclosure of the rays.

In the Divine Fire our human fathers first found the truth for all men and placed the seeds of that truth in our human heritage. The rocky mountain is the obstinate ignorance of the material world which imprisons the wish-fulfilling Cow of our soul and all her radiant herds of perceptions. Our Dawns are our awakenings to the divinity of our soul, our innate dignity, integrity and self-esteem as spiritual beings. These lead forth the nourishing herds of light from the deep recesses of our minds. The wise cleanse the doors of their perceptions and part the mountainous veil of external conditioning, and thereby come to know the truth of their own nature. They bind their perceptions; that is, they concentrate them in the singer, the soul who is the maker of the music of creation, in which all opens into freedom. The Divine speech is the declaration of the word of the soul that all is one — that the oneness which is the Divine is our own innermost nature and song also, in which all is light.

> 16. They meditated out the original nature of the milch Cow. They found the three times seven supreme planes of the Mother. Knowing that, the host roared forth. The radiant Bull was revealed by the glory of the light.

The cosmic milch Cow is the Divine Mother or receptive consciousness which is the ground of all the planes of existence. The Aryan seers always sought the nourishing power of the Divine Mother to give them the sustenance for the highest transformation. Her three times seven supreme planes are the triple Absolute of Being-Consciousness-Bliss encompassing all the seven planes of existence. The host is the group or army of the seers. The radiant Bull is the radiant Spirit, the being in consciousness. The pastoral symbolism reflects the primal nature of these great truths at the heart of life.

> 17. The impenetrable darkness vanished. Heaven shone forth. The luminous beam of the Divine Dawn ascended. The Sun mounted the vast causeway, perceiving the straight and crooked levels in mortals.
> 18. Then awakening from behind they looked all around. Then they upheld the ecstasy that is enjoyed in Heaven. In all the gated houses were all the Gods. Oh Friend and Lord of Heaven, let this truth be for the soul.

Our ancient spiritual Fathers, by the word of truth, their discovering of the Divine Word and creative power at the heart of man, dispersed the darkness of ignorance and found the Sun of knowledge, the sunlight of the unity of all things, in which the different natures of truth and falsehood within us are clear. The seers awakened and became enlightened. They saw all the Gods, the full Divine nature in each of the gated houses which are the bodies of creatures. They saw all beings in the Self and the Self in all beings. They became the Divine light.

> 19. May I speak to the shining Fire, the holy invoker who bears all things. He pierced, as it were, the pure udder of the Cow of light, as if was poured forth the pure juice of the blissful stalk.

20. The infinite Mother of all the holy ones, the timeless guest of all men, the Fire choosing the grace of the
Gods, may he be most compassionate, the Knower of all
beings.

May we ever speak to that Divine flame in creatures, through which
each being is a portion of the Divine and given back its native dignity in
being. It is this sense of the universal flame that brings grace, harmony
and understanding to all. The ancient seers proclaimed the burning bush
of Moses. The philosophers came later and found these symbols unso-
phisticated. But here we see their true power and glory.

IV.2
Seer — Vamadeva Gautama

11. Let the knower discriminate between the knowledge and the ignorance, the straight and crooked levels
in mortals. Oh God, for creativity and for splendor grant
us the infinite and protect us from the finite.
12. The inviolable seers have declared the seer, upholding him in the gated house of the living. Thus, oh
powerful Fire, may you see them visionary and transcendent through your stations according to your way.

The knowledge is what burns, what transmutes our vision, what gives
us the sense of transformation in life. The ignorance is what has no fire,
what stagnates and clings and moves in a devious manner. We must choose
the way of growth if we would live and see, if we would find the daring
freedom of the infinite rather than the secure bondage of our conditioning.
This discrimination between truth and falsehood, the eternal and the
transient, the real and the unreal, the Self and the not-Self is the essence
of the Yoga of knowledge, which here the seers first declare.
The seers are those who declare the Fire of perception, upholding it
in the gated house of the living man, the body and sense of man in harmony
with life. The Fire within us lifts those of us who would see, through its
stations or by its steps, to its vision above, wherein all things are seen
resplendent with the light of transformation as forms of the infinite. The
Fire is the One Divine Seer or our true Self that all seeings declare.

13. Bear the perfect guidance to your declarer, daring Fire, to the one ordained who has concentrated his

delight. Grant the ecstasy to the one who has labored, a
wide lustre for grace that fills the vision.

14. It is this we have accomplished through you, oh
Fire, by our feet, by our hands, by our entire being. As a
chariot driven by strength in the arms, the wise, striving,
have held to the truth.

The wise accomplish the inner alchemical work of the awakening of
the consciousness through the fire in the heart. It is not a matter of mere
thinking but a labor of action, for only when consciousness is held to in
action is its true power brought forth. This work of manifesting awareness
in action was the labor of the seers. It was bringing the light of consciousness into our very physical actions, a full consecration of all aspects of
our being.

15. And now may we be born as the seven seers of
the Mother, the original heroes of the Dawn who ordain
the worlds. May we be the flaming seers, the sons of
Heaven. May we, illuminating the substance, shatter the
mountain.

16. As our supreme and original fathers, Agni, striving for the truth, the directors of the utterance, attained
the pure insight and breaking through Heaven and Earth
revealed the radiant Bull.

The seers are not entities outside of ourselves. They are the seeing
powers inherent within us which the ancient seers opened up for all men
as our inner human heritage. These legendary seven seers are the powers
of seeing native to each of the seven planes of existence. They are the
flaming ones, the Angirasas, which in Greek is Angelos, and becomes in
English the word "Angel." The Vedic Angirasa-seers who first found the
light for man, are our angels, the divine powers within us, the lights of the
Divine Dawn of enlightenment. They are the sons of Heaven who with
the light of the Divine Word break open the mountain of darkness and
deliver the soul of man, illuminating the substance of being everywhere.
This prayer to become them is to realize our true human nature as the
angelic being in creation, the creature who sees by the flame of the
Godhead. The seers remain as the guardian angels or inner guides of the
race.

Each one of us has the power to become the seven seers, to return to
the Dawn and resurrect the Sun out of darkness by the flame of our soul.

In this way the *Veda* remains a living scripture which can transform our lives and is itself striving to speak again as we endeavor to interpret it anew.

Our birth as the seers today is as the birth of the seers of old, for the birth of seeing is eternal. Our ancient spiritual Fathers in their consciousness, with pure perception and the Word of truth, broke through Heaven and Earth and found the primordial Spirit, the impetuous Bull of the heart behind the daring dance of creation. Such is the true accomplishment of humanity compared to which our modern technological feats appear trivial and irrelevant.

17. Perfect in action, radiant God-seekers, forging the Divine births like metal, lighting the Fire and increasing Indra, encompassing a wide field of light, they attained the realization.

18. As a herd in rich fields they knew their perceptions that were the births of the Gods, oh awesome Fire. The aspirations of mortals cried, the noble ones for the increase of the inferior life.

19. We have labored for you. We have become perfect in the art. The radiant Dawns illumined the truth. The undeficient Fire, manifoldly bright, they cleansed the wonderfully lovely eye of the Divine.

The seers transmute the lead, the base metal of the unconscious into the gold of cosmic consciousness. They light the inner fires of awareness and energize Indra, the spiritual man whose sense of Self is in the transcendent. Ours is the inferior life that needs the Divine Fire to add the richness of perception to it. It compels us to aspire for the immortal.

Cleansing our Divine eye of consciousness from the dross of fear and desire is the labor of love that the seers accomplished. They realized the Divine, the infinite and the eternal in their own consciousness, by eliminating all that was limited or self-centered within them.

The White Horse is Born in the Forefront of the Days V.1 Seers — Budha and Gavishthira Atreya

1. The Fire is awakened by the kindling of men. He fronts the Dawn which like the milch Cow approaches. As if mighty rivers gushing forth in a stream, his beams spread across the vault of Heaven.

The Fire is the Divine Light that is brought into creation by our kindling of it within ourselves by the inquiry into truth. Man is the bearer of the Divine flame in creation and it is his place to bring it forth. Man is the keeper of the Divine Fire and is to increase its force on Earth and manifest it here. He is also the fuel for the Fire, as the immortal Fire can only grow by the voluntary surrender of our mortal nature to it. Animals can only follow instinct. We can surrender and give birth to the Fire or resist it and give more power to the darkness.

The Dawn is the cosmic Cow, the Divine feminine. When her light comes forth as full aspiration, the ground is prepared for the flame of awareness to mount in its full nature as the Sun of Knowledge. The rivers, the lights of the rising Sun, are the nourishing rays of Knowledge which come forth when we have been consumed in the Fire of our aspiration for the Divine.

> 2. The invoker is awakened for the sacrifice to the Gods. The Fire, right-minded, has arisen at sunrise. His enkindled power luminous is apparent. Almighty God has been delivered out of darkness.
>
> 3. When he has aroused the circumference of his powers, pure white, the Fire anoints himself with pure light. Then his vigorous discernment is put to work.
>
> Through his tongues of flame, stationed above, he drew sustenance from she who dwells receptive below.

The Fire is the invoker, for all things manifest to us according to the evocative power of the quality of our awareness. As one thinks in his heart, so he is. It is this flame of mindfulness that manifests all Divine powers, the Gods. When the Fire comes forth in full force, he becomes the Sun, the high God that is our true Self. When we are burning in full inner intensity, the Divine Self is delivered out of the darkness of our mortality. God comes forth from man.

The Divine Fire brings forth its Consort-powers, Shaktis, of consciousness-force, of which the foremost is discernment. Discernment is also the capacity to give, as one who discerns knows that there is nothing to lose. His discernment is the receptive mind spread open below like the fallow earth. His tongues of flame, also feminine in gender, are his Goddess-powers that spread forth into his main power of discrimination from his pure nature above.

4. The minds of God-seekers converge in the Fire as eyes in the Sun. When two Dawns of different form generate him, the white horse is born in the forefront of the days.

5. He was born noble in the forefront of the days, auspicious in things auspicious, radiant in the forests. Assuming seven ecstasies in every home, the Fire is placed within as the invoker, most holy.

6. The Fire as the invoker sat within, most holy, in the bosom of the Mother, in that delightful other realm of vision. He is the youthful seer, manifoldly perfect, truth-bearing, the upholder of the peoples of the work who is enkindled at the center.

The minds of God-seers converge in the Flame of Awareness, their eyes of pure perception merge in the Sun of Self-knowledge. The two Dawns are the dawn and the night of the full moon. The latter, our aspiration in the darkness of ignorance, paves the way for the former, the awakening of true enlightenment. The white horse is the pure Spirit born in the forefront or advent of the days of spiritual illumination.

On the horse of pure perception, which is the native movement of the flame of seeing, comes the beauty and radiance of the Divine days, the universe seen in the oneness. This Fire dwells within us in the receptive Mother-consciousness, transforming the world of perception by the delight of clarity.

7. They adore that perfect sage at the sacrifices, the invoking Fire, with hymns of surrender. As he pervades Heaven and Earth with truth, they cleanse the eternal stallion with clarity.

The Fire is the sage who knows him, the seer who knows himself. He is the indwelling consciousness on whom all the peoples, the mind, the sense organs and the breaths depend upon. He is the all-pervasive power of seeing, the Divine horse on which our mind flies to the beyond.

8. The pure lord of the house, he is cleansed in his own nature, the most excellent seer, our auspicious guest. The Bull of a thousand horns with the power of the Thatness, oh Fire, by strength you surpass all that is other.

The Divine Flame is the lord of the house of the body, which he rules from the heart. He is the all-powerful Bull of the Spirit who has innumerable horns, who is everywhere prominent and supreme. He is the Thatness of Being, the nature of what is or pure existence itself. As the Self of all, he transcends all that is other. Indeed there is nothing real other than him.

> 9. For whom you have been revealed as most wonderfully lovely, oh Fire, in an instant you surpass all that is other — you who are adorable, beautiful and pervasive, the beloved of the peoples, the guest of men.

When the Divine Fire reveals himself, he destroys all that is apparently other. All multiplicity is returned to unity. He merges all beings in the flame of seeing, thereby removing the illusion of the mortal and the undivine. The one who knows him becomes him by his transmutation of their nature.

> 10. For you, the youngest, the human peoples bear the offering from near and from afar. Know this right thought and highest praise; manifest, oh Fire, your vast, great and auspicious peace.
> 11. Today, luminous Agni, mount your most perfect, luminous chariot with the holy ones. Knower of the paths of the wide interior realm, convey the Gods here to partake of the offering.
> 12. Thus to the wise seer we have spoken, the victorious word to the mighty Bull. He who is steadfast in the light, by the power of surrender has spread his laudation into the Fire, as if a mass of gold in Heaven.

The Fire is the youngest for he is the being of the moment, the consciousness of presence, in which there is the great peace. His chariot that brings all the Gods is the luminous insight into the Self-nature, our nature of unity with all, in which we partake of the great offering of the One to the One. The seer of this hymn takes his refuge in the Fire and becomes a shining mass of gold in Heaven, a pure substance of knowledge in the world of light.

The Magical Invoker VI.1
Seer — Barhaspatya Bharadvaja

> 1. Oh Fire, you became the first thinker of this in-
> sight, the magical invoker. The Spirit, you made for all
> the unconquerable power to conquer all power.

The Fire is the primordial thinker of that intelligence which is our own soul, our natural and organic wisdom. Through it, he is the magical invoker of our lives, as according to our thoughts, so we become; according to the flame of our intent, so we accomplish. He is the Spirit that gives us the power to go beyond all power, to approach life in the unity of peace, rather than in the division of power and its assertion.

> 2. As the invoker, giving furtherance, you sat down
> at the place of adoration, being adorable. God-seeking
> men, becoming conscious, have followed you as the
> first for great splendor.
> 3. Wakeful men have followed the splendor in you
> who move like an army with manifold ranks — the vast,
> lustrous, visionary Fire, vibrating refulgent everywhere.

God-seeking men are those who strive to become aware, who remain wakeful in the moment of seeing, following the presence of consciousness that is like an ever-burning Fire. It is this hidden Fire of consciousness at the front of all things that we ordinarily overlook, as it is transparent. This the wise learn to follow and through it discover the way to the plenitude of the lights of consciousness which shine magically in all the myriad forms of beauty in the natural world.

> 4. Seeking by surrender the station of the Divine, in-
> spired men realized a perfect revelation. They took upon
> themselves sacred natures. They delighted in your auspi-
> cious presence.

It is through the surrender of our separative thoughts in the flame of the choiceless awareness of life that we come to the station of the Divine. In that auspicious presence where we no longer cling to ourselves and what we know, we take upon ourselves a new, sacred and sacrificial nature as an expression of the Fire of Oneness.

5. People on Earth exalt you, who have both the
splendors of men. You, the deliverer, are to be known as
the protector, the Father and Mother of men forever.
6. The Fire is to be worshipped, beloved in the peoples. The joyous invoker abides within, most holy.
Kneeling, may we reverence you with prayers of surrender, refulgent in your domain.

The Fire contains both the splendors of Heaven and Earth, which are
the beauties of seeing. The elemental Fire of perception is the Father and
Mother of all beings, as life comes forth from the inner flame. He is the
adorable one that abides within us, the beloved being in all creatures. The
seers knelt down and prayed to that Fire, offering all their thoughts into
his sacred presence of seeing.

7. Wise God-seeking men, desiring bliss, we implore you anew, oh Fire. Agni, while meditating you led
the people through the vast luminous realm of Heaven.
8. The seer-lord of the eternal people, the imperious
Bull of the people of the work, who presses on giving
furtherance, the purifier, the ruling Fire, the sacred
being of the splendors.

The flame of wakeful seeing is the light of meditation which leads all
people through the great Heavens of the higher mind. The seeing is the
true lord of man, for it is the dignity of man as a spiritual being that he
has the power to truly see, to be conscious of oneness and act for the good
of all.

9. Agni, the mortal who has worshipped you, who
has labored for you, who has brought with his kindling
fuel the apportioned offering, who through prayers of
surrender has comprehended the invocation, aided by
you he assumes all beatitude.

It is the duty of the mortal, our outer mind, to seek out the immortal
guest within, the inner Self. This worship is not a matter of some obscure
ritual. It means placing our sense of value in the eternal, the Fire, rather
than in the transient, the fuel. The apportioned offering is that of our own
life and nature harmonized by wakeful awareness. The invocation to be

comprehended is that of our true nature to aspire to the Divine, through which we assume all the beatitude or bliss of our soul.

> 10. With greatness may we worship you, the great, with prayers of surrender, oh Fire, with kindling fuel and with offerings, with the altar, son of Power, with songs and hymns. May we strive in your auspicious right thinking.
> 11. You who have spread out Heaven and Earth with light and with revelations, glorious deliverer, with vast vigor, with enduring opulence, Agni, shine out in us for furtherance.

All of our desires and strivings are to be harmonized in the flame of wakefulness. This is the labor of right thinking, which is to maintain the balance of awareness, to give proper attention to what is at hand. It is the same consciousness within us which, through its organic intelligence, has created Heaven and Earth. When we surrender to it, it will manifest them within us also and through it we will find them inside ourselves.

> 12. You who are the being of light, heroically ever assume in us abundant perceptions for the line of our progeny. Manifold and vast energies far from evil, let your auspicious revelations abide in us.

Here is a typical play on the meaning of words: perception, "Pasu," also means "cattle." The cattle or herds of the seers are their perceptions of truth which they pass on to their human successors. Perceptions, like cattle, are organic entities which grow, multiply and give sustenance. The Fire, our inner flame, is the true hero, for in the Divine alone is the fearlessness that can take us beyond all the attachments and obstacles of the external world.

> 13. May we attain manifold treasures of light from every side through you, oh Agni, the King, through your substance of light. In you who have all boons are the manifold treasures of light for the harmonious mortal, in you who are the King.

The Fire, the flame of truth in the heart, is the King of the peoples, the ruler of the light. It is through worshipping him in our own hearts as the ruler of our being that we attain all the splendors and treasures of the radiant kingdom of the infinite. The Divine is the true king and ruler of men, apart from whom there can be no real or enduring social order.

I Am the Fire III.26
Seer — Gathina Vishvamitra

1. Discerning by the mind the Fire, the Universal God who follows the truth, the knower of the Sun-world, we seers who bear the offering, seeking the fullness of light, invoke that gracious God with songs, the rapturous guide of the vehicle.

2. Him the luminous Fire we invoke for his grace, the Universal God, the adorable Spirit that grows within the Mother, the Lord of the Word for man's extension of the Divine, the inspired hearer, the swiftly moving guest.

3. As a neighing horse the Universal God is enkindled by the mothers, by the peoples of the seers in every age. May that Fire, the wakeful one among the immortals, find for us the ecstasy, the perfect heroic force and swift energy.

The Flame of seeing and intelligence within us is the Universal God who finds the Sun-world of enlightened perception. He is to be discerned within by a razor-sharp vision. All of our lives are a cultivation of the flame of our inspiration. Wisdom and happiness come automatically if we follow that flame to its true depths.

The true Spirit or inner power is what grows in the Mother of receptive awareness and motiveless attention. The Flame is the tongue of the Gods that speaks the word of light, the mantra of perception, not the mere word of mouth. As such, he is the Lord of the Word. He is the inspired hearer, the one who listens with his entire heart to the song of life.

The seers become mothers, receptive in their hearts, to conceive and give birth to the inner Flame of mindfulness. This Flame is an impetuous and irresistible energy like a neighing horse, who drives us into wakefulness, stimulating us to go ever further in our quest to know.

4. Let the vigorous Fires go forth with their consort-powers. They have yoked their spotted deer for beauty.

The Gods of flashing power, who rain the vast, the undeceivable knowers of all, make the mountains tremble.

5. The Gods of flashing power, the glories of the
Fire, the universal workers, we implore their awesome
brilliant grace. The thundering Gods of terrible power,
whose raiment is the rain, the perfect givers, roar like
lions of impelling will.

6. Army upon army, host upon host with their perfect annunciations of the Fire we implore, the intense energy of the Gods of flashing power, who have spotted
horses, whose abundance does not falter, they who frequent the sacrifice, the wise knowers in the sessions of
knowledge.

The Gods of flashing power, which is what their name the Maruts
literally means, are the storm Gods who pour down the rain of truth. They
are the sages in the sessions of knowledge who, as the keepers of the sacred
Fire, pour down the rain of light. They are our own inner powers of
perception and inspiration. Here the prayer is for their full orchestration
— the grand invocation for the thunder and lightning of inner revelation.
This great storm of knowledge leads to the coming forth of the Fire in its
highest birth.

7. I am the Fire, from birth the Knower of all things
born. My eye is the clarified light. In my mouth is immortality. I am the threefold solar Word that measures
out the realm. The unceasing transforming heat, I am
the offering, the Name.

The Vedic Fire is the Self of all beings, the Divine I am. The threefold
solar Word is OM that is the triple Godhead of Being-Consciousness-Bliss
(OM as the Sun is well known from the *Upanishads*). OM is the neighing
of the Solar Horse, as the Vedic horse is always the Sun in its inner sense.
The ancient religion of light was not merely to worship external Gods,
but to awaken our inner Gods leading to the revelation of our own Divine
Self, the Flame that is all the Gods. The great Self-realization which the
Upanishads later declared in a more clear and less symbolic language is
quite evident in this verse.

8. Through three purification filters he purified the
solar Word, foreknowing by the heart the intuition ac-

cording to the light. He made the most invigorating ecstasy by the powers of the Self-nature, then he saw all
around Heaven and Earth.

9. He is a fountain with a hundred streams that can
never be diminished, the Father, the illumined consciousness of all that must be said. The roaring delight
in the bosom of the parents, Heaven and Earth carry him
whose word is truth.

The three purification filters are the mind in its three states of waking,
dream and deep sleep, through which the solar Word, the consciousness
of the Divine I am, must be purified and sustained. This requires holding
to the foreknowledge of the heart that all is one. By this the ecstasy of the
Self-nature is accomplished and vision of our inner Flame spreads in and
around all the worlds.

The fountain of illumined consciousness is in the heart. He is the
Father who is the Divine Son that his parents, all the worlds, carry through
their love, by unfolding all their beauty for his sight.

Question the Fire I.145
Seer — Dirghatamas Auchathya

1. Question him, for he has come. He knows. He is
the conscious one. He is to be sought again and again.
In him are the guidances, in him the aids. He is the lord
of vigor, strength and power.

2. Him indeed they question, not all profoundly
question, what by his own mind the sage has grasped.
He forgets neither the superior nor the inferior word. He
follows them unpresumptuously by his own will.

3. To him these ladles go, to him these strong mares.
He alone will hear all my words. Who has manifold impulsions, the deliverer, who perfects the sacrifice, whose
grace is unbroken, the child takes upon himself a fierce
energy.

4. When they have approached him, he moves yet
nearer. Born in an instant, he travels with his companions. When loving aspirations come to his presence, he
touches the one who has labored for him with a joyous
ecstasy.

5. He is the wild beast of the Waters, the forest-goer.
He has been established upon the highest ground. He declared the ways of knowledge to mortals. The Fire is the
knower, the truth, indeed the Reality.

The Fire is the sage who knows the truth of himself as the being who
resides in the hearts of all. All of our lives are a questioning of him, of
who we are. He knows the teachings, inferior or superior, to fit our stage
of life. The Vedic symbolic language reflects both, the ritual for the
inferior mind and the practise of Yoga for the wise. The ladles are the
thoughts of offering and surrender. The strong mares are the impulsions
towards him. He knows the meaning of our thoughts and the sense of our
symbols as the Fire which sees into the depths. He is the child of our loving
aspirations that, through the ardor of our labor to be aware, is born in bliss.
He is not a mere human invention. He is the free Spirit of the natural world,
the man who contains within himself all nature. That Fire who is man and
all the world, and the man beyond the world, is the being of Reality.

May We Have the Power to Control the Stallion II.5
Seer — Somahuti Bhargava

1. The invoker has been born conscious, the Father
to aid our fathers. Who hastens the genuine light, may
we have the power to control the stallion.
2. In whom, the guide of the sacrifice, the seven rays
are extended, the human Divine eighth, the purifier directs that being which is all.
3. When he sped along to that he declared the Divine
Words of the Bird. He encompassed all seer-wisdoms as
the circumference of a wheel.
4. Together with a pure will the director was born
pure. Knowing his eternal laws, he climbs them as if
they were branches.
5. These living ones, his milch Cows, held to the
color of the guide. Is he not supreme over the three, the
Sisters who have come here?
6. When the Sisters have approached bearing the
clarity of the Mother, the master of the sacrifice delights
in their approach, as the grasses with the rain.

7. As the Self for self-sustenance let the master of the rite accomplish the rite. We have offered the laudation and the sacrifice, may we find delight.

8. As the knower accomplishes all for all the holy ones, in you, oh Fire, is this sacrifice which we have accomplished.

The stallion for us to control is the wild horse of our own minds. He is the human eighth that directs the seven levels of existence, as he directs that being which is all, the Divine Self which is man's secret power. The flying horse is the bird of all seer-wisdom which declares the Divine Word. His milch Cows are his creative powers in the world which he transcends and which offer their vision to him. It is this offering of the Self to the Self which perfects and completes the rite. This is the ritual of the knower, the unitary organic ritual of life which flows from the seeing.

The Power of the Sacrifice in the Supreme Ether V.15 Seer — Dharuna Angirasa

1. To the sage, the seer who is to be known, I bear this song — to the primordial glorious Fire made evident by clarity, almighty, auspicious, the upholder of splendor, the support of the plenitude.

2. By the truth they upheld the upholding truth, in the power of the sacrifice in the supreme ether, reverential men in the upholding law of Heaven, who by the births have attained the Unborn.

3. Who ward away narrowness, they extend themselves wide as a great unassailable life-energy for the primordial one. May he newborn cross the converging currents that have encompassed him as if an angry lion.

4. When spreading yourself like a mother, you bear all men for sustenance and for vision, when assuming all life-energies you sing, through your Self in diverse forms you revolve.

5. Let wakeful vigor guard the compass of your strength, oh God, your wide-yielding support of splendor. As a thief taking things secretly to his home, awakening to great splendor you have delivered Atri.

The great sacrifice in the supreme ether is the self-sacrifice in the ether of the heart that contains all the world, the offering of our mind, our personal intellect to the cosmic intelligence. Those who accomplish this are the men of wisdom who by the ascending births of the Divine flame of awareness within them attain to the Unborn that is its highest abode, the immutable awareness of the uncreate. These men in their wideness give birth to the Fire who delivers them from the raging currents of life and death. That sacred, sacrificial Fire of seeing is the Mother of all peoples, their Self and life-energy, their sight and sustenance, which in all forms revolves. That Fire, awakening in the inner secrecy of meditation, delivers us. Atri is the name of the seer saved from this darkness of mortality by the birth of the inner Fire, the being of the Unborn.

The Universal Ruler VII.6
Seer — Maitravaruni Vasishta

1. I declare the preeminence of the almighty universal ruler, the male of the peoples who is to be rejoiced in, whose actions are as the power of Indra. Lauding I celebrate him who breaks things open.

2. The seer, the guiding ray, our sustenance, the light of the mountain, all men give impulse to as the kingdom of peace in Heaven and on Earth. With songs I beautify the primal great laws of the Fire who breaks the cities open.

3. The soulless, false people of the evil word, the faithless, unexalting, unsacrificing traders, the Fire attacked these destructive creatures. From the east he drove to the west the unholy ones.

4. The Goddesses who exulted in the western darkness, he brought to the east by his powers, most heroic. The Fire, the Lord of the light of being I sing, the tamer of those who would assault us, who does not bow down.

5. Who forced down their walls with his deadly weapons, who made the Dawns consorts of the noble, having subdued the people who would bind us, the mighty Fire by his strength made them tribute-bearers.

6. In whose refuge all men according to their nature abide praying for his grace, the Fire as the Universal Man sits at the supreme place of Heaven and Earth, the bosom of the parents.

7. The Divine Universal Man received the foundation treasures in the rising of the Sun. From the inferior
and the superior Ocean, the Fire received them from
Heaven and Earth.

This hymn celebrates the founding of a great spiritual kingdom in
ancient Aryan India. The first enemies of the Aryans were called "Panis,"
whom some scholars identify with the Phoenicians. They were an alliance
of commercial and military power which oppressed people of spiritual
inclination. They lived in great cities in which a corrupt, idolatrous and
materialistic lifestyle prevailed along with a religion of worshipping lesser
gods or powers of darkness and indulging in black magic and human
sacrifice. At this earlier, more spiritual age, the Aryans or spiritual people
were stronger and able to drive the Panis out of India, perhaps to the west,
taking control of their cities which had become centers of unspiritual
living.

Their second enemies, the people who would bind them, were those
Aryans who themselves reverted to the unspiritual life of the non-Aryans,
who upon defeating the non-Aryans wanted to take their wealth and power
as their own rather than using it for the good of all. They were even more
powerful warriors and were only defeated by the grace of God. They were
called "Nahushas" as they were descendants of an earlier Aryan king
Nahusha. This hymn relates to the exploits of Sudas, the great Aryan king
who subdued these fallen Aryans and drove the worst of them out of India.
He conquered the whole of northern India and received tribute from both
oceans (the Arabian Sea and the Bay of Bengal). He is mystically
identified with Agni, the spiritual king.

This establishment of a spiritual kingdom on earth is symbolically the
return of the sun from the west to the east, the return of the light to the
east at dawn after traversing the domain of darkness. The Aryan kings
ruled by the power of the Fire, that is, by the power of their spiritual
knowledge and the spiritual principles they based their culture on, the law
of unselfish giving rather than the selfish pursuit of wealth. Such kings,
through their respect for spiritual knowledge, put their kingdom under the
beneficent influence of Heaven and brought the cosmic rule of light to the
Earth. In their surrender to Heaven, they became the world-rulers, ruling
by the power of universal truth, projecting the universal force and right
into the turbulent realm of social action. Such hymns, which evidence the
human capacity to create a spiritual kingdom, a spiritual government on
Earth, give us hope for the future. They show that what we so desperately
need today has been once before, and therefore is possible again. Opening

up ourselves and our culture to the mantras of the ancient seers may once more help us create that spiritual kingdom on Earth. Only in the rule of the Spirit or flame of seeing can there be any real peace for humanity.

INDRA

The original Being is the archetype of all be-ings. He knows all births and slays the Dragon.

Our guide seeking the light, singing from Heaven, the friend freed his friends from blame.
— Rig Veda III.31.8

The Beneficent Lord has become every form, fashioning magical changes around his own Self.

He has come three times from Heaven in a moment, by Self-mantras, the drinker out of sea-son, the truthful one. — Rig Veda III.53.8

He rejects all former friendships, with new friendships he continually changes.

Those who have no direct experience, he throws off. Indra crosses over manifold autumns.

He has become the counter-form of every form. That is his form for the counter-vision.

Indra by his magic wisdom power moves in manifold forms, as a thousand are his radiant stallions yoked.— Rig Veda VI.47.17–18

4

INDRA

PURE BEING, THE SPIRITUAL MAN

Cosmic Warriors in the Battle for the Light

All creation is a labor to bring forth one being, the being that is man; the sentient being or being of consciousness. All creation is struggling to produce man, is crying out for him to manifest himself. All creation is a prelude to man. Creation has been a labor in the darkness, a work of the night, to prepare the way for the sunrise in Man. Creation up to the manifestation of the true man is man hidden — the sentient being hidden in the stars, in the stones, in the trees, the birds and the beasts. Everywhere man is hidden — but who is man?

All creation is a movement from darkness to light, from death to life, from non-being to being. This is also the movement from chaos to cosmos, from the state of disharmony to that of harmony, from unconsciousness to consciousness. Man is the archetypal being who has been prepared to deliver creation from darkness to light, to manifest the consciousness of the Creator within his own creation and thereby bring the creation under his direct guidance and power of love. Man is the creature in whom is all creation, through whom the Creator can come to act and to know himself. Man is the microcosm in which the macrocosm on all its levels can be harmonized. Man need not be the product of his environment, a mere creature of material evolution. He is the being designed to take creation beyond material evolution and its unconscious mechanism. His role is to make creation a free and conscious display of the glory of the Spirit, not a dark inertia of materialistic tendencies.

The true man is the cosmos, apart from whom all is chaos. He is the supreme element in creation which harmonizes all other elements, that affords each its appropriate place in the cosmic order. He pervades earth, water, fire, air and ether as the conscious force, infusing the elements with life. He is the central or uncreate element in creation, the presence of the eternal being, the axis of the world-mountain. He is the unconditioned entity among conditioned forms, the Self or immutable mind who, transcending the inertia of nature, includes all the powers of nature within himself. He is both creation and the uncreate. He is not the inferior man who is part of nature but the superior man of whom nature is a part. He is the supreme person, the only real entity in creation, of whom all beings are expressions. He is the spiritual man which only the highest human types begin to approach, who is the ideal essence of all men, which all humanity must labor to manifest.

Our creation is still very young. It remains in the thralls of the dark cosmic night. We have yet to reach the day and only possess but a vague sense of the dawn. Man has appeared in our world but not in his true being. A shadow or reflection of man has arisen, possessing the body and the capacity of the spiritual man, but as yet has displayed only the inertia of chaos, bound by fears and desires without true consciousness or self-knowledge. Through him has been built an artificial society apart from both nature and God, allied with the regressive forces of the metallic and now even elemental realms. His action threatens to release the forces of the abyss and return the planet to the pre-life stage.

The true human type has existed and at times has had much power. Such is the type of the ancient seers and the great yogis and mystics of the world. These are not some abnormal religious or spiritual human type, but the natural man of the Spirit freed from the regressive influence of social conditioning and animal inertia. It is only through again recognizing this higher human type and giving precedence to it in our social order that there can be any real harmony in society. Otherwise we are the blind leading the blind and our cultures will rise only to fall quickly again. But this higher human type is not a mere extension of civilized man and his higher forms, such as the creative genius, artist and intellectual. This higher human type is a radically different being than conditioned humanity, including and transcending both the savage and the man of culture. He possesses a primal life force greater than primitive man and a sensitivity of awareness far beyond any development of the intellect.

The Vedic archetype of this true man is Indra. He is the presence of the unconditioned being operating in the psyche, in the unconscious, preparing the way for its manifestation in the waking mind. It is only this Divine Man clearing out our psychological resistance to truth who can manifest our true humanity. All we can do in our ordinary state is to recognize the limitations of our personal mind and will and give him the space to operate. This recognition of our limitations is the space in which the higher man can manifest. He is the Divine warrior, the Dragon-slayer, the wild man of the Spirit we must invoke for a true release of our creative energy. He is the fierce intensity of the truth consciousness, the searing heat of awareness we must face. He is not some mere pleasant and compromising acceptance and approval of the unmanly, inhumane creatures we are, which only justifies and perpetuates our weakness. As human beings, we are warriors in the world for the light of consciousness. We must deal with insidious and hypnotic elemental forces, the mythical dragon or serpent which keeps us asleep. This myth of the dragon is not some superstitious fear but an inner recognition and symbolization of the secret meaning of our lives. Our labor requires the utmost vigilance, the most uncompromising attention. The balance of good and evil, knowledge and ignorance in the world rests with us and we can take it either way. We can either further the light and foster creation as true men, or sell ourselves over to the powers of sensuality and disintegration, where defeat will be our ultimate sorrow.

We must again invoke within ourselves the unconditioned being, the great God Indra, and his consort power or consciousness-force, the great Goddess, as men and women warriors for the truth. Our enemies are not each other, not people of different religious or political views, different countries, races or sexes. Our enemy is the darkness of ignorance, the Dragon that spawns a regressive egoism in the hearts of us all. We are both the god and the demon in creation and can move in either direction. It is upon this true recognition of the enemy that our success will lie. As long as we are fighting among ourselves, human against human, we will fail. In fact, we cannot fight and win at all. All our struggle is a defeat because in our ordinary consciousness we are products of the ignorance that rules the world. We can only invoke Indra and his power within ourselves. Our human mind and ego cannot destroy the dragon of ignorance because it is a product of it. We can only arouse the Divine warrior who is our true soul.

The true warrior operates only through surrender to the Divine, not through any personal will, which is itself the real catastrophe. The true warrior is the friend of all men, of all beings. His enemy is not anything or anyone but the ignorance that divides us and draws us back into the primordial chaos and its conflicting forces. The true warrior is a presence of the cosmic being, here to win the Earth for the Divine, to deliver creation from the rule of unconscious material inertia to conscious spiritual beneficence. Man is meant to be the presence of the Divine army on Earth. It is in this battle alone that our true will and intensity are to be found, the battle of unitary knowledge versus separative ignorance. In that spiritual war we must follow the lead of Indra and once more pay homage to the seers.

The Divine Warrior III.34
Seer — Gathina Vishvamitra

> 1. Indra, who breaks the cities open, overcame the
> Destroyer with sunlight chants. Shattering his opponents
> he found the treasure. Impelled by the Word, flourishing
> in his Self, the abundant giver filled both Heaven and
> Earth.
> 2. I energize the impulse of your supreme power, at-
> tending the Word for immortality. Indra, you are the
> foremost of the peoples of men and of the races of the
> Gods.

Indra, the spiritual Man, breaks open the cities which represent the conditioned, artificial states of the ignorant mind. The Destroyer (dasa) is our own lack of self-knowledge which condemns us to the realm of death. The treasure is the inner light that our opponents, the powers of duality and hatred in life, hide in their darkness. The Word is the Brahman, the Divine Word which reveals the One Self, the supremacy of consciousness. Through it the mind is freed to extend in oneness through the cosmos and beyond.

The seer energizes the power of Indra within himself through the Word-Goddess. She is not our ordinary speech of the conditioned and mechanically operating thought process, but the declaration from the soul of the knowledge of unity it perceives.

> 3. Indra, the guide of the daring Gods, encompassed
> the Obstructer. The phantom-guide of illusion powers
> vanished. Burning in the forests he destroyed division.
> He revealed the nourishing streams of the restful nights.

The Obstructer, Vritra, literally a serpent or dragon, is the ignorance which inhibits life and perception, the inertia deep in matter that resists evolutionary growth of consciousness. This phantom-guide is the ego, which is the regressive and fixated side of our consciousness that seeks to perpetuate the past. The guide of the Gods is our Indra-spirit through which we seek unity and the destruction of the dark weight of the past on our minds. We must learn to negate the serpentine urges in our uncon-scious based on past evolutionary growth and the phantoms, the strange desires and violent passions that infect us through it. All true human evolution is the freeing of the mind from past impressions and regressive animal tendencies. Cleansing the mind in a state of pure perception and clear consciousness, our action becomes impersonal and humane. Indra is the God or archetype for this process. We must energize him in the depths of our unconscious, in which our creative streams are bound, and slay the dragon who holds them. In this occult war in the mind, we must slay all the illusions which bind us. The only way to accomplish this is to destroy the central illusion, the ego, our sense of separate self, thereby opening up to the universal life, the power of Indra.

> 4. Transcendent Indra, the winner of the Sun-World, generating the days, with his devoted friends conquered the assailants. For man he made to shine the guiding ray of the days. He found the light for a vast delight.
> 5. With vigor, Indra entered the forward-pushing forces, heroically assuming manifold heroic strengths. He made conscious these insights for the singer. He spread their luminous color.

This sense of Indra or the supremacy of our being makes the light of consciousness for the delight of bliss. The Indra archetype operating in the mind of the seer, the Indra sense of fearless awareness that faces down all opposition and duality, brings into consciousness the insights which destroy the ignorance. As mere mortals we cannot conquer the ignorance which rules us because we are a product of it. However, by opening up to the Divine light through choiceless perception, the Indra-force or Divine Warrior is activated within us on the deeper levels of the psyche to accomplish the work. The main thing for us to do is not to interfere with this force but to surrender to its grace.

> 6. They marvel at the great actions, the manifold perfect accomplishments of great Indra. Of transcendent vigor, with concentration, by magic wisdom power he crushed the crooked Destroyers.
> 7. The Lord of Being, who pervades all men, by greatness, through war, Indra made the wideness for the Gods. In the station of the rising Sun, sages and seers laud his deed with hymns.

The great action of the Indra archetype is the deed of consciousness, the act of maintaining awareness, destroying the darkness of ignorance with the light of knowledge. Magic wisdom is the wisdom of seeing all things as magic. Ignorance is being deceived by magic, taking the magic as real. All things are unreal; that is, they are not real in themselves as separate entities according to their superficial appearances. All life is magic and wonder and each thing is a great symbol of the all, a cosmic mask. As symbols all things are real, not according to form or appearance that is only a display, but according to content or meaning which is always profound. This is the magic wisdom, the Maya of Indra, that destroys the magic illusion or mysterious ignorance, the Maya of the destructive serpent. Indra is the state of mind that is not deceived by illusion because it knows that all things are illusions, not as a delusive unreality but as a profound symbolism, a cosmic theater which demonstrates the highest truths.

Falsehood is what is crooked, what dissimulates. Truth and conscious-ness is what is straight, what is as it is. Thought is crooked, for it is based on memory which is a flight from what is. Holding to the straightness of consciousness, of direct perception, is the heroism of Indra, his manly power, because it does not shrink from anything. Through war, Indra, the Divine Warrior, creates wideness for the Gods. This war of Indra that brings deliverance from ignorance is this facing of everything, all oppo-sition, bringing to light all the layers of the unconscious and conquering them by the power of pure perception. Vedic war means to ward off. It is warding off ignorance by vigilant awareness. It is discriminating between the real and the unreal, being and non-being. There can be no peace or compromise between truth and falsehood. Where one is the other is not. One must be destroyed for the other to be. It is this war to the finish, to the utter destruction of the enemy, that the Indra archetype insists upon. It is only when we are utterly opposed to all falsehood, when we have pursued it to the depths of our mind and driven it out with patient awareness, that there can be wideness for the Gods, for the Divine principles and powers within us and all life.

8. The most excellent eternal conqueror, the giver of conquering force, who has conquered the Sun-Word and the Goddess-waters, who conquered this Earth and Heaven — according to that Indra the wise rejoice.

9. Who won swift horses and won the Sun, Indra won the all-providing Cow. Gold and enjoyment he con-quered. Having slain the destroyers, he furthered the color of noble men.

10. Indra won the plants and the days. He conquered the lordly forest-trees and the atmosphere. He burst the

enclosure and drove away those of false speech. Thus
he became the tamer of the arrogant.

The Indra sense of the supremacy of the Self, of the conscious
individual over all the world, is the conqueror of everything. He is the
guiding power in evolution behind every victory of the cosmos out of the
darkness of primordial chaos. His swift horses are the transcendent
energies of the Sun of Truth, which itself is the all-providing Cow or ray.
Gold is its color or quality of value and delight. We see in this symbolism
also the victory of the Vedic Aryans, noble people of spiritual values, over
their ignoble, greedy and destructive opponents, and the dispersal of their
hoarded wealth for the good of all. This victory over evil men was seen
as part of the march of evolution, another victory of the light on Earth.
Indra is that forward power of evolution always pressing on in the
development of life and consciousness.

Indra represents the daring will of the Divine behind every evolutionary growth from rock to man, which has fashioned the marvelous and
harmonious cosmos out of the darkness of chaos. It is the place of man to
incarnate this Indra power as the guide of evolution on Earth, to further
the life and intelligence in manifestation. However, we have come to deny
Indra, thus becoming guides of devolution on Earth, with our regressive
tendencies and unconscious drives bringing the world to the brink of
annihilation. We must once more awaken the power of Indra within
ourselves and drive away those of false speech who divide humanity into
warring parties by labels of nation or belief. We must once more become
Divine Warriors and drive the falsehood from our minds, exposing all the
illusion and arrogance of our collective unconsciousness. The Indra
archetype who can do this was already seeded by the ancient seers. We
must set it in motion again.

11. May we invoke auspicious, beneficent Indra, the
most heroic in this struggle for the winning of power —
the awesome one who listens and gives grace in the encounters, who slays the obstructers, the winner of the
treasures.

We must be real human beings and invoke Indra, our own spiritual
potential of transcendence. It is this archetype of transcendence alone
which makes man, which allows us to go beyond the manipulations of our
environment to awareness, from which alone true and harmonious action
is possible. If we cannot get beyond our conditioning we are only

machines or animals, reflections of our environment, in contradiction and conflict with reflections of different environments. We must invoke the Indra will towards transcendence and thereby deliver all life from the darkness to the light, deliver all creation from the compulsion of the ignorance to the gentle guidance of the knowledge. This is our true inner role as the fosterers of evolution on Earth (which is not the evolution of technology, but that of love).

The Dragon-Slayer IV.19
Seer — Vamadeva Gautama

> 1. Indra, wielder of the thunderbolt, all the Gods
> here as well-listening helpers and both Heaven and
> Earth chose you alone, great, exalted and sublime, to
> slay the Dragon.

Indra is our sense of supreme aloneness, which is all-oneness, our awareness of the supreme Self, which alone has the power to destroy the Dragon of ignorance, sorrow and death. All Gods and all worlds do not have that power, and then look to humanity for it. Nothing external can match the Dragon, for the Dragon is the sense of the external, the idea that there is something other than the Self, something other than unity. The Gods or cosmic powers must accede to Indra. All spiritual qualities must accede to self-knowledge for victory over the ignorance.

> 2. The Gods, as if decrepit, were thrown down.
> Indra, whose source is truth, be their supreme ruler. You
> slew the Dragon who encompassed the floods. You
> opened out the stream paths which provide all nourish-
> ment.

The Gods, the plurality of Divine powers and principles, have no real efficacy in destroying the ignorance, for the ignorance is multiplicity, the sense of difference and separation. They need and provide the way for that Indra power, the power of the One only, whose source is the supreme truth. He slays the Dragon and releases the flood the Dragon has held back, the oceans of life he keeps repressed in his coils.

> 3. Extended insatiable, not to be awakened, who
> slept ever unawakening, who encompassed seven de-

scending streams, Indra where no joint was you dismembered the Dragon.

The Dragon (Vritra) is primordial ignorance, the basic inertia within
matter which resists its information by the Spirit. The Dragon is the
negative spirit of the formless waters of primordial chaos. That Dragon
of the prima materia holds in his formless coils the streams of creative
force of the seven levels of existence. It is out of this that Indra, the light
of life and consciousness, dismembering the Dragon, produces all seven
levels of creation, releasing the spiritual powers held in thrall, imprisoned
therein. The Dragon is also the Kundalini or serpent power in its latent or
sleep state that keeps hidden all the powers of spiritual evolution within
us. The wise must take power over that Dragon and release its secret
energies for inner transformation.

> 4. Indra with strength made the Earth's foundation
> quake, as the Wind with his powers drove the wavy
> floods. Heating up his vigor he smashed their
> firmnesses, he broke down the summit-peaks of the
> mountains.

Indra's appearance in the world is an unparalleled event, the eruption
into the material world of ignorance of the vast, free power of the Spirit
that breaks everything open. His appearance is cataclysmic; a power that
shakes the world to its foundations, revealing the supremacy of the Spirit
over its material creation. His appearance is apocalyptic, as it brings the
long march of evolution to its explosive consummation. His is the coming
into the world of the alien power of the Absolute, the Spirit breaking
through its material bondage and, through its power of consciousness,
shaking the world like a toy. It is an event without precedence that breaks
the very laws of nature, the manifestation of the Spirit which is the
freedom behind her laws, the supreme marvel behind her marvels.

> 5. They rushed to you as mothers to their child. The
> mountains like a row of chariots went forth all at once.
> You refreshed the spreading currents and pressed down
> the waves. Effortlessly, Indra, you set free the rivers.
> 6. To aid Turviti and Vayya, by the power of their
> prayer of surrender you halted the agitated flood, the
> great all-nourishing stream that flowed. Indra, you made
> the rivers easy to cross.

Indra is the Divine Child for whom the Mother floods flow. He is the supreme mountain range, the Himalayas, that breaks into the clouds above the lower peaks and sends the great streams spreading down through them in rows.

Indra is the Lord of the flood. He directs the waters to overwhelm the godless, who are drowned in the ocean of the ignorance, but he makes the rivers stop flowing for those who have surrendered to the Divine, those who reverence all life as sacred. He delivers them from the floods of creation, affording them easy passage across all the currents of the world. This "parting of the Red Sea" myth is common in the Vedic hymns and has various forms. The parting of the waters is one of the main demonstrations of the power of the Vedic Gods and seers. Turviti and Vayya are two mythical seers or personifications of peoples so aided by Indra across the sea.

> 7. The young virgin knowers of truth, like bubbling
> springs, like whirling fountains, he made to overflow.
> He inundated the thirsty desert plains. Indra milked the
> barren cows, the consorts of the Lord of magic.

The virgin streams are the Goddess floods which are Indra's consorts, the pure streams of the knowledge of truth which flow from the heights. The desert plains are the material realms of the ignorance below, which the waters of truth cultivate into the flowers of life. The barren cows are the material realms far removed from the creative force of the Spirit. Indra is the knowledge of the Self which alone has the power to milk them, to find the milk of truth even in the darkness of the material world. Indra is the Lord of magic wisdom who draws the light out of darkness, life out of death, reality out of unreality, the creative out of the transient.

> 8. Through manifold Dawns and grateful years, hav-
> ing slain the Dragon, Indra released wide the rivers. The
> waters which were bound and contracted, Indra opened
> them to flow in channels through the Earth.

The Dragon in his mountain cave conceals and withholds the waters of immortal life. He is the ignorance in the deepest recesses of our subconscious, our elemental egoism that binds us to the hypnosis of external conditioning, the mad rush to accumulate things or become somebody. It requires the will and perception of Indra, the Divine hero, to conquer him. When the Dragon is slain, all our doors of perception and all the nerves of our body are flooded with the immortal streams.

> 9. The child of the virgins who was eaten by ants,
> Lord of radiant stallions, you bore him from the nest.
> Grasping the serpent, the blind man saw clearly. The
> cauldron vanished; his joints were reunited.

We enter again the realm of magic symbolism. The child of the virgins is our inner Divine child or soul, the offspring of the cosmic waters, the free flowing streams. He is eaten by the ants of worldly cares and anxieties. Indra as the Lord of radiant energy takes him away, teaches him to fly. The dragon or serpent is the Serpent-power or Kundalini in its uncontrolled state. Grasping it or holding the staff is making firm the spine, awakening all the centers or chakras therein. Indra is the Divine consciousness which alone is able to conquer and hold the dragon, to control and direct the Serpent-power. It is not a matter of technique, which can always fail, but a change of nature through knowledge, an awakening of the vision of the Self beyond the domain of serpentine Maya-illusion. The cauldron is the alchemical transformation vessel which vanishes when the Dragon is slain, its work being accomplished. The Dragon is the power of ignorance which divides. Indra is the knowledge that unites. The knowledge of Indra reintegrates the dismembered cosmic Man, who is himself, and re-establishes the wholeness of our being in oneness with all. This magic of Dragon-slaying is not primitive superstition but a profound ancient symbolism of self-knowledge and spiritual reintegration.

> 10. Your primeval labors, oh Sage, the knower has
> spoken your actions to the wise. As these energies exist
> according to their nature, Self-glorious King, you have
> taken possession of all the heroic arts.
> 11. Now lauded, Indra, now sung, as a stream over-
> flow a nourishing energy for your singer. The new
> Word for you has been accomplished, Lord of radiant
> stallions. May we by the soul be masters of the vehicle
> forever.

Indra is the Self-glorious King who is the master of all the heroic arts, the inner skill and adaptability that slays the serpent, the rigid and opinionated mind. He is the Self-knowing sage, the inner hero, who has mastered the all-conquering arts of knowledge. For him the mystic Word or prayer, the Brahman or the declaration of the supremacy of the Self is accomplished. Through him we are borne on the car of the soul or the intelligence forever in the flight of the immortal to the immortal. He is the vehicle of knowledge which speeds us on the eternal journey.

In the Ecstasy of Soma II.15
Seer — Gritsamada Bhargava

> 1. I will declare the actions great and true of him, the great Truth. He drank the effused essence in the three world-vessels, in ecstasy Indra slew the serpent.
> 2. In unsupported space he up-pillared Heaven. He filled the two firmaments and the atmosphere. He upheld the Earth and spread it wide. In the ecstasy of Soma, this Indra accomplished.

Indra is the mythic archetype of the great Truth, the truth of Being that all is one Self. The effused essence he drinks is the ambrosia of bliss that comes forth from all things when we see them in the light of direct perception. When we see things as they are, observe them choicelessly, their essence comes forth and that essence is bliss. This is the inner meaning of the pressing out of the Soma or nectar of immortality.

In the ecstatic essence that comes forth from fearless perception, consciousness fills the worlds and gives them order. It is this same consciousness awakening by degrees that has fashioned and made firm the worlds.

> 3. He measured out with measures as if the front of a house, with his lightning bolt he pierced the holes of the rivers. Easily he released them by far traveling paths. In the ecstasy of Soma, this Indra accomplished.

What is measured out like a house is the body. The holes that are pierced for the rivers to flow are the sense organs for the mind streams to flow out. The power of consciousness pierces the stone of the body and makes the waters flow from it. This is Indra's great action as the lord of the sense organs (which are called in Sanskrit Indriyas, powers of Indra). It is his capacity as the power of pure or direct perception to make the inner light flow through them and reveal the true beauty of the outer world which is its creation. Normally our sensory sensitivity is limited by our conditioning based on memory and external stimulation, within which limited and repetitive nature it becomes sensuality. When we learn to observe life choicelessly, our sensory sensitivity expands until it becomes spiritual, until we see not only the form but the being of things in the unity of the observer and the observed. This is Indra wielding the lightning bolt or Vajra.

> 4. Having surrounded those who bore away the
> power of deception, he burned all their weapons in the
> enkindled Fire. He released it with light, energy and the
> power of movement. In the ecstasy of Soma, this Indra
> accomplished.

The power of deception is also the name of a mythic seer (Dabhiti) saved by Indra. This power of deception rightly belongs to the Divine as its illusion-power of creation. But the powers of the ignorance take it over, use it not to further creation, like the illusion of a great painting, but to condition the mind to the realm of desire and death. Indra is the Lord of the magic wisdom of the Gods who reclaims his Maya-power. He releases it, or the seer who symbolizes it, with cows (light or perception), horses (energy or the liberated life force) and chariots (the power of movement and change). These ancient symbols also have an abstract meaning, which is the inner meaning here.

> 5. He stopped the mighty, roaring stream from flow-
> ing. He delivered to safety those who could not swim.
> Having crossed over, they attained to splendor. In the ec-
> stasy of Soma, this Indra accomplished.
> 6. By his greatness he poured the river upwards.
> With his lightning bolt he crushed the vehicle of the
> Dawn, rending her slow horses with his swift mares. In
> the ecstasy of Soma, this Indra accomplished.

Indra stops the flood and delivers his friends who were drowning in them. He saves those devoted to him from the cosmic waters of the ignorance, Samsara. The stream of consciousness flowing downward in the ignorance, the waters of our creativity sinking into the unconscious, he drives upwards by his knowledge-power. The vehicle of the Dawn is aspiration. Indra is the Sun at the zenith, the direct lightning-perception of being that is Divine, which goes far beyond this initial inspiration.

> 7. Knowing the secret of the virgins, revealing him-
> self, the outcast stood up. The lame stood firm; the blind
> saw clearly. In the ecstasy of Soma, this Indra accom-
> plished.

The outcast is our Indra, our transcendence in the Godhead through which we are outside all the laws of nature and society. Indra is the spiritual man who is the Divine outcast in the world. He knows the secret of the virgins, the power of the pure mind. He dares to stand outside of everything, as the individual who defies the entire world to be true to the Self. It is this Divine outcast who is the real virgin, the pure being in creation, who does not consent to be violated by the rule of another, the rule of the ignorance or the sense of otherness in which the Self is lost.

Inwardly we are all outcasts, exiles from our true nature into this world of the ignorance. We must be true to our outcast being that it may manifest itself in its real scope as our transcendency, our freedom in the Absolute. We are also the lame or cripple, the one who does not have the power to stand on his own. We depend upon others and their approval for our sense of stability in life. Knowledge of Indra, our independence in the Self of all, frees us from this. And we are also the blind, deceived by external forms into losing the sense of our true Self.

Indra is the self-sight that gives us back our eyes and allows us to see things as they are. Or the cripple who stands firm is our true Self that is lame to the affairs of this world, which is not concerned about mere appearances. The blind one who sees clearly is our true Self, who, blind to all the glamour of this world, is able to see things as they are.

> 8. Lauded by the flaming seers he burst the enclo-
> sure. He broke open the firmnesses of the mountain. He
> overflowed their artificial embankments. In the ecstasy
> of Soma, this Indra accomplished.

The enclosure is the cave-like mentality of the ignorance in which we know only the shadows of our conditioning. The firmnesses of the mountain are the dark and obstinate tendencies of the unconscious, our blind compulsion to fear, desire and hatred. They are supported by the artificial embankments of our social conditioning. All this Indra, our sense of true individuality, in the ecstasy of its Divine creativity or Soma, shatters.

9. Having covered the raging demon with sleep, he
slew the Destroyer and furthered the power of deception. There the staff-bearer found the gold. In the ecstasy of Soma, this Indra accomplished.

The raging-demon, who is the demon of rage, is covered with sleep.
The ignorance, which is our addiction to the past, is overcome by
forgetting it, by being in the present. This destruction of the destroyer is
the deceiving of the deceiver, the putting to sleep of the power of sleep.
It is the ignorance which is to be ignored. Indra is the magic knowledge
which is the knowledge of all things as magic. When all things are revealed
as deception, there is no one left who can be deceived. It is the power of
deception which is our own mind, our capacity to deceive ourselves with
ideas about things, that is to be saved. It is saved when we realize that
truth is in seeing, while what is seen is only its shadow. The staff-bearer
is the one who bears himself firmly. He finds the genuine gold of his own
nature.

10. Now may your beneficent discernment, Indra,
yield in return the supreme wish for the singer. Give aid
to your affirmers. Let our share of your grace not fail us.
Full of heroic power, in the sessions of knowledge may
we declare the vast.

Indra's beneficent discernment is his consort, his Goddess-power
who as the mystic cow yields the supreme wish, the knowledge of Indra
or the Self, to the singer, to the one who sings the true wish of the soul.

I have Been Born as the Sun VIII.6
Seer — Vatsa Kanva

1. Indra, who is great by wakeful vigor like the rain
God full of rain, grows by the hymns of the child.
2. Delivering him as the Son of truth, the carrier
flames bear him, sages with the power of conveyance of
truth.
3. When the Kanva-seers with their hymns made
Indra, the perfection of the sacrifice, they called the
friend their weapon.

The child-like seers grow Indra, the Divine Child, by the power of their hymns of affirmation of the truth of oneness. They fashion him within themselves. He is the Self that is the perfection of the sacrifice, the Self-sacrifice which conquers all the worlds. He is the Divine Friend who is the weapon against all evil and sorrow.

>4. All the people of the work bow down to his Spirit,
>as rivers to the sea.
>5. That vigor of his shone brilliantly when Indra
>rolled up together as if in a skin both Heaven and Earth.
>6. He cut off the head of the boisterous Dragon with
>his mighty lightning bolt of a hundred joints.

Indra is the Spirit, the awesome Godhead, to whom all the people of the spiritual work bow down. His supreme brilliance is that he rolls together both Heaven and Earth in the skin of the human body, when he manifests his supremacy in his own creation as Man. His lightning bolt (Sanskrit: vajra) cuts off the head of the arrogant Dragon of egoism. The sense of the Self cuts off the root of all egoistic thoughts.

>7. We sing them forth, insights among the foremost
>of inspirations, lightnings like the white heat of the sa-
>cred Fire.
>8. When truths which are hidden come forth by the
>Self, when insights shine luminous, when the Kanva-
>seers move with the stream of truth,
>9. May we attain That, Indra, the splendor full of
>rays and swift energies, that Brahman for the original
>consciousness.
>10. I from my Father received the meditative mind
>of truth. I have been born even as the Sun.

The foremost inspiring insights are those of the Oneness, the supreme lightning heat of the flame of awareness. When we meditate deeply in the heart they come forth spontaneously in a stream by the power of the Self within. Following that stream, the seers come to its source, the seat of all splendors, the Brahman, the Being of the Absolute in the heart of Indra. In that Brahman we are born as the Divine Sun, the Self or Atman. That Brahman is the Divine Father through which, in the meditative realization of the enlightened mind, one is born as the Divine Son — the unitary light of creation.

This solar rebirth into the Supreme is the perfection of the ancient religion of light and sacrifice, the offering of all into the Oneness that wins the all in return. This is the great Self-sacrifice for which all the other sacrifices are symbols or a preparation. It is the desired birth that takes us beyond all birth through desire. This spiritual rebirth of the Man in the Sun of enlightenment is the summit of the ancient solar religions. The ancients sought entry into the Divine light and mergence into the spiritual Sun. This was the true Sun they adored and propitiated, of which the visible Sun is only a reminder. It is in the sunlight of Self-knowledge that we find the resurrection of the true Man into the Godhead. It is on that note, the golden tone or music of light, that the *Vedas* were seen, that the *Upanishads* were spoken and by which they shine forever in the hearts of all.

> 11. By the primal thought I beautify songs like the
> Kanva-seers, through which Indra takes on power.
> 12. By all the laudations the seers have or have not
> given you, Indra by that as my laudation increase your-
> self.

The primal thought is that of the Oneness in which we beautify songs of joy and in which we give power to the Self. In this all the songs of wisdom of the seers that have been or are to be are in our song, the heart's song of Self-being.

> 13. When his Spirit sounded, dismembering the
> Dragon joint by joint, he burst the floods to the sea.
> 14. Into the hissing Destroyer you struck down your
> firm bolt of lightning. As the awesome Spirit you are re-
> nowned.
> 15. Not the Heavens, nor the Atmospheres, nor the
> Earths could encompass Indra, the wielder of the light-
> ning, with his vigor.
> 16. He who lay prone, restraining the great Waters,
> in his own secret places, Indra, you pierced.
> 17. Who had swallowed together both great Heaven
> and Earth, with darkness you concealed him.

Indra is the wild man of the Spirit, the crazy man of knowledge, not the beast of base passions. He is the daring man of consciousness who dares to dive into the depths of the unconscious to slay the Dragon of primitive egoism hidden within it. He is not a regressive male hero with primitive macho charm that some barbarians worshipped in ancient times (as many interpretations of the *Veda* try to portray). He is the true Man of consciousness, more primeval than the savage, more refined than any cultured man. He is the man of Divine simplicity and power who stands far beyond the weak civilized male and his fear of what others think of him. He is the post-civilized man who sees the savage and the civilized man as two sides of the same coin — primitive and refined conditioning but equally bound to the external — while he himself is the unconditioned. He is an archetype our culture is desperately in need of, as we have only the primitive macho man on one side or the overly intellectualized and effeminate cultured type on the other.

Modern culture, particularly of recent years, suffers from an excess of passivity, a too great social sense, which leaves everything diffuse and group oriented, caught in external stimulation and role playing. We need again the individualistic Man of the Spirit, the eagle who flies alone and does not look back, who is not seeking approval from anyone, who can challenge the whole world, all the universe, and win — who can challenge not just the powers of human ignorance but all the darkness of the psyche going back to primeval eons — and fearlessly drive the Dragon of the ignorance from the world. Ignorance is not overcome by being passive, by being nice to it or seeking harmony with it. It requires a relentless, uncompromising pursuit of it to its darkest depths, therein negating it completely. For the real liberation of Man, we must again find a true inspiration in the great Divine warrior and hero. The Goddesses prepare the way and supply the weapons, but only the great high God can slay the Dragon. The Mother gives birth to the warrior and savior Son who wins the light. Only in him is there deliverance, the true victory of the light in the battle between the knowledge and the ignorance on Earth. That Indra-man is the real basis of humanity, without which we are just animals or machines, and need the approval of others for the inner value and power we do not really have.

18. Whatever lauds the wandering ascetics or the
keepers of the Fire have given you, hear that as my call.

19. They, your dappled Cows of the sky, Indra, yield
a well-heated clarity, pouring out the Goddess of truth.

20. They, your mothers, with their mouths have
made you as their child to sing, Indra, as the Sun, according to the law.

21. Lord of strength, the Kanva-seers have exalted
you as the effusions of blissful drops have grown you.

22. Indra, in your guidance and according to your direction, wielder of the stone, the sacrifice is to be fully
extended.

The seers, here those of the family of Kanva, are the celestial herds
which produce the milk and clarified butter of truth for the Indra-Self.
They incarnate the Goddess-powers and become his mothers. The Divine
Child is delivered by the mouth, by the utterance of the Word of truth
which is always a song, the chanting of OM with all our being. Man has
the inner capacity to sing the Sun, to make the Sun shine through his word
of truth. This capacity was incarnated by the ancient seers. Their language
is that of the Sun, the music of light, the radiance of the mantra.

23. Disclose for us a mighty energy, Indra, like a
city full of light, and a most heroic progeny,

24. And that swiftest energy which foremost shone
among the peoples of the Nahushas.

25. As the Sun for our nearest vision you envelop
the enclosure when, Indra, you give your grace to us.

26. When you put forth your consort power, you
rule the people, great and shoreless by your strength.

27. People who bear the offering address you for
grace, a wide expanse with the drops of bliss.

Indra is the all-beneficence that comes from the Supreme. The
Nahushas were great Aryan warriors and Nahusha is sometimes a generic
term for the Aryan peoples (though later it was used for Aryans who were
separated from the original culture for their excessive use of force). The
enclosure is our sensory field which like a bubble is dissolved into the sea
of consciousness, as the great Sun of awareness absorbs its tiny ray of the
mind. Power is Indra's consort, the Goddess, Shakti, the ruling force in
creation which he wields.

28. In the ascending slope of the mountains, in the
confluence of the streams, by the Goddess-understanding the sage was born.

29. Hence being conscious at the summit he looks
down upon the sea, from which vibrating he stirs.

30. Then they see the morning light of the primordial seed, when beyond Heaven it is enkindled.

The pure streams of understanding of our soul in their vast course
from the mountains of meditation to the ocean of consciousness give birth
to the sage, the man of knowledge. He knows himself as the full circuit
of existence. When the circle is completed the Sun is born shining beyond
Heaven, the solar eagle in his native freedom beyond the worlds.

31. All the Kanva-seers, Indra, increase your
thought and your masculine power, and you who are
strongest, your spiritual energy.

32. Welcome your affirmation by me. Grant me
your grace and increase your thought,

33. Which through Divine wisdom for immortal life
as sages we have fashioned for you, the exalted wielder
of the lightning.

34. The Kanva-seers, like floods speeding down a
descending slope, have sung for Indra the winning
thought.

35. Their hymns have increased Indra, like rivers the
sea, of unequalled Spirit, the undecaying.

The thought of Indra, his consort mentation or intuition, is the thought
of the Self, the mind of unity. It is not an ordinary thought at all, a reaction
of the mechanical mind, but an updwelling of Divine thought in the silent
mind. It is this deepest thought of the soul, of the heart, the intuition of
unity that wins Indra, the Divine Lord, as its spouse. This is the flood of
Divine wisdom that comes when we surrender ourselves to that free Indra
spirit within us.

36. Come to us from the beyond with your two adorable radiant stallions. Indra, drink this effusion.

37. You, the foremost slayer of the Dragon, men
who strew the altar seat invoke for the winning of
power.

38. Both Heaven and Earth follow you, as the turning wheel does the Sun's horse. The concentrated drops
of bliss follow you.

39. Delight yourself in the Man of the Sun-World,
delight yourself in the lake of reeds. Delight yourself by
the thought of the morning Sun.

Indra's two radiant stallions are the sun and the moon or the mind and
the breath. Heaven and Earth follow the man of wisdom who, through
concentration, presses out the Soma bliss from his perceptions by the
all-conquering mind of Indra. The Man of the Sun-World is the true or
cosmic man of the Sun, the sunlight presence of pure perception and
daring consciousness in creation. The thought of the morning Sun is the
Dawn, the aspiration to know Indra. The lake of reeds is the lair of the
wild Bull.

40. Exalting himself in Heaven, the Spirit, the wielder of the lightning, roared again and again, the Dragon-
slayer, the supreme Soma drinker.
41. You are the ancient-born seer, Indra, the One
ruler through strength. You radiate the treasures.
42. Let our effusions, as a hundred straight-backed
radiant stallions, convey you to the feast.
43. Her, the primeval Goddess-understanding, the
nectar of clarity and of the honey-bliss, the Kanva-seers
by the hymn have grown.
44. Let the mortal in wisdom among the mighty
Goddesses choose Indra. Let the one who would conquer choose Indra for aid.

Indra is the seer of whom all the seers partake, the Bull of the heights
whose roar is creation, the great seed syllable or original mantra OM. Our
effusive concentrations of inspiration like the numerous horses bear him
to us. He is manifested by the Goddess-understanding, the receptive mind
which gives the space for him to reveal himself. These understandings are
the most mighty Goddesses, the Divine loving aspirations which seek the
supreme. Among them, by their ascending yearning, we must choose
Indra, the sense of our Divine aloneness, the supremacy of the individual,
for the winning of the light. The hymns of the seers not only laud the Gods,
they create the Gods, who are but different forms of the Divine Word, and
bring them into functioning within us. The supreme incarnation of the
Divine Word, OM, itself is Indra.

How to Sing the Mystic Song I.62
Seer — Nodhas Gautama

1. To the conqueror, the lover of song, we meditate a
swiftly turning song of victory like the original seer. In
transformation let us sing the song of the Sun for the renowned hero, the laudable being of the chant.

2. Bear a great prayer of surrender to the great, to
the conqueror the swiftly-turning mystic Song, through
whom our ancient fathers, the flaming seers, the knowers of the region, in illumined singing found the light.

Indra is the Lord of the Divine Word, the cosmic chant that is also the
mystic Song, the great hymnal vibration of the Oneness, OM. The flaming
seer, Angiras, is the archetypal Man-Angel of the chant. It is through the
transmutation of our nature, the inner revolution or catharsis whereby we
forsake the transient and seek the eternal, that we awaken this Divine
Being of the Word. This Song of light is the Song of the Sun that finds
and illuminates our souls which are the solar rays, the Divine cows.

3. In the impulse of Indra and the flaming-seers, the
hound of Heaven found sustenance for her progeny. The
Lord of the Vast broke the mountain and found the
light, when together with the radiant mornings the heroes roared.

The flaming-seers are the rishis, the Angirasas, who are the companions of Indra. The hound of Heaven, Sarama, the swift one, is the
Goddess-intuition who searches out the way to truth. The Lord of the Vast,
Brihaspati, is the Lord of the vast word of light, the planet Jupiter, the
wisdom lord who breaks open the obstinate mountain of our lower nature
to free the light of our soul hidden in it, its secret herds. The radiant
mornings are these herds of light or nourishing notes of illumination
through which the heroes, the true or spiritual men, sing and by which
they energize all the Gods.

4. He, the solar note, by laudation and perfect laudation, along with the seven seers of the nine rays, through
the golden tone broke the mountain. Indra, Lord of
power, with the swift seers of the ten rays, you burst
open the cavern-receptacle with a roar.

The solar note is the musical sound of enlightenment. It is the essential tone or the golden tone, the universal tone of oneness, which harmonizes every voice. The seven seers of the nine rays (Navagva) are the seeing powers of the seven levels of existence in their complete ennead. With Indra they become the seers of the ten rays (Dashagva) which returns them to oneness. They are the primordial flaming-seers, the mythical Angirasa family of diverse forms (virupa), of which all the Vedic seers and their lineages are an extension. They are the original and mythical spiritual men in our true human nature as singers of Divine Oneness. The cavern-receptacle is the unconscious mind which is the receptacle of karmic conditionings that keeps us under the rule of external influences. The Divine Word clears out the unconscious with the enlightened reason of Self-knowledge, the power of pure perception.

> 5. Sung by the flaming-seers, the wonder worker,
> with the Dawn, the Sun and the radiant herds, you dis-
> pelled the blinding darkness. You spread out the summit
> of the world and made firm the region under Heaven.

Indra is the wonder worker whose great action is to make the light, to illumine the consciousness. Strictly speaking, this is no action at all. It is the action of knowing, which is something beyond the actions of the body or the ideas of the mind. Yet it is more deed than thought, as it is the transforming action of seeing. It is the action of inaction, the transforming action of stepping outside the karmic field of action and reaction and daring to see things as they are. This action is consciousness singing, or the singing that is itself the vibratory state of consciousness.

> 6. This is his most adorable deed, the most lovely
> wonder of the wonder worker: when along the approach-
> ing slope of Heaven he made four rivers overflow, de-
> scending floods of honey-bliss.

Indra, the knowledge of the Self, brings down from Heaven four floods of bliss. These are the bliss of the four Divine principles which are native to the higher half of existence, the domain of the knowledge beyond the lower sphere of the ignorance. They are the infinite streams of Being, Consciousness, Bliss and Intelligence.

> 7. Inexhaustible, from of old with laudatory illumina-
> tions he spread apart the two ancient-born Goddesses

who have a common nest. Like the blissful Sun, the
great wonder worker upheld Heaven and Earth, the
beautiful maidens, in the supreme ether.

Heaven and Earth, the dual worlds, are the twofold Goddess, the
creative dual consort of the supreme. Their real origin and abode is in the
supreme ether, in the celestial spiritual summits, the revelatory space of
love-wisdom. They are the dual archetypes of creation that manifest to
guide us back to our transcendent nature. In our ignorance we treat them
as objects and abuse them, using them only as a background or raw
material to fashion our selfish pleasures and attainments. The vision of
truth reveals them as archetypal symbols radiant with the highest truths,
the maiden form of the Godhead.

Indra's great victory, the victory of Self-knowledge, is also the
deliverance of Heaven and Earth, the world-soul, the Goddesses from
their corrupt and abused state in the ignorance to their celestial beauty in
the knowledge. He is the knowledge of Oneness that raises the Earth to
the garden of God, that reveals in the myriad forms of nature the splendor
of the Absolute. This is the vision of the blissful Sun (Bhaga) in whom
all is adoration and all the worlds are adorable as presences in the
Supreme. We have made our Goddess-powers, our creative force, servile
to the enjoyments of personal or collective egoism, using our soul talents
to make money or become somebody in the transient world. Indra, the
principle of Self-knowledge, returns them to their original purity and
transcendence as the creative beauty of the Spirit. He is the spiritual Man
whose great action it is to rescue the spiritual Female creative principle
and give it its real and true support in the Supreme.

> 8. Night with the dark beauties of her wonderful
> body, Dawn with the bright, around Heaven and Earth
> from the eternal they travel, one after the other, diverse
> in form, the young Goddesses ever born again according
> to their ways.

Night and Dawn are the dual creative powers of life, the twin rhythms
of the sacrifice. They are all that is dual — life and death, rest and action,
light and darkness, but as complementary forces. They are duality resolved into the complementary rhythm of unity. This is the cosmic order
that Indra establishes.

9. The master of the sacred art, the wonder worker,
the Son upholds by his power the most complete unity.
The ripe white essence you uphold in the raw black and
red cows.

The Divine Son, who is the child of all creation as well as of the
eternal, maintains the most complete unity, the most perfect friendship
with all existence. He holds the white essence in the black and red qualities
of nature (the cows). The white essence is the quality of knowing (sattva).
The red is energy or action (rajas). The black is inertia or resistance (tamas;
the three gunas of the Sankhya Yoga system of philosophy of later times).
The red and the black are also the Dawn and the Night or the dualistic
cycles of creation in which the white essence of the Absolute is hidden,
to be drawn out by the consciousness of Indra, the knowledge of the
supreme Self.

10. The Goddesses who have a common nest, from
the eternal their courses unchallenged, by their powers
guard the immortal laws. Manifold thousands, wives
like mothers, the sisters serve him, the imperious.

Indra, the supreme Self, is the One Lord of the myriad creative
powers, the Goddesses. They are his many thousand wives who serve him
in his Divine majesty as the Lord of all. He is the Sun and they are the red
Dawns and black Nights which revolve around him. He is the center, the
zenith, from which they blossom and expand. For one who knows the
Cosmic Male (the independent supreme Self), all creation becomes his
consort and waits upon him as the Goddess, taking the role of the Cosmic
Female (receptive creative Energy) relative to him.

11. Eternally young Goddess-thoughts, seeking substance, by prayers of surrender, with new songs of light,
rush to you, the wonder worker. As wives their husband, lovingly the loving one, the intuitions embrace
you, the conqueror.

The consorts of the Indra-Self are his knowledge, the higher thoughts
and intuitions of the Supreme. The Goddess is the soul who is our true
intelligence, wisdom manifesting as right thought and direct intuition. All
creation is their reflection, the manifestation of the ideals that they
represent.

12. From the eternal the splendors in your hands do not perish and cannot be exhausted, worker of wonders. You are radiant, strong willed, Indra, the sage. Aid us, Lord of power with your consort powers.

13. For you, the eternal one, who yokes the radiant stallions, for the perfect guide and conqueror, Nodhas rich in light has fashioned the new Word. May he whose substance is intelligence come directly in the morning.

Indra is the eternal being which conquers all things, that through time rules everything. All the powers of time are his consort powers and through him we gain their obeisance. Nodhas is the name of the seer of the hymn, rich in light or of the lineage of Gotama. The seer fashions for the Indra-Self the new Divine Word, the Brahman that is his declaration of victory — the OM, I am All.

Who Slays His Own Parents V.34
Seer — Prajapatya Samvarana

1. The ageless and immeasurable Waters of the Sun-World, according to the Self-nature, flow to the wonder worker whose opponent has never been born. Press out and cook the essence for the all lauded conveyer of the Divine Word. Further your efforts for him.

These are the infinite waters of immortal life, the waters of the sunlight of spiritual knowledge. They flow spontaneously from the Self to the Self. Indra is the being whose enemy has never been born, for he is the Self that has no opposition to anything. His only enemy is the ignorance of the Self, which, however, is unreal. To him we are to prepare and present our essence. In him we are to concentrate our energies, that he may convey the Divine Word, the knowledge of Brahman or the Godhead in which we pass beyond all opposition.

2. He who filled his belly with Soma, the beneficent Lord delighted in the juice of the honey-wine, when the seer Ushanas gave to him the mighty deadly weapon to slay the beast, the weapon with a thousand points.

3. He who presses out the Soma for him, in the heat or in the rain, becomes resplendent. For him luminous

in himself the beneficent Lord of power, the friend of
the seers, removes away his conditioning.

Indra is the spiritual man who fills his belly, his solar plexus, with the
mystic nectar, the wine of the Spirit. This Soma transmutes us from being
a conditioned slave of the ignorance into the wild unconditioned man of
the knowledge. The seer Ushanas, or the power of burning aspiration, is
what gives to the Indra archetype his deadly weapon, the thousand-pointed
vajra or thunderbolt to slay the beast of unconsciousness. It is only through
such actions of the seers that the Indra archetype, the consciousness of the
supreme, can manifest in creation. For this we were born.

For those who by choiceless awareness and pure perception are able
to distill the essence of delight out of all the experiences of life (press the
Soma), that Indra consciousness so strengthened removes his conditioning, literally "the line of his desire."

> 4. The Lord of power does not flee from him whose
> father, whose mother or whose brother he has killed.
> The maker of efforts, he arouses their exertions. The dis-
> tributer of the fullness of light, he does not flee from sin.

We find here a profound psychological statement, not the cult of some
brutal primitive god. Indra is the archetype of independence, the unconditioned mind. To discover that, to know our real Self, we must destroy
all the conditioned impressions in our mind, the mechanical stream of
thoughts which binds us to external influences and to the past. The main
bondage of our conditioning is that passed on through our parents and
family. To be a real man, an unconditioned entity, we must be able to set
aside the influence of our parents. We must enter the deep recesses of our
psyche and slay our father and our mother, their impression on our mind.
This is not to deny any spiritual influence that may come through our
family, but only to eliminate the egoistic side of their influence. Otherwise
we remain the shadow and extension of their shadow. We cannot do this
unaided because our mind or sense of ego is produced by these external
forces. We must invoke the great archetype of Indra to accomplish this
for us. He is the knowledge that mercilessly slays all conditionings, even
those that are comforting, maternal or paternal. He destroys all sense of
separative or exclusive relationship, that we may discover our true kinship
with all life. He is the wild man of the Spirit, the power beyond good and
evil which shatters the good thoughts, ideals and rationality of the mind,

showing that these are also just products of the unconscious or the ignorance.

Reason, idealism and good conditioning do not have the power to eradicate ignorance and violence from the psyche. They can inhibit it but cannot prevent its occurrence. The analytical mind is itself the product of thought and its ignorance. It functions not by a perception of truth, in which there is freedom, but by an attempt to explain things away that can only cover over the darkness and allow it to fester. What is necessary is the consciousness of the Self that is more primeval than the ignorance of the unconscious. Through it freedom is found by erasing the good and evil conditioning of the mind. All conditioning is ultimately evil and creates bondage, being a domination of the mind by external influences, not true conscious being. Whether we are conditioned for good or for evil, whether we are the barbarian or the cultured man, we are will-less products of our environment. We are reaction mechanisms according to our conditioning, not real men capable of independent perception and creative action. We need the mind of Indra, the unconditioned sense beyond good and evil, the barbaric and the civilized, for the birth of the true man.

> 5. He does not seek alliance with five or ten. He
> does not associate with those who do not concentrate
> and never provide nourishment. Fierce, he conquers and
> slays him and gives the God-seeker his share in the con-
> centration full of light.

The consciousness of the Self always goes alone. The One does not seek or depend upon alliance with the many. It is up to them to follow him. Only when we are willing to face the truth directly and alone can we find it. As long as we are seeking some comforting alliance to lead us to it, we will never find it because, bound by fear and thinking of others, depending upon their approval, we cannot reach our unconditioned Self. As long as we are forging some alliance, seeking some advantage for ourselves, not providing nourishment but seeking it elsewhere, our own soul will flee us. Our inner being will humiliate us and make us face the folly of our arrogance. It is only for the One who stands alone, concentrated in the Self as a source of nourishment for all, depending or relying on no external aids or artifices, that the true Man can manifest.

The five or ten are also the five senses and the five elements. The inner Self does not seek alliance with these outer forces. It has substance in itself and direct knowledge.

6. Skillful in the encounter he stopped the wheel, the
opponent of those who do not concentrate, the increaser
of those who do. Indra is the terrible tamer of all. According to his will the noble lead away the ignoble.

The wheel Indra stops is that of karmic conditionings, the reaction
process of the ignorant mind. Those who do not concentrate inwardly to
find their true nature, by that dispersing energy they disintegrate, losing
their Indra. Those who concentrate, who press out of their minds by inner
inquiry the archetypes that decondition the mind, themselves become
Indra. The noble are those who have the nobility of mind not to seek
advantage for themselves or cling to external support systems but rest in
the power of their own unconditioned being.

7. He collects for plunder the wealth of the traders.
He distributes the joyous wealth to the mortal who consecrates himself to him. Even in an inaccessible place
all the people cannot hide, the men who have enraged
his consort-power.

The traders (Panis) are the bartering mind that always seeks advantage
for itself, the negative side of the commercial mentality which today is
destroying the world. That mentality and the people who delighted in it
were thrown out of the spiritual kingdom of ancient India. For a new age
and spiritual civilization today we must again throw out the pursuit of
wealth as the highest goal, which in its divisiveness creates conflict
between men and causes us to violate and plunder the Earth. Those who
hoard what they have lose it to their own greed and never can accumulate
enough to give them peace or happiness. Those who give freely cannot
lose. The wealth of the Divine Spirit manifests within them and they find
all life in its great beauty to be theirs. If we enrage the beneficent
Goddess-power of the Divine by our greed for personal wealth, not seeing
the overflowing bounty of this glorious creation, where can we expect to
hide and who can we expect to share our company?

The Wielder of the Vajra III.46
Seer — Gathina Vishvamitra

1. Great are the heroic energies of you who are renowned as great — Indra, the Self-ruler, the fighting

Bull, the awesome youth, firm and daring, the undecaying wielder of the vajra.

2. Great are you by spiritual vigor, the wild Bull, the
awesome one who wins all wealth, conquering all that is
other. As the One alone you are the ruler of all the
world. Send men forth for battle and for rest.

3. He has extended beyond all measure, shining, be-
yond the Gods to every side, unequalled. Imperious
Indra by his majesty has transcended great Heaven and
Earth and the wide Atmosphere.

4. To him, the vast, profound, awesome from birth,
the all-encompassing well of intuition, the effused
streams of bliss from earlier Heaven like rivers to the
sea enter into Indra.

5. That Soma of yours which Heaven-Earth bears for
you as a mother bears her child, that the masters of the
sacrifice impel for you, that they cleanse for you for the
Bull to drink.

Indra is the warrior Bull of the Spirit, the Self-ruler who through
Self-rule rules all the universe and all levels of consciousness. He is the
wielder of the vajra, the thunder or lightning-bolt of illumined perception,
the flashing power of the Divine Word that is the solar weapon of the
enlightened Mind. In the West the vajray is more commonly known as a
symbol used in Tibetan Buddhism. But like most of the terms and forms
of Buddhism, which is also an Aryan religion deriving from the ancient
seers, it can be found in the *Veda*, where it first originates. Indra is the
vajra being of the *Vedas*, the immutable warrior power of the light. Indra
is the One only who conquers all sense of otherness and so wins freedom
for all beings. He is the sense of individuality, of the Divine dignity of the
individual human being as greater than all the world, out of which all men
strive towards the supreme. When this spiritual Man accomplishes his
Self-rule, when we gain the supreme power of self-knowledge, our
consciousness extends beyond measure, beyond all the worlds into the
Absolute. He becomes the single ruling Sun in Heaven, the all-conquering
vajra of Self-illumination through which like a wheel, he directs all
creation. That supreme being above is the profound being within, the well
of all right thinking and sure intuitive perception. All the streams of
Soma-bliss in earlier Heaven, the archetypal world, are intrinsically his.
He is the Divine Father through which Heaven-Earth is the Divine Mother
of creation through his bliss. This Soma-bliss the seers, the masters of the

sacrifice, bring forth in man for the manifestation of Indra in his own creation.

According to His Own Will He Created Himself III.48
Seer — Gathina Vishvamitra

1. At the instant of his birth the young Bull was ready to drink the concentrated juice. According to your desire, drink the original heated essence, the Soma of perfection.

2. The day when you were born with this desire you drank the nectar of the luminous stalk which dwells in the mountains. That your Mother, the maiden who bore you, poured forth first in the house of the mighty Father.

3. Having approached the Mother he implored her for food. He saw the pungent Soma on her breast. Warding off all others, the wise one wandered. Of manifold presence he accomplished great actions.

4. The awesome, swift conqueror, of transcendent vigor, according to his will, he created himself. Indra, by nature having transcended the Creator, drank his Soma in the world vessels.

The young Bull is the ever new Spirit. The instant of his birth is the moment wherein he manifests Himself. The concentrated juice, the heated essence or Soma of perfection is the essence of perception distilled by Self-knowledge. It is our vision of the Self in all beings that extracts the secret essence of delight hidden in creation. Indra is the sense of the supremacy of the Self, the unconditioned individual over all the world, including God the Creator himself. The luminous stalk is the spinal nervous system and its subtle centers or chakras that yield the Soma-nectar, which dwells high in the mountains of meditation. The Mother is the Shakti, the Goddess-power behind creation. She yields the pungent Soma of the intensity of bliss. Her breast or udder, as she is also the wish-fulfilling cosmic Cow, is the Word of truth, perceiving which the Indra-Self absorbs it for sustenance. Indra is that sense of the supremacy of the Self whereby we ward off all sense of otherness and the hostility this misconception breeds. His manifold presence is his great action, the daring deed of seeing himself in all beings and thereby destroying all opposition.

The Creator or Fashioner (Tvashtar) is the personal God of the ignorance, the Divine not as the Self of all beings but as a God different from his creation, in relationship to whom there is a sense of separation. He is the Lord of karma, action bound by desire that causes rebirth; the God who in our lack of Self-knowledge we must worship. Indra is our true Self that is one with the Absolute and transcendent to creation and all of its phenomenal vicissitudes. Energizing his archetype within us through the perception of the Soma-essence within the Mother Shakti, we go beyond the rule of this outer Creator or cosmic demiurge. We steal the wine of creative delight hidden in the worlds because in our Self we experience all creation as our own. The Indra archetype is the manifestation of our unborn essence, the integrating seed-power of transformation whereby we step beyond the domain of change, beyond cosmic law to the freedom of being behind it. Indra is the prototype of seeing within us whereby we become all that we see and the Seer of all. Through him we bring the Godhead into Self-awareness in its own creation, the Brahman manifests as Atman, the Absolute as the Self. It is this Self-creation, this re-creation of ourselves in the Supreme Self that is the highest creation wherein we win all the worlds. It is the highest birth after which there is no other and which has no end.

The house or domain of the mighty Father which yields this first Soma is the home of the Absolute, the Divine Father. Indra is the Son of the higher and uncreate Father who reclaims his domain from the lower created Father, the conditioned God of the ignorance. We see, therefore, in these ancient mythic mantras the highest truths of later Vedantic philosophy, the distinction between God the Creator and the Absolute and the transcendency of the Self.

Indra Speaks as the Hawk IV.26
Seer — Vamadeva Gautama

1. I was the father of all men and I became the Sun. I am the seer Kakshivan, the sage. I overwhelmed Kutsa of the lineage of the light. I am the seer Ushanas, behold me!

2. I gave the Earth to the Aryans. I brought down the rain for my mortal worshipper. I led the roaring floods. The Gods moved by my will.

3. In ecstasy I burst open at once the ninety-nine cities of the Dragon. Destroying the hundredth-most habitation, I delivered all beings, as I favored the servant of Heaven, of the timeless ray.

4. Oh Gods of light, let this bird take precedence over all birds, this swift flying hawk over all hawks, as, strong winged by his unmoving Self-nature, he brought to man the God-loved offering.

5. When the bird brought it to us, speeding by a wide path swifter than thought he moved. Quickly he went with the honey-bliss of the Soma. Thus the hawk found the revelation.

6. The imperious hawk, the song bird, taking the stalk, the joyous delight from the beyond, brought the Soma. Godlike, the bird grasped it firmly, which he had received from the highest Heaven.

7. The hawk took the Soma he received through a thousand times ten thousand effusions. Thus the Goddess of bountiful intelligence abandoned the ungiving; in the ecstasy of Soma, she in wisdom abandoned the foolish.

Indra as the spiritual Man is the father of all men and the Sun of the world. In our Indra-Self we are all men and their prototype. Kakshivan, etc., are various famous Vedic seers who possessed knowledge of Indra. This spiritual Man has ordained the earth for the Aryans, for noble people, the races of noble wisdom. He drowns the ignoble in the great flood of his power. The cities destroyed are all the artificial propensities of the ignorance, the perversions of lust and greed that cities breed. These events also refer to the great flood in ancient times that destroyed an earlier and spiritually fallen civilization (Atlantean) and opened the Earth for the Aryans, the new spiritual race, to spread.

This knowledge of the Self is the hawk or eagle, the bird of the Sun, the free Spirit. It carries the highest bliss, which it effuses infinitely. The Goddess of bountiful intelligence is the consort or mind of Indra, our own soul that is released through this knowledge of the Divine I am, the I am All. The first verse of this hymn is used in the *Upanishads* (*Brihadaranyaka Upanishad* I.IV.10.) as the model expression of God-realization in man. The same hawk symbolism occurs in ancient Egypt under the God Horus. The solar hawk or winged disc was also the symbol of the Aryan kings.

Generating at Once the Sun, Heaven and the Dawn VI.30
Seer — Barhaspatya Bharadvaja

1. He has grown even greater for heroic power. The one undecaying apportions the treasures. Indra has transcended Heaven and Earth, half of him is equal to both the worlds.

2. Vast I know is his almighty power. What he has upheld no one can diminish. Day by day the Sun became more beautiful, of good will he spread wide the habitations.

3. Even today remains that artistry of the rivers, when you opened out a channel for the floods. The mountains like men at a feast settled down. By you of good will the regions were made firm.

4. This is the Truth, Indra, there is no other like you, no God or mortal greater. You slew the serpent who held back the waters. You released the floods down to the sea.

5. You burst open the flood gates to every side. Indra, you broke the firmness of the mountain. You became the ruler of the world, of all men, generating at once the Sun, Heaven and the Dawn.

Indra is the spiritual man who is the Divine Being, the Lord of Light. All creation is only half his nature. The other half is transcendent, the Godhead of the Absolute. There is no other like him as he is the Self in which there is no otherness. His consciousness wins for man the light and the waters, the floods of light. He slays the serpent of the ignorance, the snake of egoism that bottles up and inhibits the flood gates of spiritual knowledge. He is the light of pure perception that breaks open the mountain of the unconscious and releases the power of our consciousness confined and inverted in it. He is our own daring soul, the being of life that is awake within us at every moment, equal to every challenge, ever ready to grow further.

Conscious with the Energy of Life in Every World-Age VI.36
Seer — Nara Bharadvaja

1. Ever have your ecstasies been all-creating, so ever-more have been your earthly splendors. Ever you

have been the apportioner of power, since among the
Gods they upheld your almighty being.

2. Men win his vigor through sacrifice and evermore
sustain it for heroic strength. To seize the rein of the impetuous war horse they concentrate their will in Indra
for the slaying of the serpent.

3. All aids and manly energies conjoined in conver-
gence follow Indra. As rivers to the sea our songs and
hymnal powers enter into Him, the all-comprehensive.

4. As you are lauded, Indra, open out the spring of
splendor, manifold delight and treasure. You have become unequalled among men, the One rule of all the
world.

5. Listen with knowledge, you who wish to work,
who like Heaven, over the Earth, stands over our
opponents' splendor. May you be with us by strength delighting, conscious with the energy of life in every
world-age.

Indra is the Being of Life, of the true life that is immortal in all men
and all world-ages, the eternal Man. He is the Man who is supreme among
the Gods, who can manifest the supreme in the material world — a feat
of daring even the Gods cannot accomplish and fear even to attempt. The
impetuous war horse is our concentrated life energy that must be released
to destroy all the serpentine obstructions of the ignorance which make us
dependent upon the external. The Indra archetype remains ever within us,
wishing to work within us, standing as Heaven above the material desires
that enslave us — beckoning us to the authentic and genuine existence
that is possible only when we are true to our Self. His is the real life, the
eternal eon, of which all else is a shadow play. By invoking him we enter
into that imperious life.

You have Conquered All Births VIII.88
Seer — Nodhas Gautama

1. The wonder worker who conquers the stream,
who enjoys the juice of light, as milch cows in their
own stalls to their calf, with songs we sing to Indra.

2. The celestial perfect giver, encompassed by his
consort-powers, like a mountain yielding manifold de-

lights, directly we implore him for the hundred thousandfold rich power full of light.

3. Indra, vast and massive mountains cannot obstruct
you when you wish to give the fullness of light to such a
singer. No one can diminish your bounty.

4. Through your majesty, through will, power and
magic, you have conquered all births. This solar Word
for aid will manifest you, which the Gotama-seers have
generated.

5. Through strength you have extended beyond the
ends of Heaven. The material region cannot encompass
you, Indra, when according to the Self-nature you have
expanded.

6. Beneficent Lord, there is no limit to your beneficence, when to your offerer you give. Be the stimulator
of our utterance, the most magnanimous for the winning
of power.

Indra is the conqueror of all births, the knowledge of oneness that
takes us beyond the stream of separative existence. He is the Divine Being,
the real entity or supreme man, who lives on the luminous juice of bliss.
He grants the infinite fullness of light to the mortal who surrenders to him,
who consecrates himself to the sacrificial life of self-knowledge. He is
manifested by the solar Word, the word which is the Sun, which is OM,
the truth vibration of the enlightened or illumined Mind. This is the sound
all the mantras of the seers give impulse to. Indra is the surrender of
ourselves to the supreme which grants the supreme beneficence and
felicity. He is the sense of universal oneness that self-knowledge brings.
We are bound to the cycle of rebirth only through the acquisitive mind
whereby we seek things for ourselves only. Indra is the state of giving
which is the Mind of wisdom that breaks this net of selfish thought.

You have Transcended All Existence VIII.89
Seers — Nrimedha and Purumedha Angirasa

1. Gods of power, move with greatness to Indra, the
supreme Dragon-slayer, through whom the Gods who
exalt in truth generated the Divine ever-wakeful light
for the Divine.

2. He blew away all curses, the curse-destroyer; then
he became resplendent. Indra, you who have the vast

light, who rule the army of the Gods, the Gods strive for
your companionship.

3. To your vast Indra, Gods of flashing power, sing
to light the Divine Word. The Dragon-slayer, whose
will is hundredfold, he will slay the Dragon with his
hundred-jointed lightning bolt.

4. Press forward with daring, you of daring mind,
your renown will be vast. Let the Mother floods pour in
torrents. Slay the Dragon, win the Sun-World.

5. When you were born without precedent, beneficent Lord, to slay the Dragon, then you spread wide the
Earth and up-pillared Heaven.

6. Then your sacrifice was born, along with the solar
Word and the laughter. Thus you have transcended all
existence, what has been born and what will be born.

7. You energized the ripe essence in the immature
cows. You made the Sun rise in Heaven. As the radiant
essence in the mystic Song, cook him through inner
transformations; as the joyful being of the vast, for you,
the lover of song.

The Gods of power or of the storm, the Maruts, the companions of
Indra, are the seers who in lauding him partake of his ever-wakeful Divine
light of consciousness. This intuition of Indra or the Supreme destroys all
the curses of wrong thinking. He holds within his possession the all-conquering Sun of knowledge, of which the Gods are the rays. We manifest
him in the fullness of the song of our soul which is Divine. Through him,
the being of the sacrifice, we transcend all birth and existence, go beyond
all rebirth. He finds the light of truth even in the ignorant and immature.
He draws the Divine light even out of mortal men. He is our Divine sense
of individuality, whose creative growth unfolds our inner Sun, resurrects
it from the darkness to the light, restores it to its true nature as the vast.

SURYA

*We meditate upon the supreme effulgence of
the Divine creative Sun, that he may give impulse to our intelligence.* — *Rig Veda III.62.10*

*When arising today, oh Sun, you declare the
truth that we are sinless to the Divine Friend
and Lord,*

*May we, oh Infinite Mother, be in the God-
head, dearest companion, your beloved singers.*
— *Rig Veda VII.60.1*

*Evermore right-minded, perfect in vision,
creative, free of weakness, sinless, with you rising as the great Friend day by day; living
brightly may we reflect you, oh Sun.*

*As you bear the great light, clear in vision,
radiant as bliss to every eye, arising from a
great force; living in truth, may we reflect you,
oh Sun.*

*According to whose morning ray all the
worlds come forth and by whose evening stars
descend to rest, golden-haired Sun, in sinless-
ness day by day arise for us more real.*
— *Rig Veda X.37.7–9*

5
SURYA, INTELLIGENCE,
THE SOLAR SELF OF DIVINE WISDOM

The Sun of Creation

In the beginning darkness was on the face of the deep. All creation lay enshrouded in the formless waters of chaos, a confused and turbulent sea of incipient forces. In the beginning was non-being, insentience and sleep. The cosmos lay hidden in the primordial ignorance. All was a dark mass of elemental forces, stagnant in their inertia, not wanting to be, not daring to be aware, afraid of life, enshrouded and contracted in a fathomless blank and endless finity. An alliance of death, darkness and unconsciousness ruled supreme in a timeless transience, a spaceless finitude, the ultimate limit of nonexistence that had only somewhere, as if by chance, a secret spark of being and consciousness wanting to manifest. Whence came this massive ignorance no one can say. The mind is still in its shadow, is the very separative intelligence of this chaos carried within it all along. Time and space come after it. Moving energy comes after it. It is originally only a frozen motion of inertia, the resistance of a blind intelligence, a mute obstinacy not to grow or to change, of which the mind is the final product as well as original seed.

This primordial ignorance is not only, therefore, the primal cosmic event, it is also the primal psychic event; as without, so within, by the dual parallelism of all creation. We are the creatures of this chaos, still caught within its sphere, not certain whether to seek to transcend it or to defend it. Ignorance or not-knowing is the limit out of which we operate, the horizon our thought and action presumes, in which dilemma we live and have our being. The only explanation for this ignorance may be that it is the latent state of cosmic existence, the darkness of unmanifest potential, life longing to be but not yet daring to come forth. Ignorance is the darkness of the beginning like the chaos of ideas and the resistance of the medium that a great artist faces. In the cosmic creative labor it is a massive chaos, an eonic resistance towards what must be the most difficult but most enduring, daring and fulfilling creative adventure.

In the beginning was the ignorance, the indefinable ground of cosmos-psyche, its burgeoning chaos. Yet even this ignorance had an intelligence, this death a life, this non-being a being, which was all it knew, or could know, as it was a boundless, self-enclosed finitude. This apparent existence was not a true intelligence, life and being, but rather a shadow or imitation of it, a resistance or mere potential for it. It was the intelligence of chaos, a self-defensive clinging to an obstinate and unjustified resistance to growth and evolution. It was the life of death, a confused energy of desire from a beginningless past, blind to the energy and vitality of an endless present. It was the being of things that could exist only insofar as being did not manifest — the divided, incomplete, disintegrating state of things, a clinging to emptiness and sorrow as that was all it knew beyond which it could only sense an even greater nonexistence. It was the being of ignorance and misconception that could only imagine true conception as self-annihilation. This ignorance must be destroyed for consciousness to manifest, just as wood has to burn to produce the flame. Ignorance is the resistance in the fuel of matter to the flame of the spirit, the blind opposition of the rock to life that has to be overcome for life to be and which defends itself mercilessly for its survival even against a higher force that would take it beyond.

This life of the ignorance, this false life and intelligence produced the first generation of creatures, the distorted and monstrous offspring of chaos, the mythological demons or titans. They are the great elemental forces of primordial fear, anger and desire that first awoke in the abyss of chaos. Their effort is to return creation to its primal state of sleep and chaos. These dark creatures of the psyche find life to be a disturbance to their sleep and to the ignorance which supports them. Such creatures have no soul or real life but are the shadowy expressions of chaos wishing to return to its original dark eon of non-being. These are the demons, the negative energy sources of false thinking and blind emotion, fear, desire and sloth that are always there to drag us down should our labor of mindfulness slacken. They are our natural enemies, the opponents of spiritual man which we must mercilessly and unrelentingly slay to discover our true Self and bring the light of truth to the world. With them is the war between light and darkness, cosmos and chaos, the mythic war between the Gods and the demons, the Divine and the undivine.

This ignorance is not itself life and creation, but only the negative background, the dark latency of potential forces seeking to be, out of which life and creation are the victorious manifestation. This ignorance is also a womb, a matrix. Even its resistance ultimately serves to temper the light laboring within it, forcing it to draw out of itself the supreme power of transformation. If it is the most difficult medium, it is also the greatest challenge, evoking the strongest and most daring Spirit. To be at all, it must contain a spark of true being, life and intelligence. As being, life and intelligence is one and universal that is enough to eventually overcome it.

What is born in these formless waters of the cosmic deep, the great world abyss and its descending currents, is the great miracle of life and creation, the Sun. This Sun is at first hidden, no more than a secret spark, the hidden presence of the fire or Agni. Then matter coalesces and densifies, becoming a massive vortex, as it defiantly, against the spirit, asserts its separative existence. The ignorance is extended to its ultimate conclusion. Separate clouds of matter condense into differentiated centers. The ignorant will that is directed towards the finite and the transient appears triumphant. Formless chaos, by its own obscure inertia to protect itself against the spiritual light, becomes the chaos of form; elemental matter. Yet precisely at this extreme point the great transformation occurs. The densified matter explodes into light. The Sun is born. The ignorance taken to its extreme limit repolarizes, is transmuted. Having reached its furthest point of contraction, its energy reverses itself and expands into a higher level. It is like a bow pulled backwards to release an arrow forwards. All of its inertia and resistance become the polar tension to force the emergence of an infinitely stronger counterforce. The cosmic Sun is ignited and explodes into light. Matter suddenly irradiated with light is restructured by its magnetic currents. Its separate centers become linked with currents of light and lines of force. Each center becomes a point of oneness, a center that is everywhere, and the inertia of division vanishes like the smoke before the fire.

Ignorance is the seeking of being in non-being, the eternal in the transient. Yet even this seeking reflects an innate knowledge of being, as otherwise why would it be sought? So at the extreme point of this search, the realization dawns that there is no being in non-being. The urge is separated, differentiated from its wrong direction. Being comes to be sought in being and is therefore found everywhere. This great revolution is the birth of the Sun and its resurrection out of darkness, the winning of the cosmos from chaos.

On the psychic plane, this extreme densification and differentiation of matter is the formation of the ego. Though hidden in all states of matter, it is in man that its ultimate development occurs, and in which its full pain is felt. The ego that is latent in nature, restrained by instinct in animals, is given a voice and a power of action in man, through which the evil of its inertia of chaos and delusion is released. This is why man, who is the highest creature in nature, is also the lowest. In him is the greatest polarity between good and evil, truth and falsehood, being and non-being, spirit and matter. This draws us into the search for transcendence, that we may

take the world soul through us to its point of repolarization, its revolution-
ary return to the Divine. At the extreme manifestation of the ego, the
futility of its entire process is understood. We see its basic blindness and
sorrow. We realize that separateness can only breed pain. Then this great
miracle again occurs. The ego ignites, explodes into light and becomes
the Sun of the universal Self. Contracted to the extreme point of selfishness, unable to go further, it explodes the other way and the great catharsis
occurs. Our separative stream of thought settles into the great ocean of
unitary awareness. Man gives birth to the psychic Sun, the solar Self, and
all creation rejoices in its deliverance into the transparent light of seeing.

In their worship of the Sun, the ancients revered not just our star. It
was the principle of light, the world sun, the cosmic sun, the central light
of consciousness in the heart that they gave homage to. The Sun symbolizes the victory of the light over darkness, being over non-being, life over
death and knowledge over ignorance. It is the immanent Divine consciousness in creation, the Divine Son who manifests the transcendent
uncreate Godhead, the Divine Father. Within man, the creature of intelligence, is his unity with all as the Divine Son. This victory of the Sun is
the victory of the Divine Person, the unconditioned entity, over his
conditioned field of manifestation, the victory of the subject over objec-
tivity, of the individual over the world, of the One over all multiplicity.
The Sun symbolizes the presence of the Absolute as the guiding ray in
creation, the evolutionary forefront of all life. It is that supremely daring,
irrepressible Will to Be, through every possibility of manifestation, however difficult and dangerous, even physical matter which is the densest
and most obstinate field of manifestation for the Divine. It is the reverence
for the supreme transformative truth of all creation as a movement from
an unmanifest chaos of dark ignorance to a splendorous cosmos, a temple
for the Godhead as its indwelling light.

To the ancients, the Sun was the visible face of all the Gods, the
universal Godhead itself. Their mantras shone like the Sun, being reflections in human language of the Divine word of light. The ancients
regarded themselves as the people, the children of this Sun, its representatives on Earth — the Sun of the secret and sacred Heart of Being, more
primal than the Earth yet manifested by her patient and receptive labor.
Its stimulating perceptive rays are everywhere for the seer, fostering and
nourishing the true life spirit and will to grow. There is only One Light
without and within. The presence of the outer light is the seal of the
presence of the inner light. Its rays are like open hands everywhere
offering the gift of wisdom and the waters of immortal life. It is our duty
only to see them, to witness them, and in so recognizing them to serve as

a channel for them for the good of all, beyond which there is no other good. May that beneficent Sun return again for all men to see!

The Solar Self I.115
Seer — Kutsa Angirasa

1. The wonderful face of Gods is arisen, the eye of
the Divine Lord, Friend and Fire. He has filled Heaven,
Earth and the Atmosphere, the Sun, the Self of all that is
stable and moving.

The Sun (Surya) is the visible presence, the vision of the Divine, the cosmic symbol for the supreme. He is the Divine light and presence that fills all the worlds. He is the world-soul, the Self, the Atman of all beings. He is the Sun in the heart by which we all live and have our being and consciousness. It is this solar Self that is the real truth and reverence behind the ancient solar religion. It is not the sun that they worshipped but the Self within the heart which the Sun in the sky parallels outwardly and symbolizes. The Vedic seers saw that there is only one light, which is life and consciousness without division. That unitary light of seeing, in all its beauty and glory, they felt within the Sun.

2. As a youth follows a maiden, the Sun follows
after the radiant Dawn, where God-seeking men extend
the world-ages, facing him who is auspicious for bliss.
3. Auspicious are the radiant mares of the Sun, wonderful, variegated, to be delighted in. Holy they have
mounted the ridge of Heaven. They travel around
Heaven and Earth in an instant.

The Sun of illumination follows in love after the Dawn of awakening. There God-seeking men extend their world-ages, spreading forth within the solar Self into the eternal. In that light of oneness all time is auspicious.

The Sun's mares are his consort-powers. They are his beneficence of love and beauty that circle all the worlds. They are his friendly and nourishing rays. They are also the planets.

4. This is the Divinity of the Sun, his greatness, that
what was extended in the middle of his work he draws
back together again. When he has yoked his radiant

mares from their station, then the Night spreads her garment over all.

5. The Sun in the bosom of Heaven changes his
form that the Divine Lord and Friend might see. Infinite
at one time, refulgent in his power, dark at the other, his
radiant mares draw it back together again.

The great glory and mystery of the Sun for the ancients is its return
to the east in the morning, its mysterious disappearance in the west at night
and its mystic transit of darkness. As such, the Sun is the symbol of the
resurrection and renewal of the soul, the promise of immortality. It is this
mystic night Sun that was their main Sun God. It is the Sun's invisible
journey through the realms of darkness, the dark realms of the psyche, its
defeat of the powers of darkness for its return to enlightenment in the east,
which most fascinated them. To them, the true Divinity and greatness of
the Sun was that he could resurrect himself. He could stop his work in the
middle, gather up his light and take his radiant mares through mysterious
interior realms in order to return renewed. It was the solar renewal at night,
the secret of the midnight Sun, that was for them the supreme light and
essence of the Sun. His radiant mares are his powers of conveyance
through the night, who hold his power compressed within themselves as
his mothers for his rebirth at dawn.

The ancient quest was how to return the solar soul of man from its
western setting in death and ignorance to its eastern sunrise again in life
and knowledge. Man must also learn to draw back in his creative powers
and let them renew themselves through the night of the quiescent mind.
Underlying the sensitivity of perception for its sustenance should be
periods of rest in the void of pure awareness. That play of day and night,
expansion and contraction, wide impersonality and concentrated compassion are the complementary rhythm of the sacrifice, in which there is
eternal return.

6. Today, oh Gods, in the rising of the Sun, deliver
us from all narrowness and blame. May the Divine Lord
and Friend increase that for us, along with the Infinite
Mother, the Ocean, Earth and Heaven.

In that return through darkness, facing all the chaos of our own
unconsciousness, is the rebirth of our soul in which we are born sinless.
This is the way of self-knowledge, to turn the light of perception within
and illumine our own interior night, exposing the elemental conditioning

that rules us in secret. This is the mystic Vedic work through mantric archetypes of the Gods, without which we are not men in the light of day but the bubbling of obscure passions out of elemental confusion.

Savitar, The Sun of Transformation I.35
Seer — Hiranyastupa Angirasa

> 1. First, for well-being I invoke the Fire. I invoke the
> Divine Lord and Friend here for grace. I invoke the
> Night that brings the world to rest. I invoke the Divine
> transforming Sun for aid.

The Fire is the flame of mindfulness which must be enkindled first in the inner ritual of the transformation of consciousness. The Divine Lord and Friend (Varuna and Mitra) are the Divine Father and Son; the first the power of stern judgment, the immutable order of the Absolute, and the second that of compassion, the creative order of the immanent Godhead. The Night, a form of Goddess, is the mystic night of spiritual knowledge which illumines the depths of our psyche. The creative transforming Sun (Savitar) is the God of the mystic night, the night wherein all outwardness and worldliness is put to rest for the illumination of the inner Sun of Self-knowledge.

The God Savitar is the Sun of transformation. In his central action he is the secret Sun at midnight that brings the light into the deepest recesses of the darkness and turns even the darkness into light. He regenerates and transforms our being in the light of Self-knowledge, taking us beyond the rule of the unconscious. He is the Divine principle that governs the course of the sun from dusk to dawn, taking it across the darkened regions for their renewal and the sun's illumination. He brings the light from its western decline back to its eastern resurrection for a new and higher day of inner awareness. This great God, the transforming Sun at midnight who brings the world to rest, was the main Sun-God of the ancients, like the Egyptian Re, who similarly is the God of the Sun through its mystic night journey. He is also the spiritual or invisible light of the Sun which feeds the plant of our soul and its subtle astral growths just as the Sun's visible light nourishes vegetation. His is the cosmic light of intelligence that sustains the vibration of spiritual harmony and peace in creation.

> 2. Revolving through the darkened region, laying to
> rest the mortal and the immortal, by a golden chariot the
> Divine creative Sun journeys, perceiving the worlds.

> 3. He travels by a descending slope, by an ascending slope he travels. Most holy, he moves with his two radiant stallions. The Divine creative Sun comes from the Beyond, driving away all evil.

The creative Sun has two complementary actions according to the twofold nature of the symbolic night. The higher night is the night of the Absolute, the great night of the unknown and uncreate Godhead, in which all the worlds, all Gods and men, all mortals and immortals are put to rest in the pure One only. The lower night is the dark night of chaos, of the unconscious, the realm of obscure, evil devolutionary forces, the primeval inertia of the cosmic swamp and the dark beings that feed on it and wish to sustain our sleep within it. The transforming Sun is the sunlight of truth perception which reveals the Absolute, breaking up the darkness of the unconscious and releasing its imprisoned creative light. Savitar illumines the lower night of the ignorance with the higher night of the knowledge, through which he prepares the way for the Divine day, creation redeemed in the knowledge of the Absolute. His two radiant stallions are his powers of seeing duality in unity, his capacity to resolve all contradictions into complementarity. He comes from the Beyond, from the Absolute, driving away all the evil of the mind confused by relativity, thereby revealing the pervasive Godhead.

> 4. Encased with pearls, possessing every form, vast with a golden pole, the adorable god Savitar, who has a wonderfully clear beam, has mounted his chariot, holding his consort power for darkened regions.
> 5. Conveying his chariot whose forepart is gold, his dark, white-footed stallions have illumined all men. All beings and all worlds remain forever in the bosom of the Divine creative Sun.

The vehicle of the Divine transforming Sun is the omniform vehicle of knowledge supported by the golden wisdom of oneness. It is the Sun in its invisible power as the secret light of knowledge that opens out the darkness of the night of ignorance. On this chariot, the God Savitar takes his consort power, his Goddess radiance, to these regions of illusion. She is the intense brilliance of his light which cherishes all beings, brightening but not burning. His stallions are dark, that is transcendent and of the Absolute, but their feet are white as they bear the light to the phenomenal worlds. All life as a constant movement is a dance of transcendence, a play of transformation. In this essence of transformation all beings remain forever in Savitar, the Being of transformation. He is the supreme light of creation that is the free overflowing of the transcendent uncreate. His is the power of the Divine creativity which underlies all creation and which recreates and regenerates us in the light of truth. The Greek Sun God Apollo derives from him as the power of creative inspiration and insight.

> 6. To the creative Sun belong three Heavens. Two are in his presence, one is in the world of Death where the heroes dwell. As on the axle-pin of a chariot, there all the immortals remain. Let him who knows this declare it here.

These three Heavens are the triple-Absolute of Being-Consciousness-Bliss, Sacchidananda. The third Heaven or the plane of Bliss also contains the world of the God of Death, Yama, who represents the power of yogic discipline (also called yama in Sanskrit). Also called the Creation of Light, it is the highest domain of the Gods and of enlightened souls, the heroes of the lower worlds (called Siddhas in later Sanskrit literature). In this triple Godhead, all the immortals in essence reside, who are but diverse forms of a common and interpenetrating substance. The higher realms are realms of pure unity, with the third or bliss-principle containing the realm of multiplicity in unity, where the pure archetypes reside in their ideal perfection, the Divine causal realm from which creation originates by descent.

> 7. The hawk, the almighty Lord and perfect guide whose vibration is profound, has illuminated the intermediate spaces. Where is the Sun today? Who perceives it? What Heaven has his ray extended?
>
> 8. He has illumined the eight summit-peaks of the Earth, three desert regions, seven rivers. The golden-eyed God Savitar has come, holding boons and delights for the harmonious mortal.

The intermediate spaces or atmospheres are the hidden interior realms, the spaces within and between things. In our ignorance, our lack of illumination of them, they become the abode for the powers of darkness and illusion. What we do not see becomes the unconscious in which the inertia of our non-seeing draws our minds down into sorrow and strife. When illumined by the light of self-knowledge, this becomes the inner space for the revelation of the Supreme. The unconscious is transmuted from an inertia of sorrow and conflict to a fountain of blissful creative energy. It is repolarized as the receptacle for cosmic consciousness to descend and manifest in its full power and extent. It is out of this inner space of potential consciousness stagnating as the unconscious that the hawk, the liberated being of free perception, through the capacity of its great depths fashions Heaven, illumines all the worlds.

The eight peaks of the Earth are the octagon of cosmic existence. They are the seven planes and their unity, perceived in the heights of the physical being, the awareness of totality on the material plane. The three desert regions are the triple phenomenal realm of matter-life-mind which are dominated by the ignorance and its dry mechanism. The seven rivers are the creative forces of the seven planes through which these deserts are flooded with life and consciousness. All this the archetype of transformation, the mystic Sun of the dark night of regeneration, makes conscious to the mortal who is harmonized to him, who has become attuned to his power that he might accomplish his Divine work within them.

> 9. Golden-handed Savitar, clear in vision, travels on
> between Heaven and Earth. He drives away violence
> and directs the approach of the Sun. Through the dark-
> ened region he unfolds Heaven.
> 10. Let the perfect guide, the compassionate al-
> mighty Self-natured Lord with golden hands approach.
> Driving away demons and sorcerers, the God is present,
> sung at evening.
> 11. Savitar, your original paths, perfectly made, dust-
> less in the interior realm, by these easy going paths
> today guard us and bless us, oh God.

Savitar has golden hands. These are his helpful and beneficent rays of knowledge, the light that gives the gift of immortal life. He is the night Sun, the secret Sun of the inner planes, who prepares and directs the approach of the day Sun, Surya, the manifest Sun of the outer planes. For the Sun of knowledge to rise in our outer waking consciousness it must first rise in the dark night of our unconscious states of dream and deep sleep, clearing out the ignorance that keeps our waking state bound by fantasy and lack of true perception. This is the transforming action of Savitar. Evening is his dawn. He is the light that remains aware and awake throughout the night. In his presence evening, dusk, is not to be feared as a return to the rule of darkness but to be welcomed as the gestation of an inner light to prepare a newer and more glorious day. Savitar is the secret presence of the light even in darkness, discovering which we can conquer all darkness and ignorance and the monsters and demons of misconception, the divisive ideas of duality or otherness, which it breeds.

Without this saving and transforming action of Savitar, there can be no real dawn or sunrise, no true day of clear awareness and open perception. Without him, even our waking state is under the dark shadow of the principalities of sleep and the evil dream of ignorance and separation. His is the sense of the Absolute and invincible nature of truth through which alone we can endure all darkness, death and sorrow, from which standpoint alone we can destroy all the misconceptions they bring when we take them as the final truth of things. Savitar is this capacity to see the light in the darkness, life in death, being in non-being and immortality in mortality, through which the contradiction between them is resolved. He is the Divine Sun that is everywhere shining, even in darkness and night. He is the light of seeing that is the true Sun which never goes out, which finds in all things seen, even darkness, death and sorrow the presence of the seer who is light, life and bliss. Without the positive being of the seer these negative phenomena could not be perceived. Remaining in his positive being they have no real power to disturb our spirit.

The Ancient Solar Yoga V.81
Seer — Shyavashva Atreya

> 1. Seers of the vast illumined seer yogically control
> their minds and their intelligence. The One knower of
> the ways of wisdom, he ordains the invocations of the
> gods. Great is the affirmative being of the Divine trans-
> forming Sun.

The transforming Sun, Savitar, is the impelling Divine archetype of the inner yogic transformation ritual. This is achieved by yoking, controlling or uniting our mind and intelligence with that of this One Seer or seeing of unity. When the mind is silent and awake in the state of seeing, the Solar Self flashes forth and the mind becomes enlightened. All the invocations of the Gods are ordained naturally by the silent yogic mind that dwells in the state of attentive observation in all things. Savitar is the great energy and aspiration, the Divine intelligence-power hidden in creation, the great evolutionary force that directs and impels the yogic process which is the way beyond ordinary humanity to the true man of cosmic consciousness. As such, Savitar is the stimulator, impeller and director of men, the archetype through which mankind seeks real knowledge and growth. He is the great power of affirmation in all beings, ever seeking to grow, to expand, to unite, harmonize and energize. He is the arising and ascent of our true will towards growth, allowing each of us to self-reliantly pursue the path of inner discovery. He is the Lord of Yoga, for it is only through arousing that great affirmative archetype of our own being and the being of Life that we can have the energy and passion for such a great evolutionary change. It is not by any effort of our own that yoga proceeds and succeeds, but through the Yoga Shakti, the Divine impulse to growth in consciousness that is at the foundation of our being and of all creation.

This verse is found in many other Vedic works including the *Yajur Veda* and the *Upanishads (Svetasavatara)*.

> 2. The seer, he assumes every form. He creates happiness for both animals and men. The adorable Sun of transformation has illumined the vault of Heaven. According to his advent the Dawns shine refulgent.

All forms are merely appearances of the seer or a movement in the state of seeing that is Divine. To see is to be and to become what one sees. This is the yoga of the silent mind, of the mind in the peace of the being of seeing. True seeing is the cosmic intelligence which by a kind of magnetization organizes the orders of creatures. This is the twofold or human order under one set of dualities, that of the mind, and the fourfold or animal order under two sets of dualities, those of instinct. The perceptive rays of that seer illumine the heavenly summit of the world and send forth the Divine Dawns, the new births of creation in the transforming light of truth.

> 3. According to the grandeur of the advent of this God, all other Gods move with strength. Who measured out the material realms, he is the variegated Sun horse, the Divine transforming Sun through greatness.

Only in the advent of the state of seeing can all the Divine archetypes manifest and function with their proper power. The light of seeing transforms the darkness of primordial chaos, the ignorance behind creation, into the light of transcendent knowledge, into the ideal creation it is laboring to manifest. To the ancients the nothingness or non-being behind creation is the ignorance or dark latency out of which creation labors as a process of transmutation. All creation was to them an evolution of being and knowledge out of non-being and ignorance. All evolution was a spiritual process, a yogic endeavor. Hidden in the ignorance dwells a Divine principle, a spark of the true light working its way out, gradually drying out the swamp of non-being and setting it afire. That spark or flame is the Vedic Fire, Agni. The Divine intelligence and power of transformation within that Fire is the transforming Sun. Savitar is thus the transforming light manifested by the Sun, and much more than an image of the Sun or a personification of it.

Spiritual growth for the ancients involved the entrance of the consciousness of the Absolute into our daily consciousness. It is only with this victory of the knowledge through man, the intelligent being in creation, that real life and creation begins — that the true cosmic Day arrives beyond the chaos of the dark night of ignorance. This is the full transformative movement of creation that Savitar impels. He is the Sun-horse (Etasha), the life energy of enlightenment in its variegated splendors, visible and invisible, manifest and obscure, apparent and arcane.

> 4. Savitar, you move to three luminous Heavens, and you are articulated by the rays of the Sun. You encompass the night on both sides and, oh God, you become the Friend according to the laws of your nature.
>
> 5. And you are the One Lord of transformation, and, oh God, you become the fostering Sun by your advents. You have wide dominion over all the realms of being. Shyavashva, the seer, has realized your being of affirmation, transforming Sun.

The Divine intelligence that fashions cosmos out of chaos moves to three luminous Heavens, the triple Godhead that underlies the threefold law of creation. All that he accomplishes in the dark interior realms is manifested by Surya, the Day Sun or enlightened awareness, according to his victory. He encompasses the cosmic night on both sides, both dusk and dawn. He is the Divine principle that voluntarily enters the darkness in order to transform it into light, the state of seeing which emerges triumphant in the enlightened human being. As such, Savitar is the Divine Friend or principle of friendship (Mitra) which through love labors in the darkness to draw it into the light.

The mystic night Sun of inner vision is the One Lord of creation-transformation. All creation represents various degrees of his transmutation of the darkness of ignorance into the light of knowledge. This he does not from the outside, but from within as the secret presence at the heart of all beings, as the Divine unknowing which is the invisible light of the Absolute. Creation is transformation. It is not a gradual growth, a movement in time, but a timeless movement, the instantaneous transformation of the eternal in its unending presence. To attune our mind to this transformative being of creation is to transform it, is to silence it in yogic concentration for unity with all life. By our ardor of seeing we come to know the glory of creation as spiritual transformation. As such we come to affirm the Divine Sun within us, the great archetype of transformative vision. Like the seer Shyavashva of this hymn, we ourselves become Savitar, we ourselves come to manifest the archetype of transformation, a vast affirmative creation for all the world.

All creation labors to produce man, the true human being, that he might deliver its secret soul, that through his realization of cosmic consciousness he may bring the creation from the darkness to the light. Savitar is the God, the Divine principle behind this process. It is our duty as cosmic beings to manifest him, to be the light that shines in the darkness and which thereby turns the darkness into light. This, our true and only really humane and manly work, is yoga. It is not to continue our material evolution in body and mind, which is only to expand on the same level of ignorance, but to initiate a spiritual evolution, an evolution in consciousness wherein we transcend the mind to true awareness. Material evolution is not transformation. It is a mechanical process based on more and more refined memory reactions. The spiritual evolution is no evolution at all, no mere gradual process of growth, but a radical revolution within. It is our place to bring creation to its true being of transformation in the seeing which has always sustained it.

Mitra and Varuna, the Divine Friend and Lord VII.65
Seer — Maitravaruni Vasishta

> 1. Present in the rising Sun I invoke you, the Friend
> and the Being of the Wideness, pure in discernment,
> whose almighty supremacy is imperishable, on every
> course aware and striving to win.

Mitra and Varuna are the dual Solar Godhead, the twofold being of the Divine as the dearest friend and most impersonal Lord. Varuna is the infinite space of Heaven personified. He comes to man as the purity of infinite consciousness that demands of us the utmost purification and reveals our mere finitude and manifold imperfections. Mitra is his complement, the Divine Friend who comes to each being with the greatest intimacy and forgiveness, stimulating our best efforts and ideals. He is the being of compassion. This is the dual Godhead present in the Sun which the seers invoke in the rising Sun.

> 2. These two are the Almighty of the Gods, they are the noble. They will make our people full of vigor. May we attain you, Mitra and Varuna, wherever Heaven and the days overflow.
> 3. These two have many bonds. They are an embankment against falsehood, hard to overcome for harmful mortals. By the path of truth, wide Lord and Friend, as a ship a flood may we cross over wrong action.

The dual Godhead is to be realized in the fullness of our knowledge, life and inspiration. It is the awe of them that brings true creativity to man.

The seeing powers of the Gods are a bondage for the ignorant, a blinding light of awareness they cannot face. Men of evil or wrong action can only hide from and try to avoid the light of truth, though it always catches up with them in the end. This is the symbolic Sun of law and justice, the Sun of ethics and morality, the light of conscience. It is this light of truth that all of us have to face in life or in death.

> 4. Wide Lord and Friend, bedew our choice offering, our field of light, with clarity and vigor of speech. Fill us here with the supreme for men, the water of Heavenly wonder.
> 5. This hymn, Varuna and Mitra, like luminous Soma for the Spirit for you is extended. Further our understandings. Awaken the Goddess of bountiful intelligence. Protect us with the powers of well-being forever, oh Gods.

Our choice offering is the open field of our own soul receptive to the Divine. This brings the Divine descent of clear thinking and creative speech. It brings the supreme waters of wonderful awareness. This our hymn, the utterance of our soul, becomes the Soma-bliss of the Spirit. The Goddess of bountiful intelligence is our own soul in the fecundity of understanding.

Mitra and Varuna are in all hymns to the Sun as the Divine Lord and Friend. The hymns to the Sun are primarily hymns to them, for the ancients worshipped the Godhead in the Sun, not the Sun itself. Sunlight itself reflects the dual Godhead of Mitra and Varuna. The Sun is intimate with and faces all beings equally, his rays illuminating each personally like Mitra, the Friend. Yet he stands aloof aloft in Heaven, his light spreading into vast space revealing our insignificance, like Varuna.

The dual Godhead, the Divine Lord and Friend, is also the Father and the Son. Varuna is God the Father, the impersonal Absolute, and Mitra is God the Son, his compassionate savior son. Our Heavenly Father of the Greek New Testament, Pater Ouranos, and Uranus of Greco-Roman mythology relate to Vedic Pitar Varuna. The peoples of the Middle East also shared this solar religion of the Father and the Son. Almighty Varuna, Asura Varuna in Sanskrit is also the Sun-God Assur, the main God of the Assyrians (Assurians) and the Ahura Mazda (Sanskrit Asura Medha) of the Persians, as Vedic Mitra is the Persian Mithra. Mithra, the Sun God, and his religion which rivalled that of early Christianity, is really a close relative of it. Christ is also Mitra, the Sun of resurrection, born on the winter solstice, the Divine Son-Sun and compassionate savior. These are all formations of the same ancient universal religion of light.

Through All the Manifold Births of Men VII.62
Seer — Maitravaruni Vasishta

> 1. The vast Sun has spread aloft his flaming rays
> through all the manifold births of men. The same
> through Heaven shining he is apparent. He has been
> formed by the will of the masters of the work, made per-
> fect.

The vast Sun is our common humanity in the supreme, the oneness of man which is only possible in our common sense of the Divine and the universal. Human unity cannot be arrived at through human terms, in terms of social, political, economic or intellectual interests, because there can never be unity on the same level of action. Unity on a common level is only possible through a transcendent factor that shifts our vision to a higher dimension. If we see ourselves as individuals operating in the human sphere of action, we will create division and conflict because the things we seek on that level, wealth and power, are limited. We must see ourselves in our true being relative to the universal, the human being as a cosmic being, if we aspire to free ourselves from the limited field of our personal and collective assertion and its disharmony. We need the ancient sense of man as a being of light, a ray of the cosmic Sun.

There is no unity or transcendence for humanity in any human leader. What is personal is what is divided and leads to opposition. True unity is in our common recognition of the Divine light, in the universal that alone can encompass and harmonize, even further to a greater unity our great differences. This is the Sun of the vast truth. He is the vision of unity formed by the will of the masters of the work — those who have accomplished the alchemical labor of consciousness, who have forged the underlying cosmic light of consciousness out of the dark depths of the unconscious and found their true being in the unconditioned.

> 2. Thus, oh Sun, facing us in the east you have
> arisen through our hymns as through your swift moving
> stallions. Declare to the Divine Lord, Friend, Compan-
> ion and Fire that we are sinless.

Our hymns and affirmations of truth make the Sun rise in creation, on Earth, in the human heart. Man makes the light through the word of truth, the song of bliss. It is this we need again to return the light to humanity. In the light of our unconditioned being we are sinless. The nature of consciousness and being is beneficence and happiness. Sin is only the ignorance of our conditioning, a fall from our true nature. When we discover the truth of ourselves we see that it has no reality.

> 3. Let the Divine Lord, Friend and Fire, the truth-
> bearers, open out for us a thousandfold richness of
> growth. Let the bright Moons extend for us the supreme
> Sun-song. Lauded let them fulfill our desire.

All the Gods are like the Moon in its manifold appearance which only serves to revolve around and give glory to the single solar Self. All time, woven by the moons, sings the glory of the Lord of Time, the eternal light, the Sun. In that great field of time and its organic rhythms is a luxuriant field for the growth of the soul.

> 4. Sublime Heaven and Earth, Infinite Mother pro-
> tect us, you who have been born of you for the perfect
> birth. May we not fall into the anger of the Divine Lord
> and Spirit or of the Divine Friend, most beloved of men.

Undivided Heaven and Earth, the Infinite Mother (Aditi), is our true source in which we are born in the perfect birth of oneness. This birth of the oneness is the birth of the Sun. The ancients were humble and reverential before the Divine, for they knew of its power and sacredness, the inviolability of the laws of the universe which brings suffering for those, such as we today, who do not heed them.

> 5. Stretch out your arms that we might live. Bedew our field of light with clarity. Make us renowned among men. Ever-young Divine Lord and Friend, listen to my invocation.
> 6. Now Divine Lord, Friend and Companion, establish the wideness for ourselves and for our progeny. May all good paths be easy going for us. Protect us with the powers of well-being forever, oh Gods.

True life is in the extension of the Divine within us. It is the dripping of the dew of clarity which like clarified butter sustains our inner flame in its pure glow. It is in that light of unity we become renowned among all, accepted everywhere as of the same nature.

The seers invoked the Divine as One and many, as two, three or more Gods in concordance. The Gods are always invoked in concordance not as separate powers but as different sides of a universal Being. This sense of universality which is the true Divine is what gives the wideness. In that all the innumerable paths of light are of easy access for us, having the key to them in the freedom of our own heart.

Flying Like a Hawk VII.63
Seer — Maitravaruni Vasishta

> 1. Up rises the auspicious universal seer, the Sun, the common being of all men; the eye of the Divine Lord and Friend, who as if in a skin has encompassed the darkness.
> 2. Up rises the impeller of men, the great guiding ray of the solar sea. He revolves a common wheel, when the Sun-horse yoked to the center drives on.
> 3. Refulgent from the bosom of the Dawns, he arises to be rejoiced in by the singers. This Divine creative Sun delights me, who does not diminish the common nature.

The Sun is the Self, the common being of all men who are the warriors for his light on the Earth. He is the eye of all the Gods. In man, in the skin of the human body, he is able to encompass and destroy the darkness as man has the capacity to manifest his universal consciousness.

The Sun is the guiding ray of the ocean of light. He turns a common wheel, a unitary nature for all, when his guiding horse is yoked to the central truth. The Sun by its circular shape and the pervasion of its light demonstrates universality and equality.

> 4. As a mass of gold from Heaven wide in vision he
> arises, swift and effulgent to a distant goal. Now men
> impelled by the Sun go to their aims and will perfect
> their arts.

The Sun of our common Self impels us to different goals according to our karma. All men must be allowed to follow their true nature. This leads to the division of levels of society, reflecting the natural and organic differences of men based on the common rights of all beings to fulfill their nature. Some men, in this way, are more suited to be businessmen, others artists or intellectuals, others seers or sages. A social order that recognizes the truth of Oneness does not force all men into the same mold, but rather allows this organic differentiation by karma to occur. True oneness and equality is universality that allows the broadest organic differentiation without interference. This was the ancient Aryan society, the social order of the Sun, in which the different levels of society were guided by the seers, harmonized according to a common sense of the supremacy of the spiritual over material goals. Later this degenerated into the caste system, which does not really reflect its true meaning.

> 5. Where the immortals have made a pathway for
> him, flying like a hawk he travels through the region. Di-
> vine Lord and Friend, may we partake of you in the ris-
> ing Sun with prayers of surrender and with offerings.
> 6. Now Divine Lord, Friend and Companion, estab-
> lish the wideness for ourselves and for our progeny.
> May all good paths be easy going for us. Protect us with
> the powers of well-being forever, oh Gods.

We live in the impulse of our inner Sun, following it to our various aims until we learn to look within and seek the Self. Then like a hawk he flies and take us into the supreme. In that rising Sun we partake of all the Gods, who manifest through him.

The Sunlight Rain of Bliss V.63
Seer — Archanana Atreya

> 1. Guardians of truth you mount your chariot, who
> possess the law of truth in the supreme ether. Whomso-
> ever you favor, Divine Friend and Lord of the Vast, for
> him the honey laden rain pours from Heaven.

The dual guardians of truth are vast impersonality, Varuna, and the most personal compassion, Mitra, the complementary being of the Divine. Those who understand and manifest this dual knowledge receive the rain of bliss from the Heavens of the higher mind.

> 2. As universal rulers you rule the world, the Divine
> Lord and Friend, who have the vision of the Sun-world
> in the sessions of knowledge. I implore the grace of
> your rain of immortality. The thunder spreads through
> Heaven and Earth.

It is this universal rule of vast impersonal friendship that we implore for the rain of immortality. Its favor is given freely for all to partake of. The thunders are our awakenings to the vast laws that govern life in which there is a free abundance for all who see objectively.

> 3. Universal rulers, awesome Bulls, Lords of
> Heaven and Earth, vigorous Divine Lord and Friend,
> with wonderful clouds you concentrate your roar, you
> make Heaven rain by the magic wisdom power of the
> Almighty.
> 4. Divine Lord and Friend, your magic wisdom
> power rests in Heaven. The Sun, the wonderful weapon,
> wanders through the clouds as light. Him with rain and
> clouds you hide in Heaven. The rain-God streams the
> honey-laden drops.

The Sun (Surya) is the Maya, the magic wisdom power of the Almighty (Asura); or she, the Goddess-Illusion (Maya), is the magic wisdom power within the Sun which makes the law that rules all life. It is the Sun of knowledge that brings about the rain of bliss by drawing up to Heaven the waters of our life for their transformation. With the Divine light comes the Divine rain, the invigorating descent of Heaven on Earth for its manifestation in the mind of man. The Divine light and waters are one, the unity of feeling and knowing that arises through the integrating power of self-knowledge.

> 5. The Gods of flashing power yoke their easy-going chariot for beauty, like a hero in the battles for the light, Divine Lord and Friend. The thunder spreads through wonderful regions. Universal rulers, anoint us with the milk of Heaven.
> 6. Divine Lord and Friend, the rain-God declares the invigorating and brilliant Goddess-Word. The Gods of flashing power will clothe themselves with clouds by magic wisdom power, when you make Heaven, radiant and spotless, rain.

The Gods of flashing power (Maruts) are the Gods of the storm, the lightning flashing in the clouds. They represent the light of truth breaking open the Heavens of the higher mind and raining them down into the waking consciousness. These are the regions of wonder and magic, the luminous Heavens of the Gods, where blissful energies weave ideal worlds of truth and beauty. The Goddess-Word (Vak) is the Divine Voice of thunder, the source of all creative energy. She is the bounty, the overflowing love-wisdom that the rain-God pours. She is the Maya, the magic wisdom power of the Supreme, which rains the Divine worlds of truth and beauty down from the Sun of enlightenment. Through her power the Earth itself is transmuted into Heaven as a symbolic revelation of the transcendent.

> 7. By your nature, Divine Lord and Friend, enlightened in consciousness, you guard the laws through the magic wisdom power of the Almighty. Through the truth you rule all the universe. You hold the Sun in Heaven as the vehicle of wonder.

The enlightened consciousness in its dual nature as the lord and friend of all rules by the law of its nature, the law of truth. That law of truth is the Maya, the magic wisdom power of the Almighty, the creative force which produces all the universe magically in the void or supreme ether.

It operates as the Sun, the vehicle of wonder, the light that is life, the causal light of creation. The Vedic rain is that of the Divine descent of wisdom and bliss, the beneficence of transcendence vibrating freely in all the worlds.

Sons of the Infinite Mother V.69
Seer — Uruchakri Atreya

1. Three luminous realms, Lord of the Vast, and three Heavens, Divine Friend, you uphold three regions, as you exalt the splendor of your ruling power, guarding accordingly the undecaying law.
2. Full of energy, Lord of the Vast, are your milch cows; full of honey, Divine Friend, your rivers flow. Three Bulls stand luminous who place the seed within the three world vessels.
3. The Divine Infinite Mother I invoke in the morning, in the middle of the day and in the setting of the Sun. I call you, Lord of the Vast and Divine Friend, in the extension of the All for splendor and for energy, for peace and happiness to all the line of our progeny.
4. You who are the dual upholders of the spiritual and material realms, Divine sons of the Infinite Mother, Lord of the Vast and Divine Friend, the immortal Gods do not diminish your eternal laws.

All the solar Godheads are called Adityas, the sons of Aditi, the Infinite Mother or indivisible consciousness from which they spring. She is present in the background in all their invocations as their essence and totality, the infinite expanse from which the Sun is born. Her two main sons are Mitra, the Divine Friend or day-sun, and Varuna, the Lord of the Vast or the night-sun. They uphold the triple creation, earth, atmosphere and heaven and the triple infinite, being, consciousness and bliss. The three bulls are the three presences of the Spirit in the three worlds who invigorate them. By this triple law all dualistic forces are balanced in the Oneness.

Varuna, The Unborn Who Upholds Heaven VIII.41
Seer — Nabhaka Kanva

1. For the preeminent Lord of Heaven, who knows
the souls of men like herds of cattle, sing to the more
knowing Gods of flashing power. Let all that is other
than him be burst asunder.

Varuna, which means, literally, the wide enclosure of space, is the
Lord of Heaven, the monotheistic One God. To invoke him we must first
invoke the Gods of flashing power, the Maruts, the Divine singers within
us. The souls of men are the herds, the perceptions, which the Divine
guards and cultivates. What is other than him is the ignorance that must
be destroyed.

2. Sing to him with a common song, with the knowledge of our Fathers and with the praises of Nabhaka,
who in the confluence of the rivers, in the seven Sisters
stands in the middle. Let all that is other than him be
burst asunder.

Nabhaka, meaning he who makes things burst, who bursts the primeval egg of the ignorance for the release of the bird of the soul, is the seer
of this hymn. Varuna is the Lord of the cosmic sea, the celestial ocean,
which as their source, receives the Goddess-streams of the seven planes
of existence. To the ancients the Heaven was a great sea, the ocean of space
or the ethereal waters, the waters of light. This ocean is everywhere in the
symbolism of the Vedic hymns, reflecting the ocean-going Aryan culture.
It is strange that the *Rig Veda*, filled with oceanic symbolism in all of its
Gods, is thought by modern scholars to be a product of a people who had
never seen the ocean.

3. He embraced the nights, the radiant morning by
his magic wisdom power he set down, who is visionary
over all. His loving consorts gave increase to three
Dawns according to the law. Let all that is other than
him be burst asunder.
4. Who sustains the summit-spaces, who is visionary
over the Earth, he measures out the primeval station.
That is the Lord of Heaven's seventh nature. He is as if

an imperious guardian. Let all that is other than him be
burst asunder.

Varuna is the spirit of the light by night and by day. His loving consorts
are the nights which in turn become the dawns and reflect his supreme
light.

The primeval or original station is the seventh nature, the seventh
plane of existence of pure Being, which is the supreme truth of Varuna.
This is the state of the unconditioned entity, the Divine Person or central
being within all.

> 5. Who is the upholder of the worlds, who knows
> the secret and mysterious names of the morning-beams,
> he is the seer, manifold by seer-wisdom. As Heaven he
> gives nourishment to the beautiful form. Let all that is
> other than him be burst asunder.
>
> 6. In whom all seer-wisdoms rest as spokes within a
> wheel. As cows to be gathered in a stall, as horses for ri-
> ding are yoked, attend on him as the Third with inten-
> sity. Let all that is other than him be burst asunder.

Varuna is the Lord of creation who knows every ray-song of the
cosmic vibration. He is the seer made transparent in every form of beauty,
in all such forms which fill his marvelous creation.

In that supreme seer or pure seeing we are to concentrate all our forces.
The cows are symbolic of our sense organs, our perceptive faculties that
are passive in nature, whose pasture is the external world. The horses
symbolize our organs of action or life-energies (pranas) through which
we move in the world. This is one of the major keys to ancient symbolism
and the yogic meaning of the mantras. The third is the Spirit as the unity
of duality, the One beyond and inclusive of duality. Inclusion of both sides
of all dualities is the way to oneness.

> 7. Who is the woven vesture in the Waters, he medi-
> tated out all their births and natures. In the ancient home
> of the Lord of Heaven are all the Gods according to the
> law. Let all that is other than him be burst asunder.
>
> 8. He is a secret sea. Victorious he ascends the sky,
> when he sets down the sacrifice within the Waters. By
> his radiant station he scattered all illusion and ascended

the firmament. Let all that is other than him be burst
asunder.

Varuna is the all-encompassing vesture that the Goddesses, the cosmic
waters, weave. He meditates all the births and natures of the Gods who in
essence reside within him. There is nothing other than him.

By the sacrifice, the law of giving which is the nature of being, he
scatters all Maya-illusion based on the sense of a separate self. It is the
sacrifice that destroys illusion, the sacrificial knowledge of all beings as
sacred oneness which dissolves all sense of duality. The sacrifice is the
truth of being in the original, primeval or radiant station of oneness. The
sea ascending the sky is the unification of the earthly and heavenly waters.
This occurs when the sacrifice is set down in the earthly waters, when the
Divine sense of giving is established in man. It is the blue sea merging
upwards into the blue sky on the ocean journey of self-knowledge.

> 9. Whose white clear-seeking powers preside over
> the three material realms and pervade the three superior
> domains, the station of the Lord of Heaven is eternal.
> He is ruler of the seven. Let all that is other than him be
> burst asunder.
> 10. Who according to his laws turns the darkness
> into a raiment of light. He measured in himself the origi-
> nal Nature, who with a pillar separated the two firma-
> ments and as the Unborn upheld Heaven. Let all that is
> other than him be burst asunder.

Varuna's seeing powers rule all the realms material and pervade the
spiritual Heavens. He is the eternal being who rules all seven domains of
existence, all the seven streams.

He is the unborn being (aja) of the original nature who upholds all
the worlds. He is the great world-pillar, the pillar being the form most
preferred by the ancients for their ritual worship of the supreme (that later
became the worship of the Shiva linga). In that light of seeing, even
darkness is light, as all things reveal the truth positively or negatively to
the inner eye. Such is Varuna, the Greco-Roman Uranus, the great father
of the Gods, the supreme Lord of Heaven.

Sailing on the Cosmic Ocean VII.88
Seer — Maitravaruni Vasishta

1. Vasishta, bear your most pure bright beloved thought to the compassionate Lord of Heaven, he who fashions here for us the vast and sacred Spirit and its thousandfold beneficence.

2. And now having come into his presence I know the face of the Lord as that of the Fire. When the Sun-world manifests in the lightning and I am blind, may he as the guardian lead me to the vision of its most beautiful form.

Vasishta, perhaps the most famous and certainly the most prolific of the seers, is the seer of this hymn. His prayer is to bring our deepest thought to the Divine to manifest the full splendor of the Godhead.

Vasishta here, like Moses, comes into the blinding presence of the Divine Light, the overwhelming vision of the Absolute. His prayer is that he may come to know its most beautiful form, the Self, in which its transcendence is no longer dreadful.

3. When Varuna and I ascend into the ship and go forth into the middle of the sea, then we wander on the ridges of the waves and swing on the swing for pleasure.

4. Varuna placed Vasishta in the vessel. Most skillful, by his greatness he made him into a seer. The sage, he made him into a singer in the clear brightness of the days, as far as the Heavens could extend, as far as the Dawns.

The seer mounts the vehicle of wisdom and rides the waves of the ocean of consciousness in the presence of the Divine. The vessel and the swing are the Sun, the enlightened mind, that goes back and forth freely through all the domains of creation. Varuna is the Heavens themselves which on the solar vessel we pervade.

The ocean-going ship is also the solar transformation vessel, the Sun. In this inner Sun is the solar rebirth wherein we are reborn as the solar Self. Varuna, the Lord of Heaven, by his wideness makes us into seers, instilling in us an infinite vision as on an endless sea. Varuna here is not a mere personal God but the seeing that encompasses all space. As in other myths the ocean journey is used as a metaphor for the spiritual quest.

5. What has become of that ancient friendship of
ours, when innocently we dwelled together? Self-
natured Lord of Heaven, I have entered your vast mansion, your temple of a thousand doors.
    6. If your friend commits transgressions against you,
Varuna, as your eternal companion he is still beloved.
Oh Spirit, may we not experience you in sin. Sage, extend a refuge to your singer.

Vasishta, in his pure friendship, enters into unity with the Lord. He
enters his mansion of the vast, the thousand-rayed Sun, the thousand-
doored temple, the yogic thousand-petalled lotus, the highest center or
chakra in the head.
    Our true relationship with the cosmic Divine is friendship eternal and
infinite. Whatever we may do to violate that is done out of ignorance and
must be forgiven. The sin is really against ourselves, as the Spirit is within
us. We only thereby damage the quality of our own life, emotion and
perception.

7. As we dwell in these eternal habitations, Varuna,
release from us the noose. As we win favor in the
bosom of the Infinite Mother, protect us with the powers of well-being forever, oh Gods.

These worlds are eternal habitations, constant domains in creation, as
they appear and disappear cyclically. The noose or perception of Varuna
is the bondage of karma, the Divine judgment of our impurity determined
within us that keeps us in inferior domains. We seek favor in the infinite
by our attempts to grow inwardly and transcend the limitations of the ego.

Mitra, The Divine Friend III.59
Seer — Gathina Vishvamitra

1. The Friend, declaring himself, brings the people
together. The Friend upholds both Earth and Heaven.
The Friend, unwinking, looks over men. To the Friend
give the offering made of clarity.

The Aryan Gods are not anthropomorphic entities. They are truth
principles. As such their main quality is abstract, to which a poetic
imagery and personification is added. The God Mitra is the personification

of friendship and compassion. His laudation is a eulogy of friendship.
Mitra is a God because true friendship is something Divine. Our sense of
friendship towards all people is a reflection in our minds of our true Self
that is one with all. It is not a conditioned reaction, but a reflection of the
presence of consciousness. The Divine is also the true friend for it is
eternally true to all beings. It is this Divine principle of friendship that is
one of the Aryan or noble truths of existence we must invoke within
ourselves and reverence with clear-thinking.

> 2. Divine Friend, let that mortal be happy who, Son
> of the infinite Mother, wishes to manifest you according
> to the law. Aided by you he is never killed or con-
> quered. No narrowness reaches him from near or from
> afar.
> 3. Free of weakness, by the energetic-word exulting,
> with bended knees on the broad expanse of the Earth,
> dwelling in the law of the Son of the Infinite, may we
> abide in the right-thinking of the Friend.

Our duty is to manifest the Divine Friend; this is the noble law for
men. In the universality of friendship which is an infinite principle, or
principle of the infinite, is our oneness beyond death, that none of the
narrow experiences of life can overcome.

Right-thinking is the friend in which all is resolved into oneness. It is
one of the laws of infinity, unbounded awareness that the Earth itself in
its broadness testifies to.

> 4. This Friend is to be reverenced, most auspicious.
> The King of good dominion, he was born the Ordainer.
> May we abide in the right-thinking of this holy one and
> in his auspicious right-mindfulness.
> 5. The great son of the Infinite Mother is to be re-
> vered with prayers of surrender. As the orderer of men
> he is most auspicious to the singer. To him most won-
> derful, the Divine Friend, consecrate this offering into
> the Fire.

The Divine Friend is the true king of all people, whom all can accept
as the ruler without any sense of servility. It is this rule of Divine
friendship that was the basis for the Aryan kingdoms. It was the unity of
monarchy and democracy, the rule of the Divine Lord who is one in all.

It is only through this sense of friendship in the Divine that there can be any true social order and harmony. The ruler, the king, has power only to the extent that he manifests the Divine Friend. Similarly, a democracy of material competition is an equality of wolves; a democracy of materialistic values an equality of greed and servility to the external. The only true democracy is in the Divine Friend, in the recognition of him among men, and the giving of precedence to those who manifest him until all men come to do so. Right-mindfulness is possible only in the state of universal friendship, when the archetype of Mitra is manifested, and in right-mindfulness is that open friendship with all.

> 6. The victorious grace of the Divine Friend and upholder of men is luminous, of the most wonderful renown.
> 7. The expansive greatness of the Friend transcends Heaven, through renown transcends the Earth.
> 8. The five races of men strive for the Friend who has transcendent power. He carries all the Gods.
> 9. The Friend among the Gods and among the living ones, for men who strew the altar seat, has made invigorating energy according to the law of sacrifice.

Friendship is the principle that carries all the Gods, that manifests all the other Divine or unconditioned qualities. Through Divine fellowship we transcend all the limitations of creation.

Vishnu, The Pervader VII.99
Seer — Maitravaruni Vasishta

> 1. No one attains your greatness, who by your self have increased beyond measure. Divine Pervader, we know both your material regions. You alone know the Supreme.
> 2. Divine Vishnu, no one born or being born attains the limit of your greatness. You up-pillared the firmament, vast and sublime. You upheld the eastern summit of the Earth.

The God Vishnu is the Divine Pervader, the pervasive principle of Divine Consciousness that measures out the wideness in the world, who gives space and freedom of motion to all beings. He is the Self in its flourishing, in its own nature beyond measure, which brings harmony and the order of freedom, the law of unlimited beneficence to the creation. We know both his material regions, Heaven and Earth, mind and body. He alone knows the Supreme, the One Self, for only one who becomes him can know it. This Supreme is the unborn that no one born can attain to, the immortal not to be known by the mortal mind. He establishes the ascending force, the spiritual vigor which upholds the world. He sustains the Earth at its eastern summit open to the light.

> 3. Heaven and Earth, be full of energy, full of nourishment, rich fields serviceable to men. Vishnu pillared wide the two worlds. He upheld the Earth with lines of force.

It is through the archetype of the Pervader that the worlds are vast and fruitful. They are the wish-fulfilling Cows that the God ordains for mankind. His lines of force are everywhere upholding all existence. Vishnu is the pervasive and expansive upholding force in creation, the sense of Self-being through which all beings are great in harmony with each other.

> 4. Indra and Vishnu, you made the wide other world of vision for the sacrifice, as you generated the Sun, the Dawn and the Fire. Heroes, you struck down in the rushing assaults the illusion-power of the strong-mouthed Destroyer.
> 5. You shattered all at once the ninety-nine massive cities of the Dragon. You slew at once the hundred thousand incomparable heroes of the brilliant and almighty demon.

Indra and Vishnu are here invoked as joint archetypes, the principles of unconditioned being and pervasive consciousness. They create that other world, the wide world of vision, the perception of the oneness. They destroy all the illusion, the Maya of ignorance, and its chief destructive demon, the illusory entity of the ego. They shatter all the massive cities of the artificial, conditioned mind and the innumerable contentious entities these dark abodes produce, our tenacious stream of false thinking which only the direct perception into the truth of the Self-nature can quell.

6. This vast intuition is exalting you with power,
vast lords of the wide stride. I offer your hymn in the
sessions of knowledge. Vishnu and Indra, overflow energy for us in concentration.

The vast intuitive hymn is the Goddess that gives increase to the dual
Godhead. The wide stride is how the immeasurable truth brings both order
and freedom to creation, the great action of Vishnu. The ancient Gods are
principles of a common Godhead, all mutually interpenetrating and any
one capable of serving the functions of all. What is offered to Vishnu, the
archetype of pervasion, is returned by Indra, the archetype of single-mind-
edness. Indra, the One only, and Vishnu, the Universal, are the same
Godhead in its center and circumference which is ever the same.

7. With my mouth I form the Word that conducts
you, luminous Vishnu. Welcome that offering of mine.
Let my well-lauding songs increase you. Protect us with
the power of well-being forever, oh Gods.

The mystic Word that conducts the God to us is the realization, "He
am I." It is the speaking of this word in truth that is the great victory of
the Gods and the great glory of man. It is this knowledge that Vishnu leads
us to, for if the Divine is all-pervasive can it be other than our deepest
Self? It is also the true Life-Spirit of the human voice which annihilates
all the demons of doubt and negativity.

The Fostering Sun, Pushan VI.58
Seer — Barhaspatya Bharadvaja

1. Two days diverse in form are yours, luminous is
one, holy is the other; you are like Heaven. You further
all magic-wisdom powers, Self-natured Lord. Fostering
Sun, let your auspicious blessing be!
2. Whose mount is the unborn, the guardian of perception, whose home is power, who invigorates the
soul, set over all the world, the Divine fostering Sun,
twirling his pliant wand, travels, perceiving the worlds.
3. Pushan, your ships that are within the sea, golden
in the atmosphere which travel, by them you go on the
embassy of the Sun, made by love, desiring glory.

4. The fostering Sun, the good friend of Heaven and
Earth, the beneficent Lord of devotion, of wondrous virtue, whom the Gods gave to the Sun-Goddess, made by
love, strong and swiftly turning.

The Fostering Sun, Pushan, is the guide of the path of light, the path
of the Sun, the path of the soul, particularly from death back to life. His
mount or horse is the goat which also means unborn. This is not an unusual
play on words which we find here in the hymns; though strange to us, it
was not so to the seers, who delighted in every sort of word-play (to the
exasperation of many translators). By the same usage "guardian of cattle"
also means "guard of perception," the perceptive rays being the cattle of
the Sun. His golden ships are also his rays in the atmospheric sea. The
Vedic Sun shines through love, is made by love. It is the love of the
Sun-God and the Sun-Goddess that produces the sunlight, which is not
only the love of husband and wife, but brother and sister, son and mother.
It is the love of the sense of closest kinship with all beings which we all
can partake of in the sunlight of unity. It is that light of love based on the
knowledge of unity which guides and fosters all beings, not by overt
direction but by a beneficent presence. Pushan is this beneficent guiding
presence of the light, the transparent Divine love-wisdom which gives life
to all the colors of the world.

The Sun-Bird X.177
Seer — Patanga Prajapatya

1. Illumined sages with heart and mind behold the
flying Bird anointed with the Almighty's magic wisdom
power. The seers discern him within the ocean's depths.
The ordainers aspire to the seat of his flashing rays.
2. The flying Bird bears the Word-Goddess with the
mind. The Angel utters her within the womb. She, the
lightning and thundering intuition, the seer guard in the
home of truth.
3. I have seen the guardian of the light who has
never fallen approaching and departing through all the
paths. Invested with the converging and diverging
forces, he revolves continually within the worlds.

The flying Bird is the Sun-Bird, the liberated Being of the solar Self.
He is the Divine Intelligence in our own hearts which bears the magic

wisdom power, the Maya-Goddess of the Almighty Godhead. The seers discern him even in the depths of the cosmic sea of creation, as the secret light of truth hidden even in the darkness. The ordaining creative powers that give harmony to the cosmos accomplish their evolutionary constructions seeking him. His consort is the Divine Word (Vak), the wisdom-Goddess whom he declares in the womb of nature, the matrix of creation. She is the lightning and thunder of intuitive knowledge which the seers protect as the high priestess at the altar-seat of truth. She is the inner wisdom behind nature, the wisdom of Life that is the real teacher. The guardian or herdsman is this solar intelligence, the cosmic mind wherein are all the laws of truth or Dharma, the laws of being. It is the intelligence which is the immanent Divine Consciousness, the Divine Son, who moves forever in creation as his re-creation. Only through the Son, the vibratory consciousness of the Self at the heart of all life, can we know the Father, the vibrationless consciousness of the Self-Absolute. Its consort, intuitive wisdom, is the means of this realization.

May We Be Infinite VII.52
Seer — Maitravaruni Vasishta

1. Sons of the Infinite, may we be Infinite, perfect, beings of light, in the Godhead and in humanity. Winning, Divine Lord and Friend, may we win you. Becoming, Heaven and Earth, may we become you.

2. May the Divine Lord and Friend, the guardians, increase that for us; peace to the line of our progeny. May we not suffer the sin of another birth. May we not do that action for which you, being of light, hold us accountable.

3. The victorious flaming-seers attained the ecstasy of the Divine creative Sun imploring. May our great and holy Father, in common mind with all the Gods, grant that to us.

May we be infinite or may we become one with the infinite Mother Aditi (the term is feminine). Our true being and home is within the infinite. In that unlimited consciousness is our perfection in the Godhead, the Divine Lord of the Vast (Varuna) and his wide vision, and our perfection in humanity is in the Divine Friend (Mitra) and his deep compassion for all. In that we are all the worlds and all the Gods in the Self. The sin of another birth is the sin of birth in the ignorance, in the consciousness which sees something other than the Self. When we are conscious in the infinite, we project no karma but only peace to our progeny, in which peace they can find themselves. The actions the Gods collect or take notice of are the reactions of the dualistic mind that bind us to the karmic stream. The ecstasy of the creative Sun is the Divine transforming light of oneness. It is this which the Infinite Father-Mother grants in accord with all the Divine powers. This hymn gives in three verses the highest aspirations of the human soul and the universal religion behind all religions.

SOMA

*The Father of the Gods, the generator wise
in discernment, the wide-pillar of Heaven, the
foundation of the Earth,*

*The illumined Seer, the leader of men, the
magic craftsman, the sage who burns intense
with seer-wisdom,*

*He found that which was most hidden, the
secret and mysterious nature of the light.*
— *Rig Veda IX.87.2–3*

*Yours is this progeny of the Heavenly seed.
You are the ruler of all the world.*

*Thus, Self-purifier, all things are in your
power.   Blissful drop, you are the original or-
dainer of our nature.*

*You are the all-knowing ocean, oh seer.
Yours are these five directions in the wide law.*

*You have extended beyond Heaven and
Earth. Yours are the lights, Self-purifier, who
are the Sun.*

*In the wide law of the region, Self-purifying
Soma, through the purification filter you are
made transparent for the Gods.*

*The original men of aspiration grasped you.
To you strive all these worlds.*
— *Rig Veda IX.86.28–30*

6
SOMA, THE IMMORTAL NECTAR
THE BLISS OF PURE PERCEPTION

Vedic Alchemy
How to Extract the Soma

Seeing is a flame. It is an energy of consciousness which penetrates simultaneously our own heart and the external world, revealing their unity. Such seeing is not mere sensation, though in it alone is the purity and vividness of sensory perception. Such seeing is not thought, which posits a division between the seer and the seen. Such seeing is direct perception, choiceless observation. In that state of seeing, there is neither the seer nor the seen. There is the seeing that is both the seer and the seen, a movement in the heart of life. This flame of perception and observation is the Vedic Fire, Agni, the Fire of wisdom. It is a God, a Divine principle. It is the God, the Divine principle which manifests all the gods, the totality of Being. Spiritual practice is maintaining and cultivating the Fire. The inner Fire burns everything. It does not change anything but makes all things transparent, infuses all things with clarity, in which purity of perception Life reveals itself.

The Flame of perception distills. The transparent white-hot heat of perception allows the spirit to come forth from what we see. It makes form transparent, clear and open. When form is transparent, irradiated with the light of seeing, it is opened up and the essence comes forth. Its being and life, the one Being and Life, reveals itself therein. The power of the transparent Flame of perception opens all things up and from that opening the essence comes forth, is extracted. Where there is direct observation the essence effuses upwards spontaneously from the heart that is everywhere. This essence is the Soma. It is the nectar of delight. The Soma intoxication is the ecstasy of pure perception in which form and consciousness are one, a radiant transparency of seeing as a constant effusion of joy and wonder. This Soma is the secret of the seers, the secret of the state of seeing, what the flame of perception distills from the plant-like growths of the world, the organic field of nature.

Drinking the Soma is a state of consciousness in which, dwelling in pure perception, we imbibe the essence of what is, we absorb the being of what we see and enter into the universal life. It is this state of mind and its mantric vibrations alone which purify the mind. These mantras are the vibrations of the Divine Word in the heart taking shape as life. They are not mere sounds to be repeated. They are what was seen by the seers, the perceptions of the state of seeing. They are not mere formulas mechanically repeated but unique perceptions. They are not mere transient sensations but the comprehension of the archetypes in things, the archetypes that came out with the effusion of the essence. These are not archetypes of thought, but the essences of being, eternal presences informing perception. They are the distilled essences of the state of seeing, rendered into sound to intimate that state for the symbolic apprehension of the soul. Repeating these mantras means dwelling in the state of seeing in which the word of truth comes forth as the essence, in which the essence comes to think in us and speak through us. This is the great declaration of the Vedic Word; through pure perception letting the essence reveal itself to man through speech. It is this word which, harmonizing man and the essence, turning man into an instrument of the essence, brings the light to the world and wins the Earth for the Divine. This again is the great victory of the Divine Warrior, Indra.

When we speak the word of truth, we declare the essence to the world. We give Being a voice and a function in which its essential delight flows to clarify and beautify the world. We become the flowing Soma, the free flowing essence of life. The effusion of our concentration in the state of seeing extracts the essence as the omnipresent universal life, the timeless movement of pure perception in the organic unity of the Spirit. It is this concentration in the state of seeing that distills, and what it distills is the Divine Word, the word of truth, the spontaneous effusion of the heart that "He am I," "I am the Self of all beings." These word-thought effusions of realization from the state of seeing are the real original mantras. To repeat them is only to dwell in their presence as the archetypal energies behind the free flow of creation. It is to enter into the vibration of the state of seeing in which all forms are forms of the mantra, vibrations of the Divine Word.

To see the mantra everywhere as the unity of the seer and the seen is the supreme absorption in the Soma. This drinking of the Soma, the extracting of the essence of life by the flame of perception, brings into the manifestation the spiritual Man, Indra. In that energy of the essence of seeing our true and unconditioned being comes forth. We become the Self of all beings. We become the being of seeing who lives on the essence. We become a true conscious entity living in unconditioned awareness, no longer a mere mechanical product of thought and matter. We find our true dignity and integrity as the Man of the spirit, the being of intelligence who acts consciously and is no longer subject to the reactions of karma. We gain our true independence and are freed from the hypnotic rule of the external. In all the experiences of life, we touch only the essence. All phenomena, natural or artificial, beautiful or chaotic, through the state of seeing become only different means of evoking the essence. This evoking of the essence is the invoking of Soma, the Word of the Heart which seeks only the pure essence in all things. This pure essence is not some rigid and artificial state of virtue. It is not found by avoiding anything, by being unwilling to see anything. It is only pure when it is found in all things pure and impure, in the facing of all life in ourselves, including above all the chaos of our unconscious which is only the chaos of our own thought that we do not wish to see. This true purity is not a material state, a discipline or set of mental judgments. It is the purity of perception that extracts the essence from everything.

When through the flame of perception the essence is effused, the mind is purified. The mind is cleansed of the stain of thought and its karmic reactions. For the purification of the mind, what is necessary is the free flowing of the essence; for the essence, like water, is self-purifying. This free flow of the essence is achieved when we come to live in the state of seeing, when we realize the state of seeing as life itself. From the heart is poured a continuous stream of pure perception. In that ever-new flow of pure perception is the renewal and transformation of the mind. It is the purifying action of the essence of life upon the mind. When the mind is immersed in the state of seeing, the Soma flows. These free flowing perceptions are the mantras of the seers.

Driving Away False Thinking IX.70
Seer — Renu Vaishvamitra

> 1. The three times seven milch Cows have yielded
> for him the warm milk of truth in the original ether.
> Four other wonderfully lovely realms of being for his
> pure raiment he made, when by the truth he flourished.

The three time seven milch Cows (Dhenus) are the triple being of the Goddess, the three muses, on all seven planes of existence. They yield the purified milk of truth-inspiration to the knower of delight, to the one who sees the essence and in seeing it extracts it. The original ether is the original space of being and consciousness in the heart. The four other wonderfully lovely realms of being are the four Divine principles of Being, Consciousness, Bliss and Intelligence, that Soma, the knower of the essence, for his immortal Nirvanic raiment makes. All this is the natural outpouring of our exaltation in truth.

> 2. Desiring to partake of the wonderful loveliness of
> immortality, he opened for himself both the Heavens
> through his seer-wisdom. By greatness he encompassed
> the most radiant Waters, when by revelation the seers
> knew the station of the Divine.

Immortality is the ambrosia of the essence hidden in transparency in all things. This is extracted by the seer-wisdom that penetrates to the essence, taking the form as only a symbol. The flaming Waters are the stream of consciousness in the most transforming heat of its free flow. This the seers find when they come to know the truth. The two Heavens are those of the Absolute and that of the Divine in their highest creative reality.

> 3. Let these inviolable immortal perceptions of his,
> by which he purified both the Divine and heroic orders,
> manifest according to both the births. It was from this
> that the thinkers grasped the King.

The perceptions of immortal truth have their archetypal being in the Divine order or in the birth of the Gods. They are manifested in action, however, only through the heroic order of men, or in the birth of men of spiritual knowledge. When the phenomenal reflects the archetypal, when our actions are according to the ideals of truth, it is then as true thinkers that we grasp the Self, the blissful King of all beings.

> 4. When he is cleansed by the ten perfect functions,
> to serve as the prototype in the middlemost Mothers,
> when he absorbs the laws of the wonderful loveliness of
> immortality, of heroic vision he reflects upon both the
> peoples.

The ten perfect functions, his sisters, are the five sense organs and five organs of action which, used in the state of awareness, help to purify the mind. The mothers are the creatrixes in whom bliss is the prototype and informing power. The laws of immortality are those of open and all-embracing creative perception. Thus the blissful Self reflects upon both the ideal and actual orders of being and furthers both.

> 5. While he is cleansed as sustenance for the power
> of perception, auspicious between Heaven and Earth he
> delights. The Spirit, by strength he drives away false
> thinking, directing his manifold growths as an archer his
> arrows.

The power of perception is the power of Indra, the spiritual Man or being of unconditioned perception. Soma is the essence of delight, the rasa, the beauty or splendor hidden in things that is extracted by silent observation and serves to further empower our perceptive faculties. This essence, like the atmosphere, fills up the space between things, revealing in the space we ordinarily do not see the transparent presence of the cosmic seer. It is this strength of purified perception, the Spirit of direct awareness and observation, which alone has the power to end false thinking, to stop the mad stream of mechanical thoughts based on memory that bind us with negative emotions and misconceptions. This seeing Spirit is able, through its vast organic growths, its ever-new intuitions, to point out all false thinking, to shoot it down by its capacity to be present in the moment. It is the chaos of false thinking that is the true enemy of the wise. This is the stream of misconceptions based on the sense of a separate self, our basic alienation from the beneficent universal stream of life.

> 6. No longer perceiving his two Mothers, the radiant
> Bull roars like the storm God's thunder. Knowing the
> original truth, the Man of the Sun-World, of good will
> he chose bliss for its instruction.

Transcending the dual worlds or the worlds of duality, the Bull of the Spirit continues roaring into the transcendence of the Godhead. The man of the Sun-World is the intelligent being of the enlightened Mind, the being of truth perception. He is the original truth, the Self of all beings. His instruction is bliss, the delight of seeing, through which our will to truth and power of awareness grows.

> 7. Clear in vision, the terrible Bull roars with his con-
> sort power, as he sharpens his two yellow horns. Soma
> is settled in the perfect source. The covering of light be-
> comes his imperishable pure raiment.

The terrible Bull is the Self whose consort-power is the Goddess. His two yellow horns, or horns of golden light, are being and consciousness-force. The perfect source is his own nature. His skin or covering is the rays or the light of archetypal knowledge. It becomes his pure or Nirvanic raiment of imperishable peace. The covering of the Cow of Light becomes the raiment of the Sheep of the Imperishable, which two are one, his dual Goddess vesture.

> 8. Pure bright, purifying his stainless Self, the
> Golden one pours through the imperishable summit.
> Welcome to the Spirit-wind, to the Divine Lord and
> Friend, the triple natured honey-wine by the perfect
> functions is fashioned.

Self-purifying Soma is purified for the Self. It is our own essence effused by the action of direct perception that purifies our own nature, clears our minds of the burden of thought, feeds us with the ambrosia of being and thereby delivers us from the non-being of our expectations. He is the Golden stallion that leaps across the highest peak into the immutable; he is our life which flows free into the deathless. This purified Self is welcome to all the Godheads as it is also their essence. It is the triple being of delight fashioned by our right actions, by our daily actions and everyday perceptions in the transforming oneness of essential awareness.

> 9. Be transparent, Soma, as the Spirit for the Divine
> advent. Enter into the Soma receptacle, the heart of the
> spiritual Man. Before we are caught, deliver us across
> wrong action, as a knower of the land declares the right
> direction when asked.
> 10. As a good swift horse, rush on for vigor. Lumi-
> nous drop, pour yourself into the belly of the spiritual
> Man. You who have knowledge, deliver us as a ship
> across the sea. As a hero in the fight, save us from
> blame.

Soma is the mind in its essence transparent as the Spirit for the joyful manifestation of the Godhead. His place is in the heart of the true man, from which he pours into the belly, uniting the vital will with the spiritual heart, and uniting action with the ideal essence. It is this combination which makes the true man, a spiritual being possessed of will, strength and the power of direct and immediate action. It is the unification of the belly and the heart that integrates our being in truth and gives it the full scope of its perceptive and creative powers and functions. It is the unification of thought and action through the perception of the essence that delivers us from wrong thought and wrong action, which are simply only thought and action out of harmony with each other; thought not grounded in action and action that does not reflect what we really think.

It is not enough for us to aspire to the heights, to cultivate the ideal and refine the sensitivity of the heart. Thereby we may flounder in a beautiful but weak imagination which cannot change the well-springs of life with their intense and disruptive energy. We must also draw the spirit out of the depths, to awaken and release the primal powers of the belly and the hand. Our being lies in the primal essence of life, in the raw energy, not the silk screen of good thoughts and positive thinking. The realization of truth is not the perfection of good thoughts, nice emotions and well organized discipline. It is the eruption of the primeval creature of the essence from the supreme ground that is higher than Heaven and beneath the Earth, above our most sensitive imaginations and below our deepest fears and passions. This primal being of the essence must be released, not the ego based on thought which, however refined, remains unauthentic, a conditioned and artificial entity empty inside and lacking any real power or decisiveness. All action based on thought, choice and motivation is wrong action. True action, the action of Soma, is a spontaneous effusion from the perception of the essence in the raw moment of living.

That perception of the essence is the true guide, the original guru and world-teacher. It is not a person, but the essential presence that ever points out the way to what is, which ever serves to disclose — behind our false thinking — and all thought is ultimately false. This free flow of the mind we must follow as our guide by attentive observation if we wish to find the truth. This spontaneous release of the essence is what frees us, not our effort to be free or our thoughts of freedom, which by their fixation inhibit the flow.

The Pillar of Heaven IX.89
Seer — Ushanas Kavya

1. By the paths the carrier has bounded forth. Like the rain of Heaven, the self-purifier has flowed. A thousand-streamed Soma with us has sunk into the bosom of the Mother, into the wood.

2. The King of the rivers has put on the vesture. He has ascended the most straight moving ship of truth. Sped by the hawk the drop grew in the floods. The Father milks him. The Father milks him as his own child.

The Soma is the vehicle or carrier of all the Divine principles, the energizing delight. The wood is the substance of delight in which he dwells, the bosom of the Infinite Mother. He is the being, the spirit, the ship that moves in the cosmic waters of consciousness. He is the Divine child who is the father of his own father, to whom even his own father must come for sustenance. This is another paradox, the father milking the child, like Wordsworth's statement that the "child is father to the man."

> 3. They unite to him, the inexhaustible Lion of the
> honey-wine, the radiant golden Lord of Heaven. The
> foremost hero in the battles, he seeks the light. The Bull
> protects us with his vision.

The lion (simha) symbolizes the power of the heart that is sustained by the mystic wine. It is the greatness and courage of the heart which comes from the sense of the unity of life that imparts heroic valor in the struggle for the light. It is to that Lion-heart, the Lord of sacrifice, that our aspirations unite in their expansiveness. He is also the Bull, the imperious one, who protects us with his vision of the supreme, his refusal to give attention to the petty emotional considerations of the mind.

> 4. They yoke him, sublime and terrible, to the wide
> wheeled chariot, the inexhaustible horse whose back is
> made of the honey-wine. His sisters and lovers, of a
> common center, groom and refresh him, the stallion.

His sisters and lovers, who all have a common nature with him and with each other, are his consort powers, his streaming intuitions. They yoke him and put him to work as their power of the spiritual work or yoga, the work of unification. The wide wheeled chariot is the Sun, the enlightened mind, in which the Soma, bliss, is the driving power. He is the inexhaustible horse of liberated life-energy, prana, whose back or essence is the mystic wine of delight.

It should be noted that the ancients generally preferred an animal symbolism over an anthropomorphic one not because they were less humane or unspiritual, but because animal symbols possess a greater numinosity for the psyche. They reflect more the unknown and impersonal spirit and its primeval qualities. They have a greater appeal to the subconscious and do not merely communicate to the surface mind. They are the language of the spirit, its creative forms which embody aspects of the Divine Word. It is in this greater sense of the universal life that we find them used in the *Vedas*. As such, they are applied fluidly and interchangeably, not as rigid idols but as a subtle and interpenetrating symbolism, as archetypal manifestations of the cosmic being in its various qualities. Their usage is to arouse these forces within us to integrate their primal vigor into our waking consciousness, to draw out the universal life from the depths of our psyche.

> 5. Four who yield clarity unite to him, who are im-
> mersed within a common foundation. They rush to him,
> purifying themselves with their surrender. They all en-
> compass him from every side.

His four clarity-yielding sisters are his consort world powers of transcendence of Being, Consciousness, Bliss and Intelligence. These principles are immersed in the foundation of a common oneness. They are purified by their inherent surrender to the Divine. They encompass truth from every side as the four levels of the infinite being.

> 6. The wide pillar of Heaven, the foundation of the
> Earth, all people are in his hands. He is the lord of your
> united powers, a fountain for the singer. The filament of
> honey-bliss purifies itself for the vigor of perception.

The pillar is the prime symbol of the great God, the cosmic masculine force, the linga of power. It is the primal line of energy, the straight truth, which in circulation spreads the sphere of truth perception. It is the central truth of oneness that upholds all beings, all creation, like the ridgepole of the Chinese *I Ching*. It is the ascending force of Heaven, the vertical impulsion of the Spirit. It is the line of seeing, the straightness of perception underlying the conscious movement of life. Bliss is both the vertical and the horizontal force of creation. It is the world's foundation and horizontal support as well as the vertical prop. In the unity of consciousness, both ascension and extension are one, a circular expansion, the wide radiating movement of the line of light and consciousness. He is the lord of all of our united powers, all the teams or concerted energies of our being, all our sensory and motor faculties and their subtle counterparts. That stalk or filament, the line of light and life, flows and clears itself for the vigor of all our perceptual faculties, all the powers of Indra, the spiritual Man. It is a fountain of force in the heart in which all life is an effusion.

7. Striving on indefatigable to the Divine advent,
Soma, as the Dragon-slayer be transparent for Indra.
Empower for us a great splendor of manifold delight.
May we be the masters of the perfect heroic force.

Free flowing, self-purifying Soma, the essential current of our mind, makes itself transparent for Indra, the spiritual Man, our unconditioned Self that destroys the dragon of environmental and social conditioning. The free flow of the essence is the clearing of the mind, its purification from the dark stagnation of thought based on memory, its becoming transparent to the Spirit and thereby manifesting it within us. This transparency of being and consciousness empowers for us all the energies of delight. It arouses our unconditioned and heroic inner being that we may know our innate transcendence over all external influences, that we may be a creative source, a fountain in life, and not a mere animal clinging to its territory or a machine repeating its programming.

The Being of Splendor IX.94
Seer — Kanva Ghora

1. When on this horse of power, as it were, all beautiful intuitions strive like people in the sun, then enveloping the floods he flows in the movement of the seer, like a concentration of perception to increase the mind.

Soma is the power of bliss on the back of which, like a strong horse, all our intuitions and understandings strive. He envelops the floods of life as he flows in the movement of seeing. He is like a concentration for our perception, symbolically, like a stall, an enclosure for our cattle, in which they can flourish and be protected. Perceptions are the cattle of the wise which are kept in the stall of the concentrated mind. It is the realization of unity, of the supremacy of the Self, that is increased.

2. From of old he opened out the nature of immortality. The Worlds spread out for that knower of the Sun-World. Overflowing insights like cattle in their stable, moving in truth, have roared to Indu.

This transparency of awareness opens out the nature of existence which is immortality and reveals our true nature, no longer reflecting the artificiality of thought and its conditioned process. In this being is the

Sun-World, the world of enlightened perception. Overflowing insights are the intuitive understandings which yield the nectar-milk of knowledge. They are like cattle in their stable, or, in the inner and more general sense, like rays of light in their own home or inherent motion, spontaneously productive of nourishing revelations. In their truth movement they roar, vibrate or lovingly turn towards Indu, another name for Soma meaning "drop" or "point," (like the Tantric bindu), the central point of the essence, the ocean-containing drop of bliss. Indu also is a name for the moon.

> 3. When the seer bears his seer-wisdom, like a hero
> his chariot, around all the worlds, then manifesting as
> glory in the Gods, as the real for discerning mortals, in
> the ever present he is the New.

His seer-wisdoms constitute his vehicle of light, his Sun of knowledge that encompasses all creation. He is the glory in the Gods, the real wealth or genuine treasure of immortality which discerning mortals seek. In the all-pervasive ever present, the eternal moment of pure perception, he is the ever New. Soma is the ever new essence in which all creation is ever renewed in the eternal, in the transparent eternity of what is. He is that unique presence which is universal and flashes forth through all time, the free flowing pure light in transformation.

> 4. He is born from splendor, from splendor he has
> emanated. He grants the eon of splendor to his singers.
> Investing themselves in splendor they became immortal.
> All encounters become truth within his measured flow.

The flowing being of the essence is the being of splendor. Splendor (Sri) is the unity of beauty, light and delight; which three ideas coalesce within the ancient language. To shine is to be beautiful; such shining beauty is lustre. Beautiful shining or lustre gives delight. This lustrous delight diffused everywhere is splendor. Splendor, Shri, is another name for the Goddess, the consort of Soma. Splendor is the consort of the essence, as the essence manifests through light, beauty and delight. Splendor is the light of delight, the Ananda. It is the perception of splendor, the soul of light, beauty and delight in all things that gives birth to the ambrosial Soma.

The ancient singers did not merely laud the Gods as external entities. Their singing was their manifestation of them in their own hearts. The being of splendor which they sing with their perceptions — and all true seeing is a kind of singing — that joyous vibration they become. The seers and singers of splendor, those who give value to the beauty, light and delight of the Spirit, in that become immortal. They enter into the higher eon, the immortal life of splendor. It is only what has no splendor, no real beauty or shine that has to die — for splendor is life. How could beauty die? It is only its forms which are renewed for the eternal affirmation of its essence. Immortality is not a state apart from mortality. It is the beauty of the present moment of ever new life. It is the essential movement of life. It is in life's stream of transformation, not in the forms which pass away for beauty to renew itself. Immortality is in investing ourselves with the splendor of life, in which all life is an overflowing. It is in giving up our petty mind that is fixated in superficial deficiencies and misses the splendor of the total movement. In that measured flow where each form is transformation, a point in the line of splendor not to be divided off or judged in itself, all things become truth. All things become steps in a Divine dance of beauty.

> 5. Flow energy and vigor for us, the beauty of the
> horse and the abundance of the cow. Make the wide
> light, gladden the Gods. All things are easy for you to
> master. Self-purifying Soma, you drive away all opposi-
> tion.

This free flow of the essence grants all the original energies and archetypes. It bestows on us the wealth and splendor of perception, the true wealth of the seer. When the ancients prayed for the horse, it was the beauty, grace and power which the horse archetype represents that they sought to bring into their own life-energy and its movement. It was the inner archetype and its invigorating power they prayed for, not merely to possess the animal. With the cow it was its abundance, its magical capacity to transform mere grass into milk and all the milk products that nourish us. They sought the archetypal cow capacity to yield nourishment in their own words and thoughts, from their own soul which is the cosmic cow. To translate these verses as mere primitive supplications for more horses or cows is quite insensitive. Yet that is what is generally done, ignoring the cosmic, mystical and magical forms these animals take in the *Vedas*.

The perception of the essence and abiding in its flow brings into us the primary quality we find in all beings; the horseness of the horse, the manliness of man. In pure perception without duality we absorb the essence of what we see. In that our own essence is restored and integrated, and we enter into the immortal life. Our life in the essence becomes the wide light of seeing, imparting to us the broadness to prevail over all opposition.

The Priest of the Gods IX.96
Seer — Daivodasi Pratardana

1. The leader of the army, the heroic Lord at the forefront of the chariots goes forth seeking the light: his
army rejoices. Making auspicious the invocations of
Indra for his friends, Soma puts on his fierce armor.

2. The golden stallions cleanse him, golden with
swift horselike reverence refined. The friend of Indra
mounts his chariot. By that the knower approaches our
right thought.

3. Divine Soma, you who are the drink of Indra,
flow for our extension of the Divine, for the great feast.
Generating the floods, bedewing Heaven and Earth, purified from the vast, extend the wideness for us.

Soma, the perception of the essence, is the leader of the cosmic
warrior hosts that seek the light of knowledge. He makes the invocation
of the spiritual man efficacious. The golden energies of the Spirit cleanse
him, the golden essence, like a charge of swift horses breaking open and
freeing our life-force. By the vehicle of knowledge he approaches our
right thought, our right awareness and comprehension which manifests
him. In that free flow of the essence in direct perception comes the
extension of the Divine, the invigoration of the spiritual man for the great
feast of awareness. In that the vast essence rains throughout Heaven and
Earth.

4. Purify yourself for agelessness and indestructibil-
ity, for well-being and for a vast universality. All your
friends here wish that, flowing Soma, to it also I lovingly aspire.

5. Soma flows, the Father of intuitions, the Father of
Heaven, the Father of the Earth, the generator of the
Fire, the generator of the Sun, the generator of Indra and
the generator of the Pervader.

6. The Priest of the Gods, the guide of the poets, the
seer among the sages, the wild buffalo among beasts,

the hawk among birds of prey, the axe among the forests, Soma pours through the purification filter singing.

Soma is the essence of our own mind, which itself is the essence of
our experiences. This essence of experience is purified when we no longer
cling to experience, when the mind flows freely in the essential state of
experiencing without accumulating any residue of like or dislike, attach-
ment or repulsion. When the essence flows freely in the state of experiencing, no longer looking back on what has been experienced, but
composed in the present, then that essential flow reveals the universal and
immortal life. It is this flow that the friends of truth long for and aspire to.
The flow of the essence of life in the state of seeing is the essential
seed-power, the Father and generator of all creation and all the Gods, the
bliss at the heart of all existence. By the transforming power of this
elixir-flow we become the spiritual man, the unconditioned mind in
manifestation.

The being of bliss is the Priest, the Brahmin of the Gods, their
executive intelligence which directs their manifestation. He is the essential form or prototype of all forms, the ideal or perfected type of all classes
of beings. Through the free flow of the essence, the liberation of the
essential energy of life, all things attain perfection. So let the Soma flow;
let the mind purify itself in its natural flow. This is to be achieved not
through any artificial effort or discipline but by being open to the essence,
being sensitive to life, being mindful and observant of the flow. It is not
a matter of resisting our imperfections, which all derive from past conditioning, but of being open to the present in which our problems are
irrelevant. The flow of life, which is revealed in the presence of pure
perception, naturally purifies and clarifies the mind into the infinite.

7. Flowing Soma has vibrated forth like the waves
of a river creating our voices, our songs and our conceptions. Perceiving the inferior powers within the enclosure, the discerning Bull ascends into the lights.
8. Intoxicated, fighting undefeated in the assaults,
pour forth vigor with a thousand seed-currents. Thoughtful self-purifying Indu, furthering the light, energize the
wave of the ray for Indra.
9. Beloved to God-bearing men, Soma flows into the
chalice to be enjoyed for the ecstasy of Indra. A thousand-streamed, a hundred-powered, the luminous drop
like a swift stallion goes to the universal.

The wave of inner bliss gives impulse to the songs and right conceptions of our soul. It is the bull of the chant that invigorates the herds of our right thinking in the enclosure of the concentrated mind. Indu is this guiding drop or central power of bliss. The wave of the ray for Indra is the wave of direct perception for the supremacy of the Self. The chalice is the receptive soul which becomes a vessel of Divine delight. The liberated energy of life in the free flowing mind naturally hastens to the universal, the common being of all.

> 10. The primeval knower of the plenitudes, when born, was cleansed in the waters and milked through the stone. The protector from the curse, the King of the universe, when purified he found the way for the Divine Word.
> 11. Through you, self-purifying Soma, our wise and ancient Fathers accomplished their labors. Fighting undefeated, open out the enclosures, be the Beneficent Lord for us with heroic energies.
> 12. As you flowed forth for the original man, assuming substance in yourself, manifest for us as the ordainer of the eon of life, the destroyer of the unfriendly, the sacred finder of the wideness. Generating your weapons, unite in Indra.

Soma is the flood of truth-light which opens out the path for the Brahman, the Divine Word, as its leading edge. Through it our ancient Fathers opened out the enclosures of darkness to free the light of truth. For Manu, the original man and father of the human race, Soma as the seer ordained this eon of life or world-age. He unites in Indra, the Divine warrior to accomplish the winning of the light, the freedom of mind and equanimity of being for the soul.

> 13. Soma, blissful and truth-bearing, wearing the waters, pour yourself over the imperishable summit. Settle in the clarity filled vessels, as the most exhilarating, intoxicating absorption for the spiritual Man.
> 14. Winning the thousands, seeking power in the Divine advent, a hundred-streamed, pour the rain of Heaven. Roar together with the rivers into the vessel and together with the radiant mornings extend our spirit of Life.

15. He is that Soma which, purified by intuition, like
a swift stallion crosses over the ungiving. Yielded like
the refreshing milk of the Infinite Mother, he is like a
wide path, like a well-disciplined horse with the power
to convey.

The free flow of the meditative, observant mind settles into clarity. It
becomes the drink of absorption, the unity of the seer and the seen that
gives the energy of ecstasy to the spiritual Man, Indra, the unconditioned
entity. He wins the plenary infinitude, the open spaces of clear perception
that bring Heaven's rain of light and bliss. He is the wild and free stallion
of life's beauteous force that delivers us across all narrowness of mind
into the wideness of unconditioned beneficence. He is the milk of infinity
which all finite things in their interrelationship exude.

16. The perfect weapon, purified by those who concentrate, overflow the wonderfully lovely mysterious nature. Like a swift horse seeking renown, overflow vigor,
overflow the Spirit, overflow the light, Divine Soma.
17. They cleanse the adorable child when born. The
Gods of power in concert beautify the carrier-flame. By
songs a poet and by seer-wisdom a seer, Soma passes
across the purification filter singing.
18. The Seer-mind, the Seer-maker, the winner of
the Sun-World, of a thousand guidances, the guide of
the seers, the wild Bull who strives to win the third nature, joyous Soma according to preeminence rules over
all.

Soma is the essence of life pressed out by concentrated observation.
It is this pressure of consciousness that extracts the Soma, the essence of
delight, out of our perceptions. In the ultimate concentration of the mind
in the perception of the unity of being is its complete effusion, its great
expansion into the universal. Soma is the concentrated essence of perception that explodes into delight. It is the perfect weapon that wards away
all darkness and duality. It overflows the wonderfully lovely mysterious
nature of the Godhead, the Brahman. It overflows the Spirit with all power
and all light. All the Gods beautify and empower this adorable child of
innocent awareness. He is the poet and seer who by the purity of his song
passes through the Divine purification filter, the narrow point of the
concentrated mind which opens up into the infinite One.

This singleness of mind is the purification filter through which all our errant tendencies, our distracted thoughts must be refined away. Yet to attain this singleness of mind requires not so much effort as inspiration. It is through the awakened song of our soul that we move into and through it. It is by the free flowing of the essence released by the natural ecstasy of the state of seeing. This free flowing essence is the seer-mind, what makes the seer, what gives true guidance and wins the light. We must let our nature flow freely; yet this is not a matter of self-indulgence but of getting the taste of seeing, the rasa of consciousness, awakening our sense of wonder and inquiry and letting it expand of itself into the deep mysteries of existence. This liberated nature is the wild Bull of the Spirit, the unconditioned being released. It is our freedom to be ourselves apart from all conditioning influences, not the pseudo-freedom to fall unquestioningly into those impulses we find pleasurable. The third nature, as indicated previously, is the nature of the One inclusive of duality, the triple being of the Spirit.

The Soma sacrifice is the sacrifice of our false sense of pleasure, which comes from the hypnosis of the external, to our true sense of delight, which stems from the magic of perception. It is to offer our subconscious instincts and self-conscious egoism, our primitive and artificial character qualities, to the unconditioned being that is both untamed and sensitive, in the intensity of unconditioned perception.

> 19. The hawk in the vessels, the song-bird widely borne, searching for the light, the Soma-drop bears his weapons. The wave of the floods uniting to the sea, the wild Bull declares his fourth nature.
>
> 20. Like a radiant youth adorning his body, like a race horse which has sped for the winning of treasures, as a male to the herds, flowing to the vessel, roaring again and again he has entered into the two world-receptacles.
>
> 21. Flow, self-purifying Indu, with expansiveness; roaring again and again, through the enclosures flow. Being purified as you play, into the two world-receptacles enter. Let your intoxicating essence inebriate Indra.

The Soma-drop is the purified disc of the mind, the point of awareness which can expand to include all creation. Its weapons are its powers of seeing that ward away false thinking, its nature of immortal life which repels the anxieties of mortal considerations. This wave of bliss of the soul unites with the ocean of the Spirit. The drop returns to the sea or rather explodes into it, as the infinite is a point of pure unity and universality. His fourth nature is his state of unity that includes all triplicities — the three worlds, the three states of waking, dream and deep sleep. Soma rests transparent in all forms, pervades the two world vessels as their essence of delight. Through the enclosures of our concentrated perception, roaring with the vibrations of the Divine Word he expands as the Godhead in creation. His supreme absorption, the bliss of unity, inebriates Indra, the spiritual man, the man of ecstasy, the unconditioned being of wild delight. Indra is the being of seeing and his ecstasy is that of seeing, a secret delight of the liberated heart, not a wild dance of some savage shaman, as it has been depicted elsewhere.

> 22. His vast Goddess-streams have flowed forth.
> Anointed with light, into the chalices he has entered.
> Perfecting the mystic song, the mystic singer illumined
> in consciousness, he continues roaring as if to the sister
> of his friend.
> 23. Self-purifying Indu, you continue driving away
> all opponents, full of song as a lover to his beloved.
> Like a song-bird who has flown settles in the woods, pu-
> rifying Soma into the chalices comes to rest.
> 24. Self-purifying Soma, your lustres come like a
> maiden, well-yielding perfect streams. The golden one,
> of manifold boons, taken into the Waters, has roared
> within the chalice of God-seekers.

The chalice of the mystic Soma-absorption is the Divine vessel of awakened consciousness, the purified sphere of awareness which contains all creation. The mystic song is the luminous vibration of bliss. The sister of his friend, the proverbial love match for young couples, is the soul of the singer, our intelligence to which the Soma unites. The luminous drop drives away all opposition and duality in the concentration that admits of no other. He settles into the forests of delight, the song-bird of the spirit in the verdant astral growths of our soul under his light and moisture. His lustrous streams flow like a dancing maiden, as the Sun of every wish roars the light within the souls of those who yearn for the Divine.

Soma is the mystic wine, the offered blood of the great God, the communal presence of the Sun. He is the being of communion, of common union in the sacrificial stream of life that is ever an offering of the one to the one. He is the substance of sacrifice, the flow of the sacred that we all partake of in the actions of breathing and seeing. Soma, delight, is the mystic body of the God, consuming which we ourselves become God. The Christian communion ritual is but another and more recent form of the ancient Vedic Soma offering.

To make the Soma flow is to open up the fountain of our own heart, to let the blood of light from our soul effuse itself in its natural intensity through all life. To partake of this essence, we must allow ourselves to be partaken of by it, taken apart by it in order to be, in essence restored. Drinking the Soma is our absorption in the universal life that can only come by the purification of our mind from all thought, all the residue of the inessential, every shadow of what was so that we might reach the essence of what is. It is the highest ecstasy which can only come when all that is not ecstatic, all that is not transcendent is erased from the mind in the effusion of aspiration. We partake of the Soma when we are willing to sacrifice all the artificial boundaries of our separate self, all the barriers we erect to shield ourselves from the intensity of life. The Soma flows when we are no longer fixated, when we have ceased to grasp, to cling or to assert, when we have begun to let life live in us as in all, when we no longer appropriate anything for ourselves but accept our place in the cosmic offering, partaking of all and being partaken of by all in endless consummation.

The Single Eye IX.9
Asita or Devala Kashyapa

> 1. The seer of Heaven, who has the will of a seer, placed between the Daughters, in effusion moves the beloved energies of life.
> 2. For a wonderful abode, welcome to guileless men, flow forth with the most delightful rush.
> 3. The pure-bright Son at birth made his two Mothers shine reborn, the great God the two great Goddesses who flourish in truth.

The two daughters are the two mothers. They are Heaven and Earth, the dual creative feminine principle. Soma is transcendent being, which is their father or seed-consciousness who enters into them as their son or first-born, the Divine consciousness immanent in creation which it is the place of man to manifest. That son of truth is the inner Sun whereby the worlds shine with beauty in the light of being.

4. By seven insights held he invigorated the guile-
less streams who have grown a Single Eye.

5. They conceived the transcendent, invincible
youth, the blissful drop in your law, oh Indra.

6. The deathless carrier-flame who takes us across
overlooks the seven. The Goddesses were satiated by
the well.

The seven insights are the insights into the unity of truth in the seven
realms of existence. They grow the single eye of the seeing Self. They are
the Goddesses who conceive the Divine youth, the child of bliss by the
spiritual man, to manifest the Spirit in its creation. That carrier-flame of
innocence of mind as the one being overlooks the seven principles of
differentiation. He is the well of bliss from which the Goddess-streams of
delight flow full.

7. Further us in our observances, oh Man. Soma,
conquer the darknesses. Purifying yourself you will slay
them.

8. Now perfect the paths for the hymn that is ever-
more new again. Make the lustres shine as of old.

9. Self-purifier, grant us a great revelation, the light
and speed heroic. Win the intelligence, win the Sun-
World.

Man is Soma, the food of the Gods. He is the being created by the
Gods for their enjoyment, that through the cosmic consciousness which
he has the capacity to manifest the Gods can become aware of themselves
as creatures, can reveal themselves in form. The human being affords the
Divine archetypes an instrumentality for their manifestation in time, in
which they find delight. Man is the vehicle for the higher Divine or
conscious creation, the manifestation of the Gods or Divine principles,
for which material evolution has merely been preparatory. To accomplish
his spiritual task we must become Soma. We must allow ourselves to be
sacrificed by the Gods, to have our consciousness crushed, as it were, with
its essence extracted and effused. We must become the crucible for the
alchemical work of consciousness, in which our being is heated, melted
and purified for its unconditioned essence to come forth.

Man is the being of the sacrifice in nature; the form nature has taken
for its sacrifice to the Spirit for the revelation of its own spiritual essence.
Man is the form the universe has taken to offer itself to the supreme and

the unborn. Man is the form creation has taken to transcend itself into its uncreate source. Man is not meant to exist for himself, to have a personal life of his own. He is the essence of the cosmos, the microcosm, through whom the universal creation is to connect itself to the uncreate, through whom the universal life is to be delivered from the darkness of matter and given a new center in the light of consciousness. He is the creature designed for the cosmic alchemical opus of repolarizing matter so that instead of resisting the light of consciousness it comes to manifest it. He is the creature through whom all creation is to be liberated and resurrected, changed from a blind instrumentality of the ignorance to a conscious instrumentality of the knowledge. As he rises or falls all creation rises or falls with him. He is to liberate creation from the dark inertia of matter that is karma so that all creation is ever-new delight and glory, responsive to the transforming presence of consciousness without resistance. For this work we as human beings must become Soma and learn to effuse ourselves through all creation, which requires that our eye must be single, in the vision of unity.

The Cosmic Atom IX.10
Asita and Devala Kashyapa

> 1. Like thundering chariots, like chargers eager for renown, the Soma-drops have marched to splendor.
> 2. Rushing like chariots they speed into the lines, like the great exertions of working men.
> 3. Like kings with benedictions the Soma-drops manifest themselves with the light, like the sacrifice by the seven ordainers.

The Soma-drops are the sphere of the mind vibrating in the stream of ever-new perception, the great charge of the liberated energy of life. The seven ordainers are the powers of cosmic intelligence on the seven planes of the universe that uphold the sacrificial order of the universe, the interrelationship of all beings.

> 4. Effused for ecstasy, the luminous drops flow concentrated in a stream through the expansive song.
> 5. Attaining the realm of the morning Sun they generate the Dawns and the adorable God. The Suns spread through the atom.

6. The ancient workers open out the doors of intuition, living ones for the intensity of the Spirit.

The soul is the atom in creation, the ultimate indivisible subtle unit
or particle. When the mind is concentrated to the atomic point of the soul,
when the mind is fully attentive in the state of observation, that point of
concentration opens out into the infinite. In this point is all the universe,
all time and space as the manifestation of a single thought, the prime
creative thought to let bliss express itself in form. The Soma-drops are the
vibratory states of the atom of the soul. When the outward going propen-
sity of the mind is curbed, its inertia or ignorance to identify itself with
the external as "I am this" or "this is mine," then the vibratory flow of the
soul is free to return to its native intensity and expansiveness. This flow
reaches its center in the realm of Vivasvan, the dawn or morning Sun,
symbolic of the original creative light. The soul in essence is this Divine
creative light. There it generates the Divine Dawns, the original creative
Goddess-inspirations, and the adorable God, the Sun of bliss. All these
Suns or supreme creative lights spread out and through the atom of the
soul which becomes revealed in its true nature as a point of universal
illumination, the point through which the Divine light is focused for its
expansion into creation.

It is the proper function of the human being in creation to be the point
through which the concentrated Divine light explodes into the world.
Man, the human soul, is the door between God and nature, creation and
the uncreate and it is his place to establish a free flow between them —
to break up the inertia of creation, its latent resistance held over from the
dark night of chaos, through the advent of the consciousness of the
Absolute, the supreme Self. This is the concentrated soul or intelligence
that absorbs all creation. This is the labor that the mystic seers and singers,
the living ones in the cosmic life, accomplish for the Spirit to project its
imperious being into the most obstinate medium of physical matter. It is
our duty as men, as the instrument of the Spirit in creation, to concentrate
our energies in pure observation, to open out and clarify the full sphere
of our soul for its atomic explosion into the infinite light.

7. Facing each other the seven kindred invokers sit,
filling the station of the One.
8. He receives their center into his center as the eye
united in the Sun. He draws out the Son of the seer.
9. The Sun with his beloved eye perceives the station of Heaven held secret by the masters of the rite.

The seven powers of creation form the circle of the One which they manifest, the supreme atom of the universal Soul. All souls, all the cosmic atoms are one in their center. In their central eye, their central being of seeing, they are united to God's center, their eye is merged in the Solar Self, into the unity of seeing, the sole Seer. The Son of the seer is the Divine or inner Son, the product of our seeing, where through the atom of the soul we are reborn in solar rebirth as the Solar Self. The Divine Self with the eye of the soul perceives the central station of Heaven, the Absolute which is the secret of the sages, the secret of the masters of the rite, the spiritual transformation ritual of self-knowledge.

The Poet-Seer IX.20
Asita or Devala Kashyapa

1. The Poet-Seer for the Divine advent flows through the imperishable enclosure, overcoming all rivalry.

2. He, the Self-purifier, infuses for his singers a thousandfold power full of light.

3. You comprehend all with consciousness, as you become transparent through the mind. Thus, Soma, discover the revelation for us.

4. Overflow a vast glory, an eternal splendor for our benefactors. Bear the energy to those who affirm you.

5. You are as if a king of wise law. Soma, you have entered into our songs, transcendent bearer, purifying yourself.

6. The bearer invincible in the floods, cleansed through the lines, Soma settles in the chalices.

7. Disporting like a liberal Lord, Soma you go to the purification filter, holding an heroic energy for your affirmer.

The Poet-Seer is the free-flowing essence of life, in which all is beauty and vision. The imperishable enclosure is the mind concentrated in oneness, through which point we pass through time and space and enter the eternal presence. That being of the essence comprehends all with consciousness, purified by the mind, made transparent by the thought of the heart that "I am the Self of all beings." The affirmers of this Soma are not mere worshippers of an external God but those who, through their inspired knowledge, manifest the Soma in their own mind, by its purification and deconditioning. Soma is the being of the essence that enters into our songs of truth, giving them the power of realization. He is the transcendent Being that bears us into his Absoluteness. He is the wine of delight which, cleansed through our sensory lines, settles into the vessels of what we see. The purification-filter is the net of truth perception in the heart. The essence clarifies itself through that and gives forth the most heroic force.

The Lord of the Mind IX.28
Seer — Priyamedha Angirasa

1. He, the stallion urged by men, the knower of all, the Lord of the mind, through the imperishable enclosure runs.

2. He has flowed through the purification-filter, Soma effused for the Gods, as he pervades all natures.

3. The God appears beautiful, deathless at the source, the destroyer of the serpent, foremost for the advent of the Divine.

4. Embraced by his ten sisters, he, the spirit, repeatedly roars. On to the vessels he runs.

5. He, the clear-seeing self-purifier, the knower of all, made the Sun reveal all natures.

6. Strong and inviolable this self-purifying Soma flows, extending the Divine, destroying the evil word.

Soma, the essence or rasa of delight, is the Lord of the mind, for it is the nature of the mind to seek delight and to dwell upon the delight it has experienced. What is necessary is to turn the mind inward through direct perception to awaken the Divine sense of delight, the delight of seeing, to free the mind from its clinging to pleasure. The imperishable enclosure is the atom of the soul or intelligence, the central point or focus of the mind. It is the door to the Divine which is closed when our mind is not thoughtful and composed, and which opens when it is attentive and aware. That point of awareness is the purification-filter, the point through which the mind is purified and cleansed of all thought and its darkness of matter and memory. His ten sisters are the five sense organs and five organs of action, his ten functions. His vessels are our various bodies or sheaths; gross, subtle and causal. He makes the Sun of the truth-consciousness shine and reveal the being of all. He destroys the evil word, our mystification by names, numbers and labels by which we lose the essence and are hypnotized by the form, the world of non-being which is only a superficial designation. The word of Soma is the word of being, the knowledge of the intelligence that "I am all."

Yielding the Milk and Clarity of the Imperishable IX.31
Seer — Gotama Rahugana

1. The wise Self-purifying drops of Soma have marched forth. They make reality conscious.

2. Luminous drop, over Heaven and Earth be the ex-alter of splendor. Be the Lord of Power.

3. For you the winds blow full of delight, to you the rivers flow. Soma, they increase your might.

4. Let yourself overflow, Soma, from all directions let the spiritual force unite in you. Manifest in the gathering place of power.

5. For you, tawny over the supreme summit, the cows of Light have yielded the milk and clarity of the imperishable.

6. You who have the perfect weapon of being, the Lord of existence, luminous Drop, we long for your friendship.

The flow of the drops of essential awareness, the stream of pure perception, makes reality conscious, makes conscious the full splendor, beauty and abundance of being — giving a vision in which all is a treasure. That point of the essence contains all the worlds and transcends them as the Lord of Power; the true power which is behind the free flow of life. In this vision of the essence, all is ever full. Everything is an overflowing of an unlimited self-contained force. The Cows who yield the imperishable are the truth intuitions, the vibrations of the Divine Word. Their milk is wisdom. Their clarified butter is consciousness distilled in purity. This purity is not of mere virtue but a transparency of perception grown through direct observation in which no stains of inattention are allowed to remain. The imperishable is our deathless nature, the receptive light our soul reveals. These meditative realizations are the highest cultivation of nature, of our inner nature, that reveals her essence, the universal Self. He is the Lord of Being, the perfect, all-protecting weapon against sorrow and non-being, darkness and death. His friendship is unity and equality in the essential existence.

Four Infinite Oceans of Splendor IX.33
Seer — Trita Aptya

1. The Soma-drops, vibrant in consciousness, move like the waves of a flood, like wild buffaloes in the forests.

2. The luminous tawny drops by the stream of truth have flowed into the vessels with a power full of light.

3. Effused for Indra and for the Spirit, for the Lord of Heaven and the Gods of Power, the Soma-drops flow to the Pervader.

4. Three voices are elevated. The mother cows bellow. The Golden one continues to roar.

5. The Priestesses, the mighty Mother streams of truth, have sung. They cleanse the child of Heaven.

6. Soma, pour for us from every side four infinite oceans of splendor.

The Soma-drops are the concentrated essences of delight which arise by nature from all things when the mind is in a state of direct perception. They are the flood of bliss. The vessels are the forms of things in the transparency of pure perception, filled with an aura of delight, a presence of clear light. The Soma is effused for all the Gods, being the nectar upon which the Gods feed. Flowing to all the Gods it reaches the Pervader, the All-God, Vishnu. They flow for the manifestation of all Divine qualities, all the higher archetypes within us. The three voices are the word of truth in the three worlds, the triple nature of delight. The mother cows are the nourishing streams of truth in which the Soma flows as their essence. The Golden one is the Sun who roars the light. The priestesses are the Goddess-powers of liberating energy, the currents of shakti which cleanse the Divine child. The four infinite oceans are those of the four infinite or transcendent principles of Being, Consciousness, Bliss and Intelligence; the fourfold higher half of existence beyond the lower triple realm of the ignorance. In the effusion of delight from the state of direct observation comes forth all the Godhead, not as some metaphysical theory but as the unity of cosmic existence.

The Spirit Effused for the Absorption IX.37
Seer — Rahugana Angirasa

1. The Spirit effused for the absorption, Soma flows through the purification filter, destroying those who guard over us, seeking the Divine.
2. Strong, clear-seeing, adorable, he flows through the purification filter, roaring over the source.
3. The Self-purifying stallion runs through the luminous realm of Heaven, the destroyer of evil, to the imperishable enclosure.
4. Over the summit of the Third, the Self-purifier made to shine, together with the Sisters, the Sun.
5. The dragon-slayer, the concentrated Spirit, the undeceivable finder of the wideness, Soma, as if to power, has flowed.
6. The God set in motion by the seer, the luminous Drop flows into the receptacles with greatness for the spiritual Man.

Soma is the essential Spirit, the being of delight, effused from concentration for the Samadhi-absorption, the mergence into the Oneness. He destroys all the powers of illusion that guard over us, the stream of our disturbed thoughts, and settles us in the source. He takes us to the center of the world in our own heart where all time and space coalesce into unity. He takes us to the summit of the world-mountain, the secret Third which is the union of all dualities, and there with his Sisters, the muses, he makes the Sun of Truth shine undiminished forever. His flow is an effusion in all directions from the source within the heart, through which, ever expanding, we settle ever more into unity. He is the Divine essence that the state of seeing sets in motion. He fills all forms as receptacles of delight, thus bringing to consciousness the spiritual Man, Indra, the sense of the universal I Am, into all creation. To drink of that essence is to be absorbed into the All. It is the supreme inebriation of the ecstasy of undivided perception, the destruction of the division between the seer and the seen.

The Essence of the Perceptive Faculties IX.47
Seer — Kavi Bhargava

1. Through this right action great Soma grew full. He puts forth his spiritual force, rejoicing.

2. He has accomplished his great deeds, crushing all destruction. Fierce, he gathers all debts.

3. When his utterance is born, then Soma, the essence of the perceptive faculties, becomes the vajra, the thunderbolt that wins the thousands.

4. The seer, in the upholding law, desires his own ecstasy for the sage, when he cleanses his understandings.

5. You who strive to win the treasures are as if a victorious mare in the battles for power.

The right action of Soma is the harmonious functioning of our sense organs and organs of action in the awareness of the essence. His great deeds are the destruction of all that is negative, the negation of the illusions of death, sorrow and violence. The debts he gathers are the wrong action, the karma born of ignorance, which by the law of truth must bear their consequences. The utterance of Soma is the declaration of the essence, the articulation of the pure, the word of truth, the song of oneness made manifest. Soma is the essence of our perceptive faculties. These are the indriyas, the powers of Indra, the spiritual Man. The spiritual Man is the power of perception and all the faculties of perception are functions of his nature. These are integrated and harmonized by the perception of the essence in choiceless observation. That essence-perception is the vajra of Indra, his bolt of light, whereby the spiritual Man conquers the light for the Divine. It is the light of being that wins the infinities, as the term for thousand in the *Vedas* has usually an indefinite sense of the innumerable. The poet-seer of the essence desires his own ecstasy for the sage who lauds him, the gift of the Self to the Self. When our understandings are cleansed, this original ecstasy shines forth. The purified soul of understanding is the mare victorious in the war for light.

Soma as the Sun IX.54
Seer — Avatsara Kashyapa

1. According to his primordial splendor, the daring ones have yielded as luminous milk the seer who wins the thousands.

2. In presence he is like the Sun. To the lakes he flows, in seven descending streams from Heaven.

3. Self-purifying, he stands over all the worlds, Soma, Divine as the Sun.

4. Self-purifying luminous Drop, you pour for us for
the Divine advent a power full of light, seeking the spiritual Man.

The daring seers by their penetrating power of truth perception milk
out the essential state of seeing which yields all delights. They draw forth
the Sun of awareness from the currents of life, from all seven planes of
existence. That essence of light is the Solar Self of all beings, which arises
forever over all the worlds. He is the light in the heart, manifesting which
we become true men, real human beings of the cosmic vision. It is this
free pouring of the essence that accomplishes the Divine advent, the
manifestation of the Divine in man. That essential drop or point of
awareness within us is the supreme point of Being, the universal Sun, the
light by which all the stars shine, the life through which all creatures live.
When we return our minds to the point of pure simplicity, the direct and
continuous awareness of Being, that supernal Sun arises within us in
splendor everywhere.

Into the Belly of the Tree IX.95
Seer — Praskanva Kanva

1. The Golden one roars being released. Purified he
settles into the belly of the tree. Held by men he makes
the light his pure raiment. Thus he generates all intuitions by the powers of the Self-nature.
2. The Golden one when free sends out, like a ship
an oar, the Path-Goddess, the Word of truth. Divine, he
reveals the secret natures of the Gods, to declare them
on the sacred grass.
3. Billowing like the waves of the flood, our conceptions stream towards the Soma. In surrender they approach and unite to him, and enter into him, loving him
as he loves them.
4. Made pure like the wild buffalo at the summit,
they pour him out as the filament, the mountain-dwell-
ing bull. All thoughts in aspiration unite to him. As the
Third he bears the Lord of Heaven in the Ocean.
5. Sending the Word as the director, purified, Indu,
release the mind of the invoker. When you and Indra for
auspiciousness rule, may we be the masters of a perfect
heroic-force.

The tree is that of our spinal nervous system, the astral tree of our soul. The Soma or mystic nectar falls into the belly of the tree, the navel center, for our spiritual rebirth at this place of power. It is the descent of the unconditioned consciousness into the vital center for the manifestation in life of the free man of the Spirit. There the unconscious is transmuted into the free flow of cosmic perception and intuition. The central Golden being of truth sends out his consort Word as his means of movement and expression. Through war, that is through warding off duality, he reveals the names and natures of all the Gods, their mysterious being in the Self. In the free flow of the essence, our thoughts and conceptions shift their orientation and come to flow from the light of perception rather than from the darkness of memory. Our transformed thoughts become means of unification with the quiescent consciousness of bliss. He is the free Spirit, the wild Bull at the summit of the world-mountain. He is the essential filament of the light, the plant of life whose sap or essence gives heat, light and nourishment.

When the mind knows this nectar at its source, all thoughts must seek it. The mind can only seek the strongest delight it knows. It must be taught where true and lasting delight can be found. This supreme Spirit is the Third, the unity of duality which bears the Lord of Heaven, God the creator, celestial Varuna-Uranus, in the cosmic sea. He is the Self of the Godhead who holds the cosmic Divine as his creative and ruling force of intelligence. By the Divine Word he releases the mind of the invoker or the invoking mind, our mind's power to create reality. Our mind is the power of conception, the Goddess who gives birth. In the ignorance she creates the false thoughts of division and duality according to our sense of delight as deriving from the external. When purified and inspired by the Divine Word, the cosmic vibration in which the delight of the oneness of perception is known, she herself is reborn and released into the infinite. Our conceptions generate a stream of right thinking that comprehends the organic nature of the universe as a movement of the One. In that Indu and Indra, the powers of bliss and unconditioned being both have their auspicious rule in us and we become masters of the heroic energy of the all-conquering Spirit.

The Secret Nature of the Father and the Mother IX.75
Seer — Kavi Bhargava

1. Placed in delight the mighty stream overflows the beloved natures in which he grows. Clear in vision he

has ascended the vast vehicle of the vast Sun which
turns to every side.

2. The tongue-flame of truth pours the beloved
honey-wine. He is the speaker, the inviolable master of
this insight. The Son, he establishes the secret nature of
the Father and the Mother in the third luminous realm of
Heaven.

3. Flashing, he has roared down into the chalices,
drawn by men into the Golden sheath. The milkings of
truth have sung to him. The being of the triple-presence,
he shines resplendent through the Dawns.

4. Pressed out by the stones, by intuition placed in
delight, he made his two Mothers, Heaven and Earth,
shine pure. He is diffused through the middle of the
fleece, the stream of honey-wine overflowing day by
day.

5. Soma, flow forth for well-being. Purified by men,
invest yourself with the commingled essence. By those
which are your expansive, struck-out ecstasies, impel
Indra to grant his beneficence.

The honey-wine is the intoxicating delight of perception. It is poured
in a great stream from the tongue-flame of truth, the flame of the Divine
perceptive word in the heart, whose vibration moves through our sensory
fields. It is the flame of beauty and power which burns as the Goddess in
all the forms of nature. He is the Son, the unity of the two parents, the
dual creative-principle. This secret nature of their unity he establishes as
the third luminous Heaven, the mysterious third region where spirit is
matter and matter is spirit, wherein all manifests the ideal. There he has
his triple presence as the triple Absolute. He is pressed out by the stones
of objective awareness. He is diffused through the middle of the golden
fleece, the imperishable filaments, the bliss spreading through the rays of
knowledge. This is the commingled essence of the milk of truth and the
wine of delight. The struck-out ecstasies are the tunes of the Divine
musician which reveal the true man of beneficence.

The Seven-mouthed Chants IX.111
Seer — Ananata Parucchepi

1. By this golden lustre purified, he crosses all duality with his self-yoked powers, like the Sun with his self-yoked powers.

The stream of concentration shines, the self-purified radiant stallion, when he encompasses all forms with his chants, with his seven-mouthed chants.

2. You found the treasure of the traders. Together with your Mothers you beautify yourself in your own domain, with the understandings of truth in your own domain.

As that mystic song from the beyond, where understandings rejoice, with his triple-natured radiant herds he has assumed the essential energy of life, shining delightful with the essential energy of life.

3. He moves conscious, directed to the east. Together with his rays he extends the visionary vehicle, the Divine visionary vehicle.

These utterances have attained to heroic force, arousing the spiritual Man in joy for victory; so you, Indra, and your thunderbolt are never to be thrown down, in the encounters never to be thrown down.

Soma is the Sun of the unitary truth that takes us across the darkness of duality. He is the solar Self who delivers all who, through the practice of yoga have united themselves with him. His are the seven-mouthed cosmic chants that pour all the levels of existence, which the stream of concentration reveals. He is the radiant stallion of the free running flow of life, the Spirit's freedom in creation. The treasure of the traders is the secret wealth of truth concealed by the bartering or commercial mind and its incessant search for selfish profit and self-advantage. We see here that even the ancients had to contend with this illusion power of the acquisitive mind bent on material enjoyment, which so dominates the world today. His Mothers are the understandings of truth through which we beautify our own nature in the home of delight. The mystic song is the Sun-song, the Om vibration of the solar Self. His triple-natured radiant herds are the vibrations of the triple-Godhead of Being-Consciousness-Bliss. In that he assumes the essential energy of life which is immortal. Through him we enter into the real era or eon of life, the true period of life in the eternal present as cosmic beings.

His visionary vehicle is the Sun of Divine intelligence, the secret organic cosmic intelligence at work in life beyond all personal limitations. The spiritual vehicle is the enlightened knowledge that leads the way to that solar Self or illumined oneness. These words for truth arouse the spiritual Man, archetypal Indra, for the great victory of the enlightened mind over the serpents of the unconscious. They energize his vajra, his bolt of lightning and thunder, Divine revelation; the satori bolt of direct perception which accomplishes the victory. The seven-mouthed chants are the voices, the tunes of the flute of the spine, the astral body of sound and light, through whose play this spiritual Man comes forth to victory.

III

THE GODDESS

Let the luminous Goddess Intuition go forth from us, well-fashioned as a stallion for a chariot.

The Goddesses know the origin of Heaven and Earth, the Waters listen as they flow.

Express your Wisdom Goddess, perfect the Word in the Godhead. — Rig Veda VII.34.1–2, 9

When the Goddess-Word, speaking to the ignorant, was seated joyful as the Queen of the Gods,

She yielded four kinds of milk for vigor, where has her supreme portion gone?

The Gods generated the Word Goddess. Perceptions of every form declare her.

Joyful, yielding vigor and energy for us, may she, the milch Cow, the Word, well-affirmed, approach us.   — Rig Veda VIII.100.10–11

The mother of the Gods of power, the daughter of the beings of light, the sister of the sons of the Infinite, the navel-center of immortality,

I proclaim to conscious men, do not slay the sinless cow, the Infinite Mother.

The speech finding Goddess-Word, elevated, with all the muses approaching, the Divine Cow from the Gods, mortals needing to elevate their minds have chosen me. — Rig Veda VIII.101.15–16

7
HYMNS TO THE GODDESS
THE POWER OF THE DIVINE WORD

The Muse

All creative expression depends on the Muse. She is the ideal, the inspiration, the beauty which alone can facilitate it, our dawn or guiding star. In fact, all creative expression is the manifestation of the Muse. Creativity is genuine only when she speaks. The only true voice is that of the Divine Word, of the Word Goddess herself. For the Muse is the creative essence of our own soul, its feminine power of true conception. All creativity is a kind of giving birth. It requires first a gestation and a labor. For any creative endeavor to proceed we must first invoke within ourselves the archetype of the Muse; that is, we must first awaken our inspiration by discovering our true passion in life, by being true to the wishes of our own deeper Self. The Muse is the presence of the Goddess within us, our portion of the cosmic feminine power which is the true creative force in life, the cosmic masculine force being more properly the supracosmic transcendent being. To create, we must all win the favor of the Muse, the grace of the Goddess. All true creation is the unfolding of the cosmic feminine energy, the release of the Goddess-energy of Life for the culmination of its evolutionary transformation. The Muse is our spirit of devotion to the Divine, our faithfulness to the cosmic vision and the creative work, our true being as human beings to bring the Divine creativity into the world for its deliverance. The Muse is our love of nature that is our openness to the cosmic creative force. She is the yearning of our life for the immortal life in which all is a play of harmony.

As with creative endeavors, so with the spiritual life. The spiritual life is the projection of our creative energies inwardly for the transformation of consciousness. It is the vertical ascent that the horizontal extension of the aesthetic mind eventually demands. The spiritual life depends as much on the grace of the Goddess as the creative life does upon that of the Muse. Yoga depends upon the Yoga Shakti, the Divine power of reintegration. Our mere mortal and fragmented mind, will and personality have no power to overcome the dark ignorance of the world. The ancient worship of the Goddess was no primitive fertility cult. For the seers, she is the higher nature of the creative Muse on the spiritual plane. She is the archetype of the higher feminine side of our nature we must manifest to energize the spiritual work.

It is only through the Goddess that one can know the Gods, for it is only by ourselves becoming inwardly receptive that we can create the field for their manifestation. We can only give birth to the Gods by becoming the Goddess, and this is only possible when we perceive the creative Goddess power in all nature nurturing the Spirit-child. This relationship between the Goddess and the Gods has little to do with the social and political considerations of ancient or modern cultures. It reflects the law and rhythm of the inner yogic alchemy of the transmutation of awareness. The Muse is the matrix of this process which works on an archetypal level. She is the inspiration through which alone these forces of the deeper mind are set in motion.

Our own soul, the receptive, devoted, intuitive feminine side of our nature is the high priestess of the inner art. She has the intuitive knowledge, the spontaneous sense of it. She knows the way and she is the door, the gate and the altar. We have only to let her stream of transformation flow. She will pour on us the great inner ocean of light. All spiritual growth is not through our personal effort, but through her aspiring force. This requires letting her force gestate within us. Our labor is the labor of patience, creating the depth of mind and character to allow the eonic Shakti or spiritual force to grow within us towards her great birth of Self-awareness, the Divine child. Our work is to create the vision that surrenders to Being and allows it to open up the stagnant currents of our mind to uncover the pure spring of the Muse behind it. It is the labor of non-effort, non-manipulation and non-interference in which we let the essence of life speak for itself. No artifice can aid in this work, which is the labor of abandoning all artifice. This inner purity, not of cultivated virtue, but of the receptive mind, the motiveless heart, is the beauty of the Muse and Goddess. To win her, we must speak the truth, live in right-thinking and right-action. She is the wisdom archetype who demands and inspires the greatest nobility of our nature.

Behind all the great mantras of the seers is this primary sense of the Muse, the Divine Word, the Goddess. The mantras are her transformations which manifest the Gods. Her rhythms are the mystic chants which reveal the Divine names and natures. She dances and the Gods come forth as the story of her dance. She is their secret power which is the true inner power that works without outer display or seeking personal credit. This homage to the Muse is the root of all creative growth. We invoked her at the beginning of this book as the Dawn. Here we explore her manifold forms as our litany draws to a close.

The Goddess Intelligence X.11
Seer — Angirasa Havirdhana

1. Young and undeceivable, the Spirit has yielded
for the Spirit by the milking of Heaven, the milk of the
Infinite Mother. As the Lord of Heaven through the Wisdom Goddess he knows all. Most sacred let him sanctify
the sacred seasons.

This is a hymn to the Fire, Agni. The Spirit yields the milk of the
Infinite Mother, Aditi. The Bull of Being yields the milk of the Cow of
Consciousness. The two supreme cosmic powers are only one. In that
unity of the twofold nature, our flame of awareness has the power to make
all things sacred, perceiving all things as the play of these two holy
principles. Intelligence or Wisdom was to the ancients a Goddess, a power
of receptivity, caring and loving attention. It also meant insight, understanding and conception. It is the insight engendered by reflecting the light
of our awareness receptively on things. It is not what we call conceptual
knowledge, which is merely projecting the veil of our preconceptions on
things, not opening up to their real being, life and presence. It is conception
in the sense of a woman bearing a child, a taking into ourselves the essence
of what we see and letting it grow organically within us. It is letting the
being of what we see affect us, allowing ourselves to be touched by life
without protective barriers or separative discriminations.

2. Let the angelic Lady of the Waters speak. In the
roar of the river may she shelter my mind. May the Infinite Mother hold us in the center of all wishes. Let our
eldest Brother, who is the foremost, decide for us.

We must seek the maiden or the Lady of the Waters, the feminine
being of creative sensitivity and inspiration, in order to find the secret of
our souls. She is the beautiful energy of the life-giving waters of consciousness. She is the Lady of the stream of Life, the caring feminine
consciousness who shelters us in her flow. She is the creative stream of
our soul which declares the word of truth. She is the Infinite Mother who
holds us in the center of reality where to think is to become, to wish is to
attain. She is the being of wishes, the ideal that underlies the actual, the
Divine archetype behind creation. Though the material world is slow to
manifest this ideal, it must do so eventually, and that ideal is a truer reality,
a higher plane of existence in its own right than our physical world. If the

228 — Wisdom of the Ancient Seers —

actual fails to meet the ideal, it is not because the ideal, the wish of the heart, is wrong, but because the world is still ignorant and not conscious of its true and ultimate being.

The Goddess is the inspiration that holds to the ideal regardless of all the inadequacies of the actual, which sees the ideal even in the un-ideal, which finds all things to be the declaration of truth and the searching of the soul. These are not the conditioned ideals of thought, memory and programmed education. They are not blind concepts that prevent us from understanding life as it is. They are the essence which is trying to take shape in all things as their true being. They are the deeper sensitivities of the soul, its expectations of truth, goodness and beauty in all life. They are not a shadow of life, but the power behind it. This Goddess of the ideal is the Muse who motivates us all to find the truth. Our eldest Brother is the Fire, the flame of wakeful awareness. Through his consort, intelligence, he is able to decide for us the nature of truth, the disposition of our being.

> 3. As this auspicious abundant and glorious Dawn,
> she has shone out for man, bearing the Sun-World;
> since the Goddesses, according to the will of those who
> aspire, gave birth to the aspiring Fire as the invoker for
> the sessions of knowledge.

That Intelligence shines out as the Dawn of Divine awareness, the Goddess Dawn for men, bearing the Sun-World of enlightened perception. Its thoughts and insights generate the upward moving flame of consciousness and bring us to the sessions of knowledge, the real and inner labor of our deeper mind.

> 4. Then the delegated bird, the hawk, brought the
> pervasive drop of clear-seeing into the rite. When the
> Aryan people chose the Fire as the magical invoker,
> then the Goddess Intelligence was born.

The hawk is the Spirit as the messenger, herald and harbinger of truth. He brings the drop of clear perception, the purified and clarified point of concentrated awareness which contains all space and time. The Aryan people are the Goddesses who are the thoughts of wisdom (most Vedic words for people are feminine, as the feminine is the principle of multiplicity and of multiplicity in unity). When our noble thoughts choose the Flame of mindfulness, then the Goddess, the receptive power of true conception, of spiritual intelligence, is born. The installment of the Fire as the priest-lord of our mind in the ritual sacrifice of life is the birth of intelligence that gives birth to all the Gods. It is the awakening of our true creative principle which is the Goddess and is of unlimited capacity for understanding. The ancient priests were, in this sense, only outer representatives of the truth powers within. The ancient ritual was an outer image of the ritual of life and awareness, the sacred movement of transformation life naturally is. The Goddess is the creative power of this process, the receptive mind that is the matrix, the womb of this great transmutation. She is the open consciousness which alone has the power of true conception.

> 5. Agni, you are ever delightful, with you as with pasture there is nourishment, by your consort invoking-powers you are the master of the rite of Man. Or when calmed by the utterance of the sage, having conquered all power, with more abundance you approach.

The flame of Awareness by its consort powers of true invocation, the invocation of truth by the receptive mind, is the master of the rite that is Man. The human being is the culminating phase of the evolutionary ritual through whom life comes to manifest the cosmic being, matter gives birth to the spirit. It is the truth utterance of the sagely mind that calms the fire of our mind and emotions and brings it to its native state of delight. Through this calm is gained all power which brings the approach of the great abundance of life.

> 6. Raise up your Parents as a lover to delight. Our adoration requests it; the impulse is from the heart. The carrier-flame speaks; the sacrifice is perfected. The almighty Being puts forth his consort power and vibrates with the knowledge.

The flame of Awareness raises up his parents, Heaven and Earth or mind and body, and renews them with his vision of delight. In that seeing, Heaven and Earth overflow with the transparency of bliss. This is the renewal of all creation in the consciousness of the Self that is the perfection of the sacrifice — the offering of the all to the all. The carrier-flame is the flame in the heart. This almighty Being comes forth by the power of his knowledge, the wisdom Goddess, who manifests his grace and concern for all beings.

7. Fire, Son of strength, the mortal who has attained
your right-thinking is far renowned. Taking on an energy conducted by swift forces, he appears luminous
and imperious throughout the days.

The right-thinking of the Fire is the right attention of the state of
seeing. It is another name for his consort power, through which all his
splendor is attained. It is our capacity to perceive and give value to the
light in all beings.

8. Flame of the sacred, when the Goddess, sacred
among the Gods, appears as the unification rite; when,
Self-natured Lord, you apportion the ecstasies, there extend our share of the plenitude.

The Goddess is the coming together of all the Gods. She is the
unification rite or the assembly of the Gods. She is the place wherein they
meet, the field of their manifestation. It is by the Goddess power of
common aspiration, right-thinking, receptivity and devoted intelligence
that diversity can be resolved into unity. It is the feminine sense of
harmony and equality, of mutual acceptance without separative assertion,
that integrates and empowers the Divine principles of our higher nature.
It is only through this point of balance and mutuality that the circumference of Divine archetypes can manifest. She is the secret to the manifestation of the Gods. She is the receptivity, the right disposition in mortals,
through which alone the powers of immortality can come forth.

To know the Gods we must become the Goddess. To give birth to truth
we must become the wisdom Mother. The manifestation of the Gods is
the power of the Goddess. The hymns that invoke the Gods are her
thoughts. She is the Word through which they declare themselves, of
which they are the expressions. She is the body of which the Gods are the
movement. The Word is the Self of all beings, the universality of the I
Am, in which all beings partake of the Godhead. She is the recognition
of this Self in all beings that brings all together in a common oneness and
gives each being its share of the Godhead. This share of the plenitude is
no mere portion. It is the equal presence of the Divine everywhere, the
share through which we partake of everything and everything partakes of
us in the communal bliss of oneness.

9. Oh Flame, listen to us in this common dwelling.
Yoke the swift vehicle of immortality. Bring to us

Heaven and Earth whose children are the Gods. Do not
manifest other than as Divine; come into being here.

The common dwelling is the unitary mind. This mind of oneness is
the swift vehicle of immortality, for through the oneness immortality
manifests directly. Heaven and Earth are the twin Goddesses to be
conducted to us in their true and Divine nature by the flame of seeing.
Through it they become the generative powers of the Gods. That Flame
manifests the Divine here, in life, not as some metaphysical theory or
emotional belief but as the clarity of unconditioned perception and the
right-thinking it engenders.

The Forms of the Goddess III.57
Seer — Gathina Vishvamitra

1. My discernment has discovered the intuition, the
milch Cow who wanders free without a herdsman. Who
immediately yields abundant sustenance, thus Indra and
the Fire give praise to her.

The milch Cow (dhenu) is the main symbol of the cosmic feminine
power. She is the intuition, the conception which reflects the truth of
things. She is the Infinite Mother, Aditi, the independent, self-sufficient
principle of consciousness that functions of its own nature without the
need for any external guidance. She immediately yields abundant sustenance for as we think in our hearts, according to the wish-fulfilling Cow
of consciousness, so we are. Indra is the spiritual man, the unconditioned
being. The Fire is the wakeful awareness. These give praise to that
receptive consciousness which is their mother, upon whom all their power
is based. It is the self-sufficiency of the cosmic feminine, her capacity to
give nourishment to all, her nourishing receptivity which responds to the
needs of all beings, that is lauded here. It is not the self-sufficiency of
isolation, of pride, of withdrawal and aloofness. It is that of openness,
responsiveness and universality, the self-sufficiency of the mother principle.

2. Indra and the Sun, mighty and skillful, joyfully
have drained the inexhaustible Goddess of Heaven.
When all the Gods have delighted in her, there, beings
of light, may I attain your bliss.

All the Gods, the powers and principles of light, milk the inexhaustible sky in which they move, the infinite Goddess of receptive consciousness who is the medium of their manifestation. When that receptive awareness is fully extended, fully open, then all the Divine principles and archetypes are able to delight in her and manifest through her. Then we attain the bliss which is our innate share in the all-giving Divine.

> 3. The Sisters who desire the power of the Spirit, in
> their surrender come to know the seed in him. The
> milch Cows come lowing to the Son who bears expan-
> sive forms of wonder.

The Sisters are the Goddess-Powers. They seek or wish to become the power, the Shakti of the Spirit, which is their essence. They gain this by their surrender to the Spirit, which is also their reception of his force. The power of wisdom is the energy of surrender to the Divine. It is the power of receptive love which, seeking no power for itself is able to convey the universal force. That Spirit which is the Father is also the Son. His Sisters are also his Mothers, as in receiving his seed they give birth to him again. The milch Cows are the symbols of the powers of the Divine Mother. Again, the animal image is used for its greater power of psychic evocation, its greater appeal to our subconscious. He is the Divine Child, the immanent spiritual being, the soul in creation who incarnates all the magical beauties of the natural world.

> 4. I speak to perfectly formed Heaven and Earth, as
> through intuition I employ the pressing stones in the
> rite. These flames of yours that have abundant boons for
> man, manifest aloft visionary and holy.

Heaven and Earth are the dual Goddess, the world medium in which the great God moves and has his birth. The stones are the states of objective consciousness, stone-like awareness in the intuitive labor of the inner transformation ritual. The tongue-flames are the Goddess-powers of the Fire, his means of manifestation and expression.

> 5. Your tongue of flame, oh Fire, honey-like, medita-
> tively wise, is called the Wideness among the Gods. By
> her make all the holy ones sit here and drink the honey-
> wine.

The Fire of seeing has for its instrumentality the tongue-flame of blissful wisdom, the means of articulation of the word of light. It is the prime flame of perception of the Fire of mindfulness that extracts the essence of delight from the forms we see. It is the capacity, the penetrating power, through receptive openness to absorb the essence of life, the truth of what which beckons to us in all the actions of life. She is the concentrated flame of perception that results from the wideness, the concentration that comes through openness and non-resistance. She is the power of absorption, the most refined sensitivity of perception, through which all the Divine archetypes are manifested and by which they are satiated.

> 6. Divine Fire, she who is your stream like that of a
> mountain, let her overflow wonderfully variegated and
> inexhaustible. Knower of all births, Being of light, yield '
> her to us, your forethought, your right-thinking who is
> universal to all beings.

The Goddess is the stream of the flaming water of consciousness, its course of movement, its means of dispensing beneficence. She is the right-thinking, the forethought through which we arrive at true awareness. She is the sense of universality, the mother-like compassion of right attention for all things. It is through the Goddess alone that we can know the God, for she is the wisdom which reveals and expresses him. To give birth to him we must become her. There is a perfect balance in the energies of the soul, without which no true transformation can ensue. Each opposite is contained within the other and each is attained through the other. The way for man is to become the Goddess that he might know the God. It is for us to take the role of the Goddess in our actions, as the Goddess is the Divine power of action and expression, that we may take the role of the God in our being and in our will. Working through the Goddess, taking the receptive role in action, we realize the God, we become active in being. We become a presence of the immortal Spirit in life that need not assert itself, but which accomplishes all things by being what it is. It is this right recognition and union of the male and female sides of the soul through which the transcendent Self is known.

We may find the forms of the Goddess mentioned in this hymn to be vague or imagistic — streams, flames, Heaven and Earth, the milch Cow of Heaven, forethought, right-thinking, universality. Were it not for the feminine case endings, we would take them as neutral terms and not relate them to the Goddess at all, as most translators usually do. Yet the Vedic Gods are of the same vague, imagistic and sometimes abstract nature.

Their symbolism is only anthropomorphic on one of many levels and more characteristically naturalistic. The God and the Goddess to the ancients were not just men and women, the human male and female reflected onto a mythic plane. As such we could say they do not primarily refer to a sexual division, though they also embody that duality. They are the dual being of existence, the complementary powers at work in all life. They are the dual cosmic energy, the power of polarity which is symbolized by the male and female human being only on one level. The ancients saw this duality at work on all levels. We find them giving a masculine or feminine sense even to abstract terms, to inanimate objects, to inner faculties, to qualities within the Divine nature. All this had little to do with an obsession with sex. It was expressive of an organic intelligence that saw the complementary powers of the cosmos on all levels of their manifestation. It is not a polarity of difference in which there is love and hate. It is a complementary polarity which demonstrates an all-embracing oneness. It reflects not an obsession with duality but a profound sense of unity which embraces all sides of dualities, through which duality leads to unity. It is an organic sense of complementarity far more intuitive than our artificial intellectual sense of equality or our emotional sense of sexual attraction and repulsion. In that organic intelligence, the two powers appear everywhere, on all levels of the mind, in the great unitary dance of life.

The Goddess of the Waters VII.47
Seer — Maitravaruni Vasishta

1. Goddess Waters, may we win that pure and stainless, clarity-distilling, honey-filled wave of refreshment of yours, which God-seekers made as the primordial absorption for the spiritual Man.

2. Goddess Waters, let the Son of the Waters, of swift impulsion, further that most blissful wave of yours. In which the spiritual Man and the beings at light will delight; God-seekers, may we attain that wave of yours today.

3. With a hundred purifying currents, delighting in the Self-nature, the Goddesses enter into the region of the Gods. They do not diminish the laws of the spiritual Man. To the rivers bestow the clarity-filled offering.

4. Whom the Sun with his rays has extended, for whom the spiritual Man opened out the wavy channels.

Let the River-Goddesses found the wideness for us. Protect us with the powers of well-being forever, oh Gods.

The Waters (Apas) are the cosmic waters of consciousness. Their essential wave or vibration is the being of bliss, the Soma. This is the primordial absorption, the state of meditative dissolution in the cosmic ocean of oneness that is the portion or nature of the spiritual Man of unconditioned intelligence, Indra. The Son of the Waters (Apam Napat) is the Divine Son, the Self which is the creative essence of all the Gods and Goddesses. He is the Vedic form of the Roman God Neptune. He is the being of depths that God-seekers come to realize. The Goddess-Waters of Consciousness have infinite purifying streams of clarity-filled blissful awareness that clear out the conditioned chaos of the unconscious mind. They are the spontaneous free flow of consciousness delighting in its own Self-nature, pervading all the Divine realm of unbounded creation. These are the rivers of bliss in the soul that the Sun of the enlightened Mind extends, that the unconditioned being of the Absolute, the supreme Person opens up.

Aryan culture grew up in various river valleys and saw in the flow of the rivers the great flow of life and consciousness. The seers saw the Divine presence in the life around them. This is quite different and far more evolved than the simple pantheism usually ascribed to them.

VII.49
Seer — Maitravaruni Vasishta

1. Whose foremost is the ocean, from the middle of the sea, they go on purifying themselves, unresting. Whom Indra, the wielder of the thunderbolt, the Bull opened out — let the Goddess-Waters further me here.

2. The Waters which are celestial or those which are flowing, those which are dug up or those which spontaneously arise, whose goal is the ocean, the bright purifiers — let the Goddess-Waters further me here.

3. In the middle of whom the King of Heaven abides, observing the truth and falsehood of men, who are the honey-distilling bright purifiers — let the Goddess-Waters further me here.

4. In whom is the King of Heaven, in whom is the Soma, in whom the Universal Gods take delight, into

whom the Fire, the Universal Man has entered — let the
Goddess-Waters further me here.

The Waters (Apas) are the primary form of the Goddess, as fire or
light is that of the God. The Vedic Goddesses are not primarily women.
They are Waters, flowing movements of consciousness and its creative
energy, of which the female is the manifestation in the human world. They
are the free flowing stream of the mind that ever purifies and clears itself.
They are the pure mind clarified by its own free flow. Indra, the spiritual
Man, by his truth perception opens out their channels. These are the
Waters, the flowing movement that is everywhere in all things, which, if
we open up our minds to them, purify our thoughts in their unceasing
flow. Varuna, the King of Heaven and Lord of the ocean abides in the
waters as their clarity that discriminates the truth from the falsehood, the
eternal from the transient. In them is the Soma, the honey-wine of bliss.
In the free flowing Goddesses, the Goddesses of the free flow of the mind,
are all the Gods, the Universal Gods which are the Divine principles of
being, pervasive everywhere.

In these Divine Waters dwells the Fire, the flame of the holy Spirit,
the Universal Man or cosmic entity. The Waters are consciousness as
object, as media, as world. The Fire is consciousness as subject, as
indwelling entity or spirit. In true awareness both are one. The Fire grows
and burns in the Waters. The Waters are the flaming waters of pure
awareness. The unity of the Fire and the Waters that the ancients sought
is the unity of consciousness, the unity of both subject and object, the
being and the world. That unity is the real basis, the universality of the
human being. In duality man is only a beast or a machine caught in
conditioned reaction patterns of love-hate, the disturbed contradictions of
the alienated mind. In unity, man is nature and nature is man in the higher
nature of the Spirit which is unconditioned and free. Man is the essence
of the Waters, the being behind the floods of creation, life and consciousness. He is the flame that grows in the Waters, the power of seeing thriving
in the free flow of the floods of life.

For the energization of the true human being, we need to seek the
grace of the Goddess, of the Divine Waters. We need her free flow and
exhilarating dance to cleanse the mind of its stagnant desires. We need to
open out the channels of our thought for the floods, for the Goddesses to
move within us with their creative streams of beauty, wonder and delight.
It is this free flow of the mind that purifies and clarifies, not any artificial
effort, discipline or technique. All we can do is to remove the obstacles,
the obstinate inertia of our nature which inhibits her flow. This we can

only do by seeking her grace and her furthering power. It is not our place to oppose the current of our mind. This only serves to fragment us against ourselves. What is necessary is to find the higher currents that can flood out the lower currents which bind us with their obscure desires and fears from the long night of time. It is these Waters we have to invoke within us, to enable the full flood of the Goddess to clear out her stagnant lower waters against which we labor in vain. It is only when the mind-Goddess flows freely that the enlightened being, the true man, can manifest through her. The flowing free of the Waters is the manifestation of the Universal entity who has nothing to resist, being the openness of the All. All we can do is be open to the effusive perception of life that lets everything flow to its true nature.

The ancient Aryans followed the rivers out to the sea and colonized many lands. They saw in the image of the many rivers uniting to the single sea the many streams of the mind uniting into the great ocean of consciousness, the grand metaphor of liberation itself.

Sarasvati
The Goddess of the Flowing Stream of Inspiration VI.61
Seer — Barhaspatya Bharadavaja

> 1. To her humble worshipper she gave the fierce
> debt-removing servant of Heaven. Who for our further-
> ance ever destroy the petty mind, Sarasvati, these are
> your powerful gifts.

The servant of Heaven, Divodasa, is the archetypal Aryan king who overcomes the power of the older, evil race and its alliance with powers of destruction and unspiritual commercial interests. Sarasvati is the Divine stream of power which destroys the inhibiting influence of the bartering mind, replacing petty human calculation for profit with Divine beneficence. She is also the great river on which the ancient Aryans lived, which once flowed between the Ganges and the Indus to reach the Arabian Sea at the Rann of Kachchh, through what is now the desert of Rajasthan. The Sarasvati went dry around 2000 BC, marking the end of the Vedic age. Like the Gods, the Vedic Goddesses are awesome beings of power, fierce primordial truth-forces not to be opposed or compromised with.

> 2. She with her strength, like one who digs for lotus
> stalks, bursts open the ridge of the mountains with her

powerful waves. Who for grace destroys the distances,
Sarasvati we adore with transforming insights.

Sarasvati is the stream of inspiration which, seeking the essence
hidden in the depths, breaks open the bounty of the summits. Coming
from afar she destroys all sense of distance, making all things accessible.
We should adore that supreme muse with the insights of truth, with the
perfect chants of transcendence, with the catharsis of understanding, the
inner revolution her profound current brings.

> 3. Sarasvati, tear down those who scorn the Divine,
> the progeny of every delusive sorcerer. You found the
> streams for the people. Full of vigor you flowed the poi-
> son away from them.

This supreme muse of Divine creativity rends away the delusive
progeny of our false thinking, the self-centered conceptions we make in
ignorance of the unity of life. She opens the channels of understanding
between man and man and her stream carries away the poison of the sense
of division and separation.

> ⁴ Let the Goddess Sarasvati, with the power of all
> power, the furtherer of our understanding, give us fur-
> therance.
> 5. Divine stream of inspiration; he who calls you
> when the wealth is placed becomes like Indra when he
> slew the dragon.
> 6. Goddess Sarasvati, like a strong mare aid us in
> strength. Like the Sun open out our victory.

In the Goddess stream of inspiration is all true power and vigor; the
power of understanding, creative insight and furtherance, which proceeds
not by personal effort but by Divine impulsion. He who has that gains the
archetypal status of the Dragon-slayer and overcomes all the negative
conditionings and obscure unconscious forces which rule us. For him the
Sun of truth opens out the victory of the light.

> 7. And this awesome Sarasvati, golden in course, the
> dragon-slayer, loves our hymn of affirmation.
> 8. Whose infinite, unfluctuating, brilliant and tremu-
> lous Ocean impetuously continues to roar,

9. Truth-bearing she has spread beyond all duality,
past all her other sisters. She has extended the days like
the Sun.

The spiritual muse is the Yoga Shakti or power of Yoga. She is the infinite, inexhaustible, unfluctuating ocean of light, whose vibrating overflow is all creation. She is the limitless ocean of the Divine Word of truth. She is the oceanic stream that encompasses all the world. She is the pouring down of the sea of consciousness infinite above. Hers is the course of golden light, the central light of truth that slays the obscure dragon of ignorance. She is the unitary sea of truth that spreads beyond all duality, all her other sisters who are her powers of manifestation and differentiation. She is the cosmic ocean of the Sun and spreads out the clear light of the radiant days of unbounded cosmic awareness. Such is the full power and beatitude of the muse hidden within us who inspires us to the discovery of the depths of our being and its powers of expression.

10. And beloved among the beloved, she of seven
sisters, most gracious, Sarasvati is most laudable.
11. May Sarasvati, pervading the material regions
and the wide realm of inner space, protect us from limi-
tation.
12. Who has three stations and seven planes, who
gives increase to five orders of being, in all our strivings
for power she is to be invoked.

Sarasvati is the stream of inspiration of the Divine Word, the foremost creative power and muse of the universe. Her seven sisters are her powers or appearances on the seven planes of existence. She pervades all the material regions and the wide inner space of the spiritual realm. Her three stations are that of the Absolute or transcendent, that of the causal or archetypal realm and that of the phenomenal realms. In the striving for inner power that is the labor of all life she is ever to be invoked. The five orders of being are the beings of the five realms of creation or the five races of men. All the prime archetypal form-patterns of existence are resolvable into the One Sarasvati, a single flowing stream of inspiration.

13. Who is the great Goddess that shines forth
among the great Goddesses, by splendor beyond all that
is other, the most artful of the graces, as a vehicle vast

for pervasiveness made, She of the stream of inspiration
is to be lauded by those who are conscious.
14. Sarasvati, lead us to reality. Do not turn away.
Do not fail to give us your milk. Welcome our
friendship and our habitation around you. May we not
go away from you to foreign lands.

Sarasvati is the Goddess of the goddesses, the Muse of the muses, the
most artful of the graces, in the splendor of oneness beyond all that is
other. She is the mystic vehicle made for the pervasion of consciousness.
She is the stream of inspiration that feeds those who are conscious with
the milk of knowledge. She is the Goddess of wisdom who leads us to the
Godhead. It is around her alone that is our true friendship, our loving
equality in the Divine creative work, and our true habitation by the eternal
waters. She is the stream of Self-being in which all is creative beneficence.
May we never leave her boundless shores for the foreign lands of duality
and otherness in which is the desert of sorrow, the dreary round of karma
with no muse to provide true beauty and vivification. All true spiritual
sessions are done on the banks of the Sarasvati, along the mystic river of
the creative movement of conscious insight.

Sita, The Goddess of the Plowed-up Earth IV.57
Seer — Vamadeva Gautama

1. Through the Lord of the field, as with a friend,
through his fostering care may we win the cow and the
horse. Let him be compassionate to such as we.
2. Lord of the field, yield to us, like the milk of the
milch Cow, the wave of honey-bliss that distills in pure
drops of clarity the honey-wine. Let the Lords of truth
be compassionate to us.

The field is the natural world, the garden of nature that it is our duty
as human beings to cultivate. The Lord of the field is the indwelling Spirit,
the soul (see *Bhagavad Gita* XIII for its discussion of the field and the
Lord of the field). Through his fostering care we win the abundance of
nature symbolized by the cow and the horse, which inwardly symbolize
knowledge and energy. The Lord of the field is the Spirit or the Self as
the Lord of nature, the beneficent intelligence behind her workings. He
yields the wave of honey-bliss, the blissful wave of the natural mind, life
in harmony with nature. He as the seer yields the clarity of pure perception

that distills the ecstasy of beauty from the natural world. This is the natural living of spiritual awareness, not the rule of instinct but of organic cosmic intelligence. This is the original life for man: living in the beauty of nature by his spiritual gift of perception. In that life of open perception is spontaneous action and instantaneous transformation wherein the true power of life is revealed. This is the unconditioned life of the seer, far beyond that of the savage conditioned by instinct or the civilized man conditioned by society. It is the naturalness of life in the clarity of the present, not that of the obscure rule of unconscious impulse or civilized stimulations and inhibitions.

> 3. May the plants, the Heaven and the Waters be full
> of honey-bliss for us; blissful may the inner realm be.
> May the Lord of the field be full of bliss for us. May we
> move according to him unharmed.
> 4. May the draught animals be auspicious, auspi-
> cious the men who pull them. Auspicious let them draw
> the plow. Auspicious let the traces be bound, auspicious
> may they apply the goad.
> 5. Cherish this Word, auspicious plow and plow-
> share, as you made the milk in Heaven. By that milk fer-
> tilize the Earth for us.

In the natural life of unconditioned perception all is full of delight. The transparent being of consciousness, which is bliss, is found every-where. That secret Lord of the field reveals the true beauty inherent in the movement of the field.

The spiritual life as a kind of cultivation is often compared to agriculture. It is the organic harmonization of our nature by the auspi-ciousness of our inner being. The traces are the straps on the animal used for drawing the plow. The goad is the sharp stick used to drive the animal on. The plow-share is the cutting-edge on the bottom of the plow that opens the furrow. They are only metaphors here. The Spirit is the farmer, the Lord of the field of the natural world. The plow is the Wind or life-force, the plow-share is the Sun or enlightened mind. By the power and being of the Spirit, the rays of the Sun of Divine intelligence open up the field of nature for the higher life. Just as the outer rays of the Sun nourish the material life, the inner rays nourish the spiritual life.

The Word is the Goddess. She is our own soul opening up to the Divine. The solicitation is for the Spirit to cultivate the field of our own inner nature, the field of our psyche, to open up the field of our mind and fertilize it with the milk of truth that it may come to nourish us with truth. For our inner growth we must let our minds become a field for the Divine. We must surrender them and let them be opened, be plowed up like the Earth for an inner crop, a Divine harvest. When the field of matter in its receptivity is opened up by the power of the Spirit it becomes the Word-Goddess, the magic wisdom symbol of the supreme. What opens up and transforms matter is discovering its true Lord, bringing in the higher nature of the Spirit. It is only a higher naturalness and freedom that can change our lower nature. All else is artificial and leads eventually to a reversion. The Earth of our nature plowed up by the Spirit becomes the Goddess and bears most fruitfully.

> 6. Most auspicious Goddess, approach us. Sita, we
> adore you. For us may you be most auspicious, for us be
> most fruitful.
> 7. Let Indra press down the furrow. Let the fostering
> Sun direct her. Full of milk may she yield well for us
> through every succeeding year.

Sita is the Goddess of the furrow, the Goddess of the plowed-up Earth. In the *Ramayana* she is discovered in a furrow in the ground while King Janaka is doing the first plowing of the year. Sita is the inner Earth of our psyche receptive to the Self. She is the receptive mind that bears all things, in which is renewal, which out of the depths yields the milk of the heights. It is only when our mind is laid open, divested of its arrogance of knowing, that we can find the truth. Our true Self can only manifest when we understand that our mind or thought process is not our self but only its field of manifestation, when we no longer confuse our true identity, which is imageless, with the images of the field of our perception. Sita represents this surrender. Indra is the Spirit-Lord of the summit who by his reflection within us, his penetration into our psyche, sustains Sita, the Goddess of the furrow or the valley. Indra is the Lord of the field. Sita is the openness of the soul necessary to embrace the breadth of the spirit. She is the openness of the depths necessary to hold the summit-height. Sita is the abandonment of loving surrender that is the way our nature, our cosmic feminine, responds to the Lord of nature, the unconditioned natural being which is our true Self. She is the plasticity of our nature which is necessary to sustain the spirit and its great force.

Any resistance to the Divine removes it from us. Sita is the non-resistance that yields all things through yielding, that in yielding draws into itself the highest power. She is the surrender in which our psyche is furrowed, is opened up into its proper creative order to allow its hidden latencies, its symbols of the supreme to manifest. She is the impression of the Spirit-Self upon us. She symbolizes the opened channels of our psyche directed by the rays of the Sun of Divine intelligence, the responsiveness of our nature that reflects the sunlight of truth perception. She is the Earth transmuted into light in unity with the Sun, the Earth of receptivity united to the Sun of perception. Overflowing with the milk of truth she yields well for us through every succeeding year or to a higher and higher oneness and equality, taking the inner meaning of the term ("sama" or year also means sameness). This Goddess-spirit of the valley or the furrow is the key to the power of the Divine Word, the word that invokes the Divine within us. She is the secret power of the *Veda*, the soul that invokes all the Gods and manifests them within herself. She is the receptive soul whose open nature draws down the Gods, the Divine archetypes, for their manifestation and realization. The way to find the highest truth is to become Sita. Once the depth is yielded, all must come into it and be transformed within it.

> 8. Auspicious let our plows plow up the Earth. Auspicious let our cultivators press on with their oxen. Let the rain-God with milk and honey be auspicious. Auspicious plow and plow-share, hold in us what is auspicious.

Sita, the valley spirit of the Earth, is the key to all that is auspicious. She is the humility and reverence that guarantees good fortune as it follows the sacrificial order of the universe which grants all things. The power of inner plowing is the power of inquiry. To open up our nature, to find our Sita, we must turn the layers of our psyche over with deep inquiry into the truth of what we are. The cutting-edge of that plow, the plow-share is the question, "Who am I?" In that our psyche is opened and we surrender our egoism while discovering our deeper creativity. Sita is this openness and receptivity through which alone inquiry can proceed. She is the receptive mind on which all inquiry rests. To find truth we must first find our Sita. Otherwise we will not have the ground to hold it and allow it to grow. This process of inquiry is the natural means for the change of our nature from the consciousness of mortality to that of immortality. Any other such process is artificial and limited in its results and leads eventually to a reversion. Man is meant to be the cultivator of the Earth of the mind by the process of inquiry. In this is our true and inward fruitfulness.

For it we need both Indra, our sense of the supremacy of the Self, and Sita, our receptivity to that truth.

Vedic Sita later became Sita, the wife of Rama, and the heroine of the famous epic, the *Ramayana*. Rama in this Vedic hymn is the Sun, the Lord of the field. He is Indra, the Divine or spiritual man. We learn from the *Ramayana* that once we lose our Sita, the cosmic feminine of loving surrender and innocent modesty, we lose everything. There can be no spiritual path for us and our whole civilization will come apart at the seams.

Today, having lost our Sita, we have lost our way. The way of our culture is not that of modesty but the way of exhibitive egoism. It is not the way of surrender to the Divine but assertion of the personal ego. It is not the way of yielding and nourishing but of taking and destroying. Having lost contact with the spirit of the Earth we are destroying the Earth. Ours is the way of personal right, not collective duty. We seek outer freedom to pursue personal pleasure but will not follow any outer discipline to produce internal freedom. We each want to get what is due to us but do not realize that our only duty and dignity in life is to give. In being so wary of being taken advantage of we give advantage to no one, and so we all must struggle for advantage. Those who have shame and modesty, who are shy and retiring, we look down upon as incapacitated, while we laud those who exhibit and display themselves, who will go to any lengths to get the attention of others. We no longer take joy in giving but each insist that we get what is rightfully ours, our separate share of wealth and power. There is no real happiness in acquiring or achieving, for these are the stagnation of our own ego. Happiness is only in giving, not in the recognition of being one who gives but in the realization of unity that comes through providing for another.

Modern men have lost their sense of Indra, the glory of their unconditioned being, and have become slaves of society, its numbers and machines. Modern women have lost their sense of Sita and, instead of the inherent joy of giving which is theirs in the cosmic feminine, they are also trying to find happiness in acquisition and achievement. Such a state of affairs cannot endure. The true archetypes of our nature cannot be suppressed. Sita, without whom there can be no Indra, must be found again. Without the manifestation of the Sita archetype there is no real love or understanding, no true humanity or universality. To really prepare a New Age for mankind we must first become the plowed-up Earth. We must learn to adore Sita, to see the summit hidden in the depths through which alone the Divine heights can manifest.

Rodasi, The Goddess of Transformed Heaven and Earth I.167
Seer — Agastya Maitravaruni

> 1. A thousand, Indra, are your aids for us, a thou-
> sand, Lord of radiant stallions, are your most gracious
> energies. A thousand splendors to give delight, a thou-
> sandfold let your powers approach us.

Indra is Shiva, the Lord of Power, the Lord whose Lady is the
Goddess, Shakti (Vedic Shachi). He is also the Lord of the Maruts, the
Gods of Power, the mighty children and companions of the Goddess
Power. Along with the invocation of the Goddess and the Maruts, he is
lauded.

> 2. May the Gods of Power, perfect in magic wis-
> dom, come to us through the vast Heavens with their
> great grace, as their supreme united energies speed to
> the other shore of the sea.

The Gods of Power are the powers of consciousness, the supreme
Maya, magic wisdom of the Divine. They bring us the plenitude of Divine
forces, the full awakening of inner power, to speed us to the other shore
of the cosmic sea, to deliver us across the waters of the world-illusion.

> 3. Among them she clings, well-placed, full of clar-
> ity, the Goddess-Word, wearing a golden raiment, set
> behind like a spear, moving in secrecy like a man's
> wife, the woman of wisdom who frequents the assem-
> blies of the learned.

The Goddess-Power is the Goddess-Word, the power of the word of
truth. She clings to all the Gods and is placed behind them as their spear,
their prime weapon. She is like the wife working in the home, for whom
men work in the world and in whom alone they find a real home. She is
the wife of all the Gods who tends their home in secret, the Divine Word
which is their sustenance and power of manifestation. She is the high
priestess, the woman of wisdom in the assemblies of the wise, the wife of
men of knowledge in whose presence alone the session can be convened.

> 4. On the other shore the luminous, inexhaustible
> Gods of Power cling to the young Goddess as if a com-

mon wife. The terrible Gods did not drive Rodasi away.
They welcomed her to grow in friendship.

The Word-Goddess (Vak) is the common consort of all the Gods, the
supreme and single Divine Feminine power which has the capacity to
delight, nourish and satisfy all beings. She is the woman who is all things
to all men, the master of appearances, as she is the primal beauty-power
of life. Rodasi normally means Heaven and Earth, or Heaven-Earth, the
two worlds as the twin Goddesses. Here there is a change of accent. It is
not the two ordinary worlds of the ignorance that are meant but Heaven
and Earth transformed in the light of knowledge. The Gods do not seek
to abandon or destroy creation. They only wish for its full exaltation as a
Divine manifestation. This requires the destruction of the inertia of
ignorance through which it fails to meet its Divine archetypal ideal. The
vision of the seer destroys the ignorance and transforms Heaven and Earth
into the world of knowledge. This transformed Heaven and Earth as the
Word-Goddess incarnate is Rodasi, the common consort of all the Gods,
the one world of knowledge of which they all partake. This is the world,
the creation from which the Gods do not seek to escape from but wish to
make flourish. It is the real world of creation struggling to emerge through
the darkness of the cosmic night. It is this world that is the new Earth we
find on the other side of the cosmic sea, beyond the waters of unconsciousness and ignorance, as the conscious ideal behind the world, fashioned
originally by the Divine Word.

> 5. When the celestial lady accepted to follow them,
> Rodasi as the Sun-Goddess with heroic mind and dishev-
> elled hair mounted the chariot of worship, fierce in as-
> pect, in movement like a cloud.

Rodasi, who represents the transformed state of creation as a conscious display of the Divine Word, is also our soul in its awakened state,
our portion of that word. She is the human soul who elects to follow the
Gods and is accepted into their company by her secret kinship with them.
In this sense, awakening the consciousness of Rodasi within us is the key
to our inner unfoldment. Her hair, like that of the Goddess Kali in later
Hinduism, is dishevelled as she is free of all outer laws and a law unto
herself. It is by her nature of freedom that she follows the Gods who are
free. She has an heroic mind or the mind of a man, as she is the feminine
spirit who has found within herself the power of the inner male. She is the
feminine soul who has surrendered to the masculine spirit, the two sides

of the inner nature. Her aspect is fierce by the power of her Self-knowledge in which she knows herself as the One being and power of all the Gods. As such she is the Sun-Goddess, the Goddess-Self, the one light and aim of all the Gods. She is the Self that moves in secrecy within all the Gods, through which alone they have beauty and power.

The ancient cultures were not only aware of outer power, the social offices generally occupied by men, but also recognized inner power, the supreme power that moves behind the apparent forms of things. It is this power they saw in women and symbolized as a feminine force. Until we recognize and give the right place to both these forms of power we will not understand the ancient cultures or produce a harmonious culture of our own. This truth of inner power, the force of inaction, surrender and openness which the ancients valued so highly, is the essence of the secret exaltation of the Goddess contained within these hymns. We must not only read the hymns in terms of their evident meaning but be sensitive to their inner currents of force which may follow a different logic.

> 6. When, Gods of Power, your adorer chanted the
> word, when the presser of the Soma sang the song of the
> Sun, youthful Gods you helped the young Goddess to
> mount the chariot, she who is wedded to beauty, the
> power of fertility in the sessions of knowledge.

The young Gods place the Word Goddess in their vehicle and drive her on the chariot of the Sun to all the worlds. She is the Divine sense of Self which comes from surrender, the modesty which is supremely exalting. It is this powerful and all-encompassing sense of Self arising from the modesty that nourishes all and seeks nothing for itself which is the secret supremacy of the Cosmic Feminine. It is the valley-spirit of Lao Tzu which inherits the heights. She is the secret Self of Indra, his feminine counterpart and reflection. It is by the power of human worship which manifests her that she mounts the supreme vehicle, delivering the human soul and through it the world-soul and all creation back to the transcendent.

> 7. I speak forth what is to be spoken of them. The
> majesty of the Gods of Power is the truth, when together
> with them, of spiritual mind, seeking the Self, resolute,
> she leads auspicious women.

The majestic truth of the Gods that is to be declared is their joint consort, the spiritual mind that seeks the Self, or the supremacy of oneness for all. This is our feminine soul uniting with the masculine spirit and asserting the supremacy in the Self. It is the woman with the mind of the male, the soul of the Bull, the spirit. It is through her that all women, all souls, all the Goddess-powers are led to the Gods. The union of the Gods and Goddesses is their oneness in the Self, in which each finds its appropriate complement. This is the union of surrender and exaltation in the Self, the receptivity in which there is transcendence, the secret action of inaction in which there is the transforming birth of the supreme. In that Self is the complementary resolution of all dualities in which each being becomes all.

This is a hymn of the great seer Agastya, renowned not only for bringing the Aryan religion to south India, but also for instituting the worship of the Goddess, aided by his wife, Lopamudra. We see the basis for the legend in this hymn. The Goddess is especially connected with the Gods of Power, the Maruts, who are also the Gods of beauty. The Maruts are also called the Rudras and the famous Vedic hymn, the Devi Sukta (*Rig Veda* X.125), which proclaims the Goddess as the Self begins with "I move with the Rudras." The idea for that great hymn is found already in this.

Like Women in Childbirth V.61
Seer — Shyavashva Atreya

> 1. Who are you, most glorious heroes, who one by one have come from the Supreme beyond?
> 2. Where are your horses and their reins? How are you empowered, how do you move? The seat was in the spine. The restraint was in the nose.
> 3. The whip was on their flanks. The heroes stretched their thighs apart like women in childbirth.

The heroes are the Maruts, the Gods of Power or Divine principles of energy, flashing truth forces which come from the Supreme Godhead to prepare the manifestation of the spiritual Man, Indra. In the typical multi-leveled expression of the seers there is here a combination of three metaphors: the riding of a horse, a woman in childbirth, and the practice of yoga. These demonstrate the action of the Maruts. The riding is of the horse of the breath, our life-energy or prana. The seat for this journey is on the back or in the spine. The restraint, the control of the reins is in the nose with yogic breathing practices or pranayama. The whip, the impelling force, is on the flanks, by controlling the lower nature with the Godward ascension of will and energy the Maruts symbolize. In this yogic transformation of life-energy, the Divine archetypal forces become like women in childbirth. They labor and they expand to give birth to the One Force, the power of the Self. As the Gods of Power or Shakti, the Maruts are the forces of being of the Goddess, her manifold sons or multiple husbands. The many Maruts, which number up to one hundred and eighty, have only a single wife. They are the complementary masculine plurality through which the single Goddess of Power works.

> 4. Youthful heroes who have an auspicious bride, depart, as you will become the heat of the Fire.
> 5. She won the hundredfold energy, knowledge and grace, whose arms passionately embraced the hero praised by Shyavashva.

The birth that the Gods of Power generate is also their marriage. It is the unification, the alchemical conjunction of opposites that is the mystic birth, the mystic marriage and the mystic death. It is the birth within us of the Divine child of unconditioned being. It is the marriage of the Gods, the Divine archetypes, with our own soul representing the cosmic feminine, the Divine Shakti through which they manifest. She is their common consort for whom they descend, to take her back to their transcendent home in marriage. She is the lower form of the Goddess hidden in man whom the Gods descend to deliver back to her higher nature, the storybook peasant girl whom the princes reveal to be really a queen. Gaining her, the Gods return to the beyond, their work in man being accomplished with the dissolution of mortal consciousness in the immortal. As such, they become the heat of the Fire, the creative ardor of the eternal flame of Awareness, the flames of the Holy Spirit.

Their consort is the awakened human soul, our cosmic feminine nature. She wins the perception of the essence, the all-possession. She wins the herds of horse-like life-energy, cow-like receptive capacity of consciousness, and the hundredfold sheep-like gentleness and grace. Here we see again how in the ancient language abstract ideas are clothed in symbolic forms. She does this by passionately embracing the hero, the spiritual Man, Indra, praised in this hymn by the seer Shyavashva, with her arms, with the open sphere of her being, thus surrendering to the Supreme, the Self. It is this direct and open surrender to the Supreme which immediately wins the Divine that the cosmic feminine represents, and which is far more simple and efficacious than elaborate practices and contemplations.

> 6. And many a woman is more praiseworthy, more generous than the man who has no consciousness of the Godhead, no beneficence.
> 7. He who discerns those exhausted, those thirsty and in want, places her mind in the Divine.
> 8. And indeed, many mere bargainers who have nothing real about them are called men. They are living manslaughterers.

Those women who manifest the receptive and nourishing power of the cosmic feminine are far more praiseworthy than men who, having no sense of the Divine and its nature of giving, have no beneficence and only seek their own advantage. By their intuitive sense of the cosmic feminine, the Divine Mother, women are usually more gracious, giving and nourishing than men. The male's sense of the cosmic masculine, the independent Spirit, can become distorted into a selfish seeking of personal power, prestige and advantage, regardless of the cost to others. This feminine principle of compassion discerns those in want, and in the height and broadness of its openness, its view of oneness and universality, leads the mind into the Godhead that itself is pure compassion, beneficence and reverence.

Many men are men in name only. They use their power to control others, having nothing real or true within them. They have only a commercial self-seeking mentality and do not really perceive others at all, or their joys and sorrows. They have nothing really to give, save what they have cunningly prepared in order to deceive others into giving them more in return. Their gifts are not free and beneficent but given only for the sake of their own greater gain. Their minds are not centered in the clarity and openness of giving but in the darkness of petty calculations of gain and loss. They only praise what brings them profit, for which they are insatiable. These men are living manslaughterers. They live in the denial of what is truly manly, the cosmic masculine force. To become true men again we must revere once more the cosmic masculine force and its power of guidance, protection, responsibility and integrity. We must be willing to sacrifice ourselves for the good of all, to strive unrelentingly and uncompromisingly for truth and beneficence in the world, to take on the labor ourselves and let the comfort, advantage and fame go to others.

9. Young and ecstatic she told to me, Shyava, the
way.

The seer relates his guidance on the path to his instruction by this
spiritual woman, this wife of a sage. The way itself is the Goddess, and
the all-embracing movement of her nature, the stream of her compassion.
The Goddess is the path for the manifestation of the Gods, the circuit that
encompasses them. To travel along the way of truth we must become that
way ourselves. To reach the journey's end is to become the path. To attain
the heights is to discern the depths. This is the complementary wisdom
that constitutes the all-fructifying yet secret power of the cosmic feminine,
the glory of the Gods.

IV

APPENDICES

GLOSSARY
OF TERMS

This glossary gives the meaning of the Sanskrit terms used in the book.

Aditi	the Divine Mother, infinite space, the indivisible, the origin or genesis, that which consumes all things, the Mother of the Gods, particularly the Sun Gods
Aditya	the Sun God, the original power or primal intelligence, which derives from the infinite origin (Aditi)
Agni	the sacred fire
Ananda	bliss or ecstasy in the spiritual sense
Angirasas	the main family of Vedic seers, cognate with our word angel
Apas	the Waters, a Vedic Goddess symbolizing the pervasive presence of consciousness and its nurturing powers
Aryaman	the Divine as the friend, helper, moderator
Aryans	noble or cultured people, people of spiritual knowledge
Asura	Vedic name for the Divine as almighty, cognate with Persian Ahura and Assyrian Ashur
Atharva Veda	last of the four *Vedas*, composed of various hymns and chants with deep mystical meaning, not as integrated into the ritual as the other *Vedas*
Atman	the Divine Self or pure consciousness
Bhaga	the Divine as the power of love, joy, bliss, Bhagavan, another form of the Sun God
Bhagavad Gita	the teaching of Krishna to Arjuna found in the *Mahabharata*; perhaps the most famous Hindu scripture
Bhrigus	old Vedic seer-family like the Angirasas, possessors of both spiritual and occult knowledge

Brahma	the Hindu Creator, originally called Prajapati in the *Vedas*
Brahman	the Divine or Absolute, the Divine Word, also a priest or performer of the Vedic ritual and the spiritual class ruling Vedic society
Brahmanas	Vedic ritualistic texts, containing also some yogic practices
Brihaspati	the Lord of prayer or the Divine Word, the foremost and original of the Rishis, particularly of the Angirasa lineage
Dharma	principle of truth
Indra	the Divine Self or Person, Purusha, prana
Indu	Soma as the primal drop or point from which all creation springs
Jatavedas	name of Agni or the sacred fire as the knower (veda) of all things born (jata)
Kakshivan	famous Vedic seer who has knowledge of all the seers and their lineages
Kali	Hindu Goddess of destruction and transformation, originally the first of the seven flames of the sacred fire
Kanvas	seers of the eighth book of the *Rig Veda*
Karma	the effect of our own actions, particularly those done in previous lives, in the Vedic sense the ritual nature of all action
Kavi	Vedic term for seer-poet, cognate with Persian Kavi, meaning king, literally "one who has the right design or purpose"
Lakshmi	Hindu Goddess of beauty, devotion and prosperity, originally symbolizing the benefic power of the sacred fire
Mahabharata	epic text of late ancient India, containing much mythology and spiritual teachings, including the story of Krishna
Mandalas	the different books of the *Rig Veda*, ten in number
Mantra	the language of the Divine Word, the basis of the Vedic chant
Manu	the Vedic original man and founder of the Vedic religion, a flood figure like Noah
Maruts	the Storm Gods or Gods of Power, sons of Rudra, companions of Indra, who symbolize the seers

Maya	magic power, either of wisdom or the ignorance, of the gods or the demons
Mitra	the Divine as the friend or power of love and compassion, another form of the Sun God
Nirvana	the realm of Absolute peace that transcends the mind and its desires
Panis	peoples of commercial and materialistic values, enemies of the Vedic people and their spiritual life and path of sacrifice
Prana	the life-force or spirit
Puranas	Hindu spiritual texts and mythological books of the later ancient period
Pushan	Vedic form of the Sun God as the Lord of the Path, the fosterer or nourisher who serves life on Earth
Rama	ancient Hindu avatar or incarnation of God
Ramayana	epic story of Rama
Ribhus	Vedic deities associated with magical productions
Rig Veda	largest, oldest and original of the *Vedas* containing the mantras of the seers or Rishis
Rishis	the seers or sages who envisioned the *Vedas*, usually seven in number i.e. Atri, Gotama, Vasishta, Vishvamitra, Jamadagni, Kanva, Bharadvaja
Rodasi	Heaven and Earth as the dual or twin worlds, a Goddess who represents them
Rudra	Vedic name for the God Shiva, the Divine Father, Lord of power and wrath
Rudras	the Maruts or all the Gods as sons of Rudra/Shiva
Sama Veda	*Veda* of song, music or ecstasy, composed almost entirely of Rig Vedic verses put to a musical chant
Samsara	the cycle of rebirth
Sarasvati	the Goddess of the Divine Word and Divine river or river of heaven, river on which the ancient Aryans lived, which once flowed from the Ambala Hills in the Punjab to the Arabian Sea at the Rann of Kachchh
Savitar	the Sun as the father, generator, inspirer, Vedic equivalent of Greek Apollo
Shakti	the power of consciousness, one aspect of the Vedic and Hindu Goddesses
Shiva	Hindu deity representing transcendent being and consciousness, derived from Vedic Rudra

Sita	Vedic earth or agriculture Goddess, symbolizes the receptive mind
Soma	the immortal nectar or mystic wine, Bliss or Ananda
Surya	the Sun as the basic power that creates and generates all things, the Solar Self
Svar	the Sun-world or realm of enlightenment
Tantras	spiritual teachings of the medieval era in India, generally emphasizing various energetic techniques, often centered around Vedic mantras and rituals
Tvashtar	form of the Sun or Moon God, Divine Father, demiurge
Upanishads	spiritual texts that show the inner or esoteric meanings of the Vedic teaching and its mantras
Ushas	the Dawn Goddess, the Goddess in general, the Divine daughter, the power of aspiration, particularly human aspiration to the Divine
Vaishvanara	name of Agni or the sacred fire as the universal deity or conscious power
Vajra	the thunderbolt of Indra that destroys the dragon or serpent, symbolizes the power of the enlightened mind or pure consciousness
Vak	the Divine Word, symbolized as a Goddess
Varuna	the Lord of Heaven, Divine Father and judge, literally "what contains or encompasses everything," a Sun God, Moon God, ocean God, God of the heavenly sea or cosmic waters
Vasishta	one of the seven Vedic seers or Rishis, seer of the seventh book of the *Rig Veda*
Vipra	another name for the rishis, particularly as the illumined ones
Vishnu	the Divine as the pervader or the all-encompassing Godhead, a form of the Sun God
Vritra	the dragon or serpent slain by Indra, represents the obstructing power of ignorance or illusion that blinds us to the reality of our inner Self
Yajña	sacrifice, ritual, methods of making things sacred, practices of giving, offering or surrendering to the Divine
Yajur Veda	*Veda* of sacrifice, ritual or yoga practice

Yoga   practices aimed at spiritual realization; the Vedic
                            yoga, which is the original form of the system and
                            the text wherein the term yoga first appears in its
                            inner sense, works through mantra or speech,
                            breath or prana, and mind or meditation

KEY TO TRANSLATION
OF VEDIC TERMS

This section explains the Sanskrit terms of the *Vedas*. It is mainly for the benefit of those who know Sanskrit and are wondering how the various terms have been translated in this book. This glossary explains the terms primarily according to their etymology. It is my attempt at an etymological key to the *Vedas* and a thesaurus, much like the traditional *Nighantu* and *Nirukta* of Yaska.

The following lists and definitions are meant to be indicative rather than exhaustive. Many other terms and variants on these terms could be given, this being a short version of what could be a much longer work. These terms are treated more extensively in my other books and articles that focus more directly on the Sanskrit.

AXIOMS OF THE INTERPRETATION FOR THE RIG VEDA

1. All terms, in their inner sense, mean the Divine, except those terms that mean the undivine.

2. All masculine terms, in their inner sense, refer to the God, to the cosmic masculine being.

3. All feminine terms, in their inner sense, refer to the Goddess, to the cosmic feminine power.

4. All neuter terms, in their inner sense, refer to the impersonal Godhead, Brahman.

5. All terms, in the inner sense, mean the Self, or the degrees of its manifestation, the stages of its realization.

6. The language of the *Rig Veda* is diverse and diffuse. There are no few key terms that dominate it. The usage is creative and fluidic. There is no literal or invariable usage of terms.

7. There is a dual nature to the terminology and terms have both higher and lower, inner and outer, beneficent and maleficent potentials according to context.

Corollary

Even terms which are mere pronouns (sah, sā, tat), mere objects or instruments (vajra, ṛṣṭi, adri), natural phenomena (agni, sūrya, uṣas), animals (gau, dhenu, aśva) or abstract terms (vāk, manas, kratu) have inner meanings in terms of Self-knowledge. All terms, generally speaking, have both abstract and concrete connotations, general and particular meanings, cosmic and psychological implications.

GLOSSARY OF VEDIC SANSKRIT TERMS

The order is according to the Sanskrit alphabet and standard rules of Sanskrit transliteration.

aṁhas	narrowness, distress, sorrow, anxiety
agni	the inner guide (agra netar), the indestructible (a-gni), the power of fire or transformation
aghas	narrowness, harm, sin, ego
aṅgiras	seer, angel, flame, ray, ember
aja	a goat, executive power, the leader, the unborn
aṇu	what is subtle, atom, bindu, tanmatra, soul, causal body
atithi	a guest, what is timeless or undivided (a-tithi), eternal
atya	a fast horse, what transcends or goes beyond
aditi	indivisible, infinite (a-diti), the mother, primal reality, original light or substance (adi-ti), the Earth, a cow, a ship
adhvan	spiritual path, sacred time, primal call or offering (ad-hu)
adhvara	sacred movement, ritual, journey, rite of passage, the cycle or course of the sacrifice, return or atonement (ad-hvṛ)
adhvaryu	master of the sacrifice, master of time and action, rite as right action
antarkṣa	atmosphere, inner or interior realm, the region between the stars
apas	work, art, artistry, weaving, creativity
apsarasas	angelic creatures who further the Divine creative work
amṛta	immortality, bliss, ambrosia
ayus	life, spirit, affirmation, eon, aion, term of life
araṇi	kindling sticks, Heaven and Earth, mind and body, what is prepared, fit or harmonized

arka	sun, song, sun song, worship, the primal vibration, Om
arvan	horse, stallion, charger, what possess pre-eminence or primal power (ar-van)
avyaya	wool, a strainer, what is imperishable (a-vyaya) and therefore clears the mind of the transient
aśva	swift horse, power, prana, mind, the sun, what is not self (a-sva)
aśvini	the twin horsemen, the masters of the breath or the life-force
asu	spirit, life-force, breath, soul, what survives death
asura	almighty being, nature of power, the Divine (asu-ra)
ahi	what is narrow, a serpent, dragon, egoism (ahamkara)
ātman, tman	Self, spirit, breath, soul, nature, what is spontaneous or natural
āditya	primal light, original substance or intelligence (adi-tya), the sun-companion, common being
āpas	waters, what waves or is woven, creativity, the stream of consciousness
indu	luminous drop, point, center of bliss, bindu
indra	lord of light and power, the spiritual man, Self or Purusha, independence, transcendence
ilā	Word of inspiration, love, revelation or energization, the Goddess, the Earth, daughter of Manu
iṣṭi	impulse, furtherance, grace (abhiṣṭi, transcendence)
iṣ	energy, essence, will, impulsion
uktha	hymn, utterance of the soul, the original words of truth (the mahāvākyas)
ukṣan	bull, oxen, spirit, Purusha
uru	wideness, the vast, freedom, space
uṣas	the dawn, full moon night, burning, blossoming, aspiration, devotion, arousing, awakening
ūrj	energy, vigor, urge, vitality, fertility
ṛk	chant, sound-light vibration of the Divine Word
ṛtam	truth, right, law, cosmic order, harmony
ṛtu	season, law, rite, harmony
ṛtvik	a priest that sacrifices by season or intelligence that operates at the right moment
ṛbhu	magic craftsman, a group of Gods or seers

ṛṣi	seer (dṛṣi), one empowered or energized, awesome, sublime, lord of the law
etaśa	sun horse, power of instantaneous movement, pervasive light
ojas	vigor, wakefulness, power, strength
oṣadhi	plant, light receptacle (oṣa-dhi), the worlds, creatures, peoples, the various sheaths or bodies
kavi	seer, poet, singer, one who has the right aim or design, director, guide, king
karma	labor, ritual, sacrifice, spiritual work, action of transformation, knowledge (kṛ, to know, discern, organize, accomplish)
kāru	singer, worker, artisan
kośa	vessel or sheath, body
kṛṣṭi	cultivators or what is cultivated, peoples or sheaths
kratu	will, spirit, intelligence, discrimination, capacity
kṣā	Earth, world, land, dominion, the worlds, existence
kṣaya	abode, habitation, dwelling, nature
kṣiti	inhabitants, peoples, sheaths or bodies
gabhasti	fingers, rays, lines of force, tanmatras
gau	a cow, a ray of light, sunlight, light, perception, the sense organs, knowledge, wisdom, the soul, consciousness, the Earth, the sky, a singer, a song, note number, word, archetype, value, substance, the mystery (guh)
gāyatri	means of going, Vedic meter aimed at taking us into the Divine
gīr	song, word, the Goddess, conceiving, grasping, comprehending (gṛ, gṛh), a river, the Earth, to be open, receptive
guhā	what is hidden or mysterious, secret, a cave, the Self within the heart
gopā	herdsman, guardian, lord of light or perception (gopā)
gharma	heated and purified essence (of consciousness)
ghṛta	what has been clarified, clarified butter, clarity
cakra	wheel, circle, center, chakra
carṣaṇi	people, working or moving powers, sense organs
cāru	wonderfully lovely, bliss of immortality
citti	perception, knowledge; acitti — ignorance
cetas	mind, consciousness, wisdom

chandas	meter, Divine vibration or cosmic law
jagatī	Vedic meter of twelve syllables, by which the world or jagat is encompassed
jātu, janus, janimā	birth, being, nature
jātavedas	the knower of all births, a name of Agni
jīva	life, immortal life
tanaya	creative extension, progeny
tanū	body, self, Self
tapas	creative fervor, ardor, consciousness-force
tavas	executive power; tavīṣi — shakti
toka	creative force, children
triṣṭubh	Vedic meter of eleven syllables aimed at affirming the Divine
tvaṣṭar	the maker of form or the builder, a Sun or Moon God and father figure
dakṣa	discernment, skill, capacity, intelligence, spirit, right distribution
dama	home, nature
dāsa, dasyu	destroyer, negator, destructive power of ignorance
durga	wrong movement or wrong action, a fortress
dūta	messenger, worker, doer
deva	God, Divine, luminary, being of delight, playful being
devatā	Divinity
devatra	Godhead
devatāti	extension or realization of the Divine
devavīti	advent or enjoyment of the Divine
dravina, dravya	wealth, worth, substance, quality
dhana	wealth, value, substance
dharma	law, truth, nature, support, pillar
dhāma	nature, realm, dominion, law
dhiṣana	intelligence, receptivity, the world-vessels
dhī, dhīti	intelligence, insight, impulse, understanding, conception, song, wisdom, receptivity, a vessel, the Goddess
dhenā	nourishing stream, intelligence
dhenu	milch cow, intelligence, power of conception, the cosmic feminine
dveṣa	enmity, opposition, duality

namas	prayer of surrender, reverence, to bend towards, to take into, turn towards
nāma	name, Divine name, nature
niṇya	what is secret or mysterious, the Self
nirnik	raiment of the purified essence
nṛ	man, male, hero, soul, spirit, Purusha, one who dances or has power
nau	ship, word, invocation, the means of deliverance
pavamāna	self-purifier, becoming clear or transparent (the mind)
pavitra	purifying presence, filtering power of pure awareness, pure perception
paśu	what is bound or fixed, cattle, the bound soul, the sense organs, perception
pīti	drink, absorption, samadhi
purohita	what is placed before all things, the fire or Brahmin priest who has precedence over all action by the power of his silent knowledge
pūr	city, citadel, what is perfect, the plenitude (pūrṇa), the various bodies or states of existence
pūrvapīti	original absorption into Brahman
pūrvaciti	original layer of Brahman consciousness
pṛśni	dappled cow or mother, the sky
pṛstha	present, prominent, to be questioned
prajā	progeny, creativity, inner child of Self-knowledge
prāṇa	life, breath, soul, original Spirit
barhis	what is strewn or scattered, the sacred grass, the stars, the sky, field of light, the sacred
bṛhat	vast, sacred, the Godhead, Brahman
brahma	vast, sacred, expansive intelligence, the Divine word, Brahman
bhaga	the Divine, the blissful Sun, our portion of light, knowledge and delight
bhārati	the Word that bears the Divine truth
bhuvana	world, realm of being, principle or plane of existence, creature
makha	what is supreme, beneficent, holy or joyous
magha	beneficence, greatness, power

mati	mind, thought, emotion, consideration, attention, resolve, affirmation, measure, formation, nourishment; sumati — right thinking or mindfulness, care and attention; pramati — forethought; anumati — care, love; aramati — perfect thought, worship, devotion
mada	ecstasy, inebriation, immersion, absorption
madhu	honey, honey-wine, bliss, ananda
manas	mind, thought, emotion, consciousness
maniśa	intuition, insight
manma	thought, mentation, realization
marut	power, flashing power, the storm Gods, the Divine, liberated sages, wandering ascetics
mahat	great, vast, law or truth
mahi	great, spacious, the worlds
māyā	magic wisdom power, illusion (adevīr māyā)
mitra	friend, love, balance, harmony, a form of the Sun God and Divine Son
medhā	meditative intelligence, wisdom, mental equipoise, the sacrifice
yajña	the sacred, the sacrifice, the Divine, the Lord
yajatra	the sacred Godhead
yahu	strength, power, sanctity, a son; yahvī — mighty stream, grace
yuga	world-age, plane or hemisphere of existence, couple
yuj	friend, companion, one united to the Divine
yuddha	war, warding off duality, darkness and destruction
yoga	work, integration, harmonization, yoga
rajas	world or region, particularly the atmosphere
ratna	what gives wealth or delight, ecstasy
ratha	chariot, ship, vehicle, rite, chant, knowledge
rayi	splendor, wealth, substance, richness, reality
rāti	blessing, gift, beneficence, value, reality
rādhas	fulfillment, felicity, perfection, reality
rudra	awesome, terrible, Divine, Shiva
rodasī	heaven and earth as a single divinity or Goddess
rocanā	heaven, realm of light
loka	realm of vision, space, freedom
vaiśvānara	the Universal Man or God, a name of Agni

vajra	thunder or lightning bolt, power of discrimination between the real and the unreal
vayas	life, spirit, term of life, eon (synonym for ayus)
vayuna	knowledge, way of wisdom
vara	a boon, what is choice or has value
varuṇa	the encompasser, heaven, a Sun or Moon God, the Divine Father
vasu	light, substance, being, plenitude, treasure, the Divine
vahni	carrier, carrier-flame, conductor, catalyst
vāk	Divine Word, word of power, command, the Goddess, wind, ocean
vājas	power, vigor, plenitude; vājī — stallion, horse of power, being of power, soul
vāra	enclosure, point in space, moment in time, atom
vipra	seer, sage, inspired, aroused, awakened, illuminated
viṣṇu	pervading light, intelligence and energy, a Sun God
viśvedevā	the Universal Gods
vī	bird, being, soul
vīra	hero, one who has conquered ignorance and egoism
vṛjana	concentration, gathering, enclosure
vṛtra	dragon, serpent, veiling or obstructing power of ignorance (āvaṣaṇa śakti)
vṛtrahan	the dragon-slayer, Indra or the Divine Self as the destroyer of the ignorance
vṛṣṭi	rain, grace
vṛṣan	man, male, bull soul, Self, Spirit, Purusha, spiritual
veda, vidyā	knowledge, wisdom, perception, realization
vaiśvānara	the Universal Man or Person
vrata	law, dominion, domain, nature, observance
śam	peace, what is auspicious, Shiva
śaci	power, Shakti, the Goddess
satyam	truth, reality
saramā	intuition, the hound of heaven, a Goddess
sarasvāti	she who abounds in intuition, the flowing stream of inspiration, a Goddess
sarvatāti	the all, wholeness, totality
savitar	the force of will, inspiration or guidance, the Sun
sasa	Peace, joy, the essence
sahas	power to endure or overcome the ignorance

sakhi	friend, lover, united to the Divine
sāti	victory, winning realization
sādhana	perfection, completing the spiritual labor
suta	concentration, effusion, libation
suvita	happy journey, blissful movement, perfect advent
suvrkti	catharsis, transmutation, transforming word or worship
sunrta	perfect or happy truth
sūkta	what is well said or articulated, Vedic hymns
sūrya	the Sun as the animating and activating intelligence in creatures
stoma	affirmation, laudation, realization, affirmative knowledge (all is Brahman)
svadhā	self-nature, Self-nature
svāhā	self-affirmation
svar	Sun-world, world of truth-perception
hari	golden, radiant, adorable, capitivating, dual case represents the two horses of Indra which symbolize mind and breath or inhalation and exhalation
hava	invocation, call, challenge, question
hūti	invocation or offering to the Divine within
hotar	invoker, challenger, warrior, questioner

THESAURUS
Terms for the Self and Brahman

ātman:	self	ātman, tman, tanū, sva, svar, svadhā, svadhāvan
	soul	vayas, ayus, asu, prāna, jīva, manas, kratu, daksa, aśva, vājī, arvan, haya, sapti, gau
	spirit (purusha)	vrsa, vrsabhā, uksā, nr, vīra, pūms, sah, purusa (rarely)
brahman:	godhead	brahman, deva, devatā, devatra, devatāti, devavīti, yajña, yajatra, pūrvacīti, pūrvapīti
	being, truth	sat, satya, tat, rtam, brhat, mahat
	substance, reality	rayi, rādhas, dhana, dravina, vasu, vāja
	nature, law	dhāma, dharma, nāma, vrata, pada, dama, ksaya
	mystery, transcendence	guhā, ninya, apicya, nirnik, adbhuta, cita, abhibhuti

brahman:	negative terms;	amṛta, amartya, akṣara, akṣiti, acyuta,
	infinite, immortal	acaran, aditi, atithi, aja, avi, avyaya
	one,	eka, advaya, adveṣa, aprati, asama, kevala
	incomparable	
	as supreme realm	dyau, svar, rocanā, loka (uru u loka),
		antarikṣa, viṣṭap, nāka, pradiva, paramam
		vyoma, paramam padam, parama janitra
	the supreme	vara, vāra, para, parama, uttama, jyeṣṭa
ānanda:	bliss	madhu, mada, matsara, ānanda, cāru, vāma,
		amṛta

Terms for The Goddess

Terms for the Self, the Divine, the Godhead

tanū, svadhā, aditi, guhā, pūr, aghnyā, devī, devatā, devatāti, devavīti, sarvatāti, viśvāci, pūrvacīti, pūrvapīti, uruci

Terms for the Word, intelligence, the soul, the muse (Sarasvati)

dhī, dhīti, dhiṣanā, svadhīti, purandhi, dhenu, dhenā, gau, gavyuti, mati, sumati, anumati, aramati, pramati, manīṣa, māyā, medhā, mā, upamāti, vāk, vāṇi, gīr, ilā, ṛk, hotrā, suvṛkti, sūnṛta, nau, sarasvatī, saramā, stuti, ṣasti, kīrti, śruṣṭi, nīti, hūti, samidh, vedi, samvid, citti, samdṛṣ, ākuti, dakṣinā, āpas, nadi, dhārā, yahvi, avani, sītā, nivat, pravat, jihvā, bharatī, mahī

Terms for power, energy, transformation (Kali)

taviṣī, saci, śakti, īṣ, ūrj, tviṣ, śavasī, vidyut, didyut, iṣṭi, abhīṣṭi, jūti, abhibhūti, prabhṛti, prasiti, prayati, iśu, śaru, heti, senā, aśani, ṛṣṭi, rīti, sāti, pṛśni, pṛsati, vājinī, śyeni, aśvā, upamit, rodasī

Terms for splendor, grace and delight (Lakshmi)

śrī, svasti, rāti, rayi, ūti, aśis, puṣṭi, yaśas, vṛṣṭi, śubh, bhā, ruc, amati, harit, dyuti, kṛp, añji, nirnik, pṛkṣ, sadhamād, vīti, pīti, dhasi, uṣas, uśati, pathyā, revati

Several other categories of feminine terms exist; the major terms for the worlds, peoples, multiplicity, the directions, terms for light and darkness, dawn and night, terms of relationship and terms for evil, illusion and conflict.

BIBLIOGRAPHY

Aurobindo, Sri. *Hymns to the Mystic Fire.* Pondicherry, India: Sri Aurobindo Ashram, 1971.

Aurobindo, Sri. *The Secret of the Veda.* Pondicherry, India: Sri Aurobindo Ashram, 1971.

Aurobindo, Sri, compiled by M.P. Pandit. *Vedic Symbolism.* Wilmot, Wis.: Lotus Light, 1988.

Frawley, David. *The Creative Vision of the Early Upanishads.* Madras, India, 1982.

Frawley, David. *From the River of Heaven: Hindu and Vedic Knowledge for the Modern Age.* Salt Lake City, Utah, Passage Press: 1990.

Frawley, David. *Gods, Sages and Kings: Vedic Secrets of Ancient Civilization.* Salt Lake City, Utah, Passage Press: 1991.

Frawley, David. *Hymns From the Golden Age.* Delhi, India: Motilal Banarsidass, 1986.

McClain, E.G. *The Myth of Invariance.* Boulder, Colo: Shamballa, 1978.

Pandit, M.P. *Aditi and Other Deities in the Veda.* Madras, India: Sri Aurobindo Study Circle, 1958.

Sastry, T.V. Kapali. *Lights on the Veda.* Pondicherry, India: Sri Aurobindo Ashram, 1968.

Sriram Sathe. *Bharatiya Historiography.* Hyderabad, India: Bharatiya Itihasa Sankalana Samiti, 1987.

Tilak, B.G. *The Arctic Home in the Veda.* Poona, India: Tilak Bros., 1983.

Tilak, B.G. *The Orion or Researches into the Antiquities of the Vedas.* Poona, India: Tilak Bros., 1986.

Waradpande, N.R. *Aryan Invasion — a Myth.* Nagpur, India: Baba Saheb Apte Smarak Samiti Publication, 1989.

Yukteswar, Sri. *The Holy Science.* Los Angeles, Ca.: Self-Realization Fellowship, 1984.

SANSKRIT TEXTS

Atharva Veda
Bhagavad Gita
Mahabharata
Ramayana
Rig Veda
Upanishads
Yajur Veda
Yaska. *Nighantu and Nirukta*

Index

274 — *Wisdom of the Ancient Seers* —

O

ocean 26, 54, 76, 109, 120, 122, 132, 156, 171, 175, 177, 178, 184, 188, 200, 207, 215, 226, 235-237, 239
Om 222
Ouranus 168
outcast 126

P

Panis 109, 141
Phoenicians 109
pillar 11, 54, 55, 78, 84, 124, 149, 177, 181, 182, 188, 198
plow 47, 49, 241-244
Prana 85

R

Rama 22, 24, 242, 244
Ramayana 242, 244
Rig Veda 11-15, 17-19, 22-31, 34, 35, 41, 42, 44, 46, 49, 50, 52, 67, 72, 73, 112, 152, 175, 188, 189, 224, 248
Rodasi 245, 246
Rudra 19, 248
Rudras 248

S

Sacchidananda 67, 161
Sanskrit 17, 18, 24, 29, 41, 45, 49, 50, 124, 128, 161, 168
Sarama 134
Sarasvati 14, 26, 27, 50, 237-240
Savitar 29, 159-163, 165, 166
Self 17, 24, 32, 33, 37, 38, 40, 41, 49, 53, 54, 57, 61, 68-70, 75, 77-82, 84, 87-89, 93, 94, 96-99, 101, 104, 105, 107, 108, 112, 113, 116, 119, 120, 122-124, 126-129, 131, 132, 135-148, 154, 156, 157, 159, 162, 163, 169, 171, 178-186, 188, 191, 193-195, 199, 201, 204, 207, 209, 211, 212-219, 221, 222, 225, .

226, 229, 230, 233-235, 240, 242-244, 247-249
serpent 115, 116, 118, 121, 123, 124, 146, 147, 213, 222
Shakti 54, 97, 131, 143, 144, 164, 225, 226, 232, 245, 249
ship 17, 18, 20, 25, 31, 32, 34, 38-41, 82, 88, 89, 101, 102, 104, 109, 112, 130, 137, 139, 143, 144, 148, 156, 157, 165, 167, 168, 172, 177-181, 183, 184, 195, 197, 205, 210, 213-215, 218, 225, 226, 237, 240, 246-248
Shiva 54, 177, 245
Shyavashva 163, 165, 166, 248, 249
Sita 240, 242-244
Soma 19, 69, 70, 84, 106, 124-127, 133, 138, 139, 142-145, 167, 188, 190-197, 199-219, 220, 221, 235, 236, 247
Son, Divine 32, 54, 57, 77, 78, 105, 128, 137, 156, 168, 185, 235
Sri 24, 50, 200
Stallion 106
Sumeria 30, 32
Sun 19, 29, 31-33, 37, 41, 48, 49, 54-64, 69, 70, 72, 78, 79, 82, 83, 93, 95, 97, 98, 103, 104, 109, 117-119, 125, 127-138, 142, 144-146, 148, 149, 152, 153, 155-174, 178, 179, 182-186, 188, 194, 197, 199, 200, 203, 205, 208, 209, 211-218, 220-222, 228, 231, 234, 235, 238, 239, 241-244, 246, 247
Sun-world 64, 103, 172, 178
Surya 69, 70, 157, 162, 165, 172

T

thunder 104, 120, 139, 142, 172, 173, 184, 185, 194, 210, 217, 221, 222, 235
Turviti 121, 122
Tvashtar 143